WITHDRAWN
UTSA LIBRARIES

SWORDS AND ROSES

SWORDS & ROSES

JOSEPH HERGESHEIMER

Essay Index Reprint Series

BOOKS FOR LIBRARIES PRESS
FREEPORT, NEW YORK

Copyright 1928, 1929 by
Joseph Hergesheimer

Reprinted 1972 by arrangement with
Alfred A. Knopf, Inc.

Library of Congress Cataloging in Publication Data

Hergesheimer, Joseph, 1880-1954.
   Swords & roses.

   (Essay index reprint series)
   CONTENTS: The deep South.--The pillar of words.
--The rose of Mississippi. [etc.]
   1. U. S.--History--Civil War. 2. Confederate
States of America. I. Title.
E468.9.H54 1972   973.7   70-167355
ISBN 0-8369-2650-1

PRINTED IN THE UNITED STATES OF AMERICA
BY
NEW WORLD BOOK MANUFACTURING CO., INC.
HALLANDALE, FLORIDA 33009

DEAR BLANCHE

Here is a book of swords, now wholly discarded, and of old-fashioned dark roses — vanished objects and flowers we both regard with an especial deeply personal regret. Well, they have existed for us only in imagination; unhappily we have been delivered to very different and far less engaging realities; and so we must write books, we must publish books and read them, in order to return, and only for a little while, to the simpler loveliness of the past.

TO
BLANCHE W. KNOPF

CONTENTS

THE DEEP SOUTH	3
THE PILLAR OF WORDS	35
THE ROSE OF MISSISSIPPI	67
MILITARY FIGURE IN BRONZE	101
THE LONELY STAR	139
SHADOWS ON THE SEA	173
THE GOOD FIGHTER	205
BELLE BOYD, OR THE FEMALE SPY	235
GOLD SPURS	267
THE FOOT SOLDIER	297

THE DEEP SOUTH

THE DEEP SOUTH

It is usual but not correct to regard the American Civil War and Virginia as synonymous. It is usual, in regarding the South at all, to think of it in the terms and within the bounds of Virginia, and that as well is far from comprehensive. The Civil War began, a great part of it was fought, in the deep South; the heart of the Confederacy was first held in Alabama. Later Virginia became the principal theatre of war; operations and the public mind were mainly concerned with the cities of Washington and Richmond; Generals Lee and Grant ultimately were placed above all other soldiers; but the War for Secession was born in the deeper, in the deepest, South. It is a commonplace to think of it beginning in South Carolina, with the State Convention which, in December, Eighteen-sixty, at Columbia and then Charleston, repealed the Constitution of the United States; but that, in turn, was largely due to the insistence of Mr. Hooker from Mississippi and Mr. Elmore of Alabama. They were firm in the belief that if one state seceded it must automatically gain the consideration, the approval and support, of the whole South. And this, Mr. Robert Barnwell Rhett, for South Carolina, was largely able to bring about.

He had, in reality, in Eighteen-fifty, presented almost the same course to his commonwealth; but Andrew Pickens Butler was then alive; Mr. Butler opposed his extraordinary gifts to secession and it failed. In Eighteen-sixty, however, with Mr. Rhett as active as possible, supported by the urging of Mississippi and Alabama, South Carolina withdrew from the Union. Mr. Rhett was very radical, very bitter in his attitude toward the Republican victory that elected Mr. Lincoln—and, by inference, ended slavery in all the territories of the United States—and for that reason he was not raised to be President of the Confederacy. A convention of deputies from six Southern States met in Alabama, at Montgomery, the February of Eighteen-sixty-one; they honored Mr. Davis and made Alexander H. Stephens Vice-President; and drew up a constitution almost precisely like the one from which they had indignantly withdrawn. The right of secession was completely ignored and, in the face of the declaration that the Southern States were acting in their sovereign and independent character, the Confederacy was declared to be permanent. Mr. Davis was driven to his inauguration in a carriage resplendent with white horses, he took his oath on the steps of the capitol building, a cannon was fired by the granddaughter of President Tyler. Later there was an illumination and a ball.

Jefferson Davis was known to be moderate in his views, a military figure rather than a statesman; and Mr. Stephens, from Georgia, had been opposed to secession. He was, at the very least, pessimistic—an incredibly emaciated gentleman with the voice of a girl. It had, though, no accent of doubt in it when Georgia left the Union. His allegiance, he considered, was not due to the United States, or to the people of the United States, but to Georgia. He was not very gay about the new Confederacy. Robert Toombs, who was Secretary of State, fought against demanding the surrender of Fort Sumter. It would, he said, be fatal. None of the principal figures in the South were gay—the South was not prepared for war; it didn't, the truth was, expect war. It had no arms. It had no ammunition. It had none of the materials of war. It was without the means of transporting armies. The North, the convention at Montgomery optimistically thought, must allow the Southern States to withdraw peacefully under their construction of the rights sacred in the Constitution.

The absurd mistake, the ridiculous and fatal siege, of Fort Sumter followed. General Pierre Gustave Toutant Beauregard opened with his cannon at daybreak, April twelfth, Eighteen-sixty-one; Major Anderson surrendered for the Union, mid-day of the thirteenth; Mr. Lincoln called for his volunteers; and then Virginia was irrevocably dedicated to the Confederacy. In the deep South the deputies to the new confederation of states found Montgomery badly supplied with hotels and the incidental comforts and pleasures of administration, and the capital was transferred to Richmond. There began then, there began at once, the endless internal struggle inseparable from government and the rights of individual states and men. Mr. Rhett and Mr. Rhett's supporting paper in Charleston, the Mercury, began their ceaseless attack on the Presidency; Mr. Davis at once disposed of William Lowndes Yancey, the pillar of words of the South, by sending him on a pointless mission abroad.

In November, at Richmond, Jefferson Davis was confirmed to be the first President of the Confederacy, with a term of six years, and his military characteristics became clear. Mr. Toombs had already left the cabinet, complaining that he was no more than a clerk, and the government was considering a Conscription Act. Mr. Davis, the truth was, refusing to regard the Confederacy in any light but that of war, was pursuing the only course open to success. Due to his single-minded persistence he almost succeeded. The first battles were very far from being Union victories, so far that they frequently had the look, the substance, of Confederate victories. Mr. Davis fought factions in his government: not only the Charleston Mercury but the Richmond Examiner—Edward A. Pollard—attacked him with a relentless personal vindictiveness; he never had the support, the weight, of the political South; and yet the bitter singleness of his being at least twice brought his army, his land, within sight of freedom.

He never had sufficient political support but he did have in and about him the bright power of Southern spirit. It too, in essence, was military; that is, it moulded superb leaders of war. The North and the South, where the ranks were concerned, fought with an equal and persistent and splendid resolve; but the captains of the South were more notable, at once more able and flaming, than those of the Union. The South almost won because of its commanders; the North was victorious because of the multiplication of its troops. Material resources brought about the fall of the Confederacy; it was upheld through the brief period of its being by an immaterial, a transcendent, power. It was, in addition to protecting what the deep South held to be its social and spiritual integrity, defending its adoration for the actuality of a land —for fields and rivers and mountains, villages and gardens and houses, a living past. Compared with that the incentive of the North was hardly more than theoretical. The position of the Union was a negative position.

The South had at least the form, the military advantage, of an aristocratic tradition, a tradition of leaders; its courage, its views, were personal, better than that they were local. It had never been a region of cities but of localities; the institution of slavery had at best given it the habit and responsibility of superiority. Slavery, the further truth was, had never, until the Civil War, generally occupied or troubled the West or the North. Emancipation gathered its visible nobility, its consuming power as a cry, in the person of Mr. Lincoln. Before that it had been the property of fanatical individuals, politicians, and of a single and small abolitionist paper. Yes, the Confederates were defending an actuality and the Union an abstraction. The abstraction, with the assistance of an overwhelming material superiority, won; the actuality, defended until the end by no more than spirit, lost. The spirit of the South, the deep South, vanished except in memory; but the beauty of its memory easily transcended the successful established fact of the North.

* *
*

The deep South was wholly different from what, at the beginning of secession, formed the northern tier of Confederate States. Its difference lay in perhaps the greatest of all physical influences—in climate. It was, in the wide regions of its lowlands and bottoms and river banks, almost tropical. Over a great part of it there was no winter whatever. As a result of this its land and its people owned a definite appearance and character. The beauty of the deep South was sombre; its land was more indifferent to humanity than a temperate land; there was often no shade, no grateful transition, between the darkness of its forests and the crushing light of its cotton fields; it was violent and oppressive and passionate. That is the effect of continuous heat. As a result the temper of its people was at once indolent and passionate, a people of violent emotions and universal valor. Alabama, the Alabama of the Confederacy, was entirely rural; it was more rural than Virginia or South Carolina; a state of small isolated communities and wide lonely plantations.

Its people came together only for court days and sales days, at the musters of the militia, and for the Agricultural Fair held on a plateau above the Alabama River near Montgomery. Prizes, silver cups, were given for the tallest cotton stalks, the stalks that bore the greatest number of cotton bolls, and for those with the best leaf. Aside from that there was a general fox hunting, dove shoots in October, and the running of deer hounds. The concerns of men still living between planted fields and a wilderness. For the most part the houses were small, built in the shadow of the woods, on secretive streams, or in communities of small people. The great plantation houses, of course, were formal in design and spacious in manner. A wide hall led from front to back, there was an immense hanging lamp resplendent with prisms, and when, late in the afternoon, a faint air stirred there was a faint cool music from the stirring glass prisms. A gallery on the front supported a small balcony above; at one side of the lower hall was the double parlor and perhaps a library, on the other the dining room and smaller chambers; there might be a glass flower pit.

There were excessively fine houses, houses with the woodwork, the stair rails, of rosewood; with marble columns and classic ballrooms, elaborate marble mantels and Florentine mosaics; with all the door knobs and window catches and light brackets run from pure silver. The kitchen, because of the heat, was built separately, with the house servants above; the left wing of the mansion itself held an office for the instruction of the slaves. Fragile chairs with reeded legs and pianos inlaid with tortoise shell and cut brass, burnished metals and Irish crystal, high wax candles, dark mahogany beds with solemn canopies and feather mattresses, linen fragrant with lavender. Smokehouses and feed houses—where the screenings of the wheat were kept for the chickens—dairies with shallow pans for skimming cream and deep pans for curds, spring houses with watermelons cool in summer. The wells were so deep that the water, drawn in a cedar bucket, was cold as ice water. Perishable food was lowered into them. The wells were haunted, they were the subject of negro legend; but the legends were all beneficent; when the slaves slowly drew up the water they commonly sang. Their songs and the sound of the winding chains were a part of the early spring morning. There were dippers at the wells

—gourds for the negroes, beautifully wrought silver for white people. The negroes, it is conceivable, were not more unhappy than the whites; they were negroes, remember, on plantations, in the country; in a country that was seldom cold. They worked in the fields, or in the house, and slept in small cabins. They were, within the rigid fact of their slavery, free—they had no responsibility, they had no debts, and when they were old they were safe: they cleaned the ornamental brasses, they tended the making of tallow candles, polished and filled the lamps, and with soft cloths rubbed brilliant the cut prisms, the teardrop prisms and the pendentive prisms of the girandoles and crystal chandeliers.

That elaborateness, however, was limited to the great plantations; for the most part Alabama was rural in the common experience of that condition; small villages, cabins on water or in little clearings, habitations gathered into the region of a water mill, a grist mill. The dusk of the mill dam was momentarily bright with fish, with mill pond chub; there were flights and settling flocks of water birds, water lilies and snake doctors and, more ominous, cottonmouth moccasins. The grain was hauled on the backs of mules, piled high around the negro riders—water-ground meal was richer, cooler from its slowly revolving stones, than any other kind. The forests and canebrakes and swamps that separated the cultivation, the living, deepened and made absolute the loneliness. The swamps, hushed with Spanish moss, held triangular cypress trees and water oaks; flowers—white iris, trumpet vines and bay blossom—grew; there were Spanish bayonets and pampas grass; and, moving through the unsubstantial tangles, cane biters, catamounts, opossum, vindictive squirrels and snakes.

The deep South, like a conservatory, was sweet with flowers. The isolated burial grounds, approached by avenues of cedars, and shaded with willows and live oaks and linden, were planted with white flowers—Cape jasmines, bridal wreath, white japonica, sweet alyssum and white althea. In the strange white radiance of Alabama moonlight white flowers—Cherokee roses, the night-blooming cereus, moon flowers and honeysuckle—were sweeter than at any other time. Perhaps they were sweeter in the moonlight of Alabama than anywhere else. There were camphor trees and ivy and the new dark red Jacqueminot rose. In the earliest spring snowdrops were followed by jonquils, hyacinths and narcissi flowered in bright groups along the south walls.

The elaborate gardens were laid out in formal walks, with prospects and labyrinths and fountains, leaden statues and marble urns, with magnolias and bay and laurel, crape myrtles and oleanders; but the little gardens were simple with flowers—cross vine, yellow jasmines, seven sisters, snow-on-the-mountain, banana shrub, verbenas and spiced pinks. There were trees with an especial romantic significance: the catalpas, Indian cigar trees, tulips, hackberry trees and palma Christi. In the Black Belt there were sweet gum, red oak and willow oaks and evergreens; the sandy lands had willow and bay, spruce pine and cottonwoods; in the red hills there were loblolly pines, magnolia, dogwood and holly. Haws were common and giant pecan trees, pomegranates and mulberry trees; mulberries and sugarberries and china berries; and everywhere lavender.

Yet, against all that tenderness of beauty, in spite of an apparent transcendent peace, the intense heat bred its intensity of emotion, a dangerous bitterness of conviction, hatred together with loyalty and a fatal pride. The deep South reacted deeply, darkly, from its heart; its passions were not tempered by deliberate intelligence. It had, together with its fineness, an unrestrained brutality of act destructive like the blaze of its sun. It had an integrity but it was not the measured dignity of mind. Its integrity, as I have said, lay in the virtues of extreme loyalty and unassailable courage. It was magnificent in battle, in battle rather than in war. It was, after all, General Lee, Virginia, who led the South; but he had Alabama tigers to lead; men born for fighting, capable of fighting throughout all their long or short lives. They made the four years of the Confederacy possible. Then they too vanished.

* *
*

The first battle of Manassas was fought in July, Eighteen-sixty-one; it was the result of political impatience in Washington, and ended in a potential Confederate victory. The victory, however, came only with the late arrival of reënforcements after a threatened disaster to the Southern army. Joseph E. Johnston, who had been guarding the Valley of the Shenandoah with nine thousand men, eluded the Union commander, Patterson, who had twenty thousand men, and joined Beauregard at Manassas. Manassas or Bull Run. The Confederates, actually, were in flight when they encountered Thomas J. Jackson's brigade standing on the Henry House plateau; it was Jackson's calm idea that the time had come for the bayonet; almost immediately the retreat occurred in the opposite direction. Mr. Davis, in Richmond with his government, took a train for the battle. At Manassas Junction he was overwhelmed with disordered fragments of his army; the air was thick with the dust from retreating wagon trains; there was a continuous thunder of cannon; and the conductor refused to go further. Mr. Davis, with an aide-de-camp, continued on the locomotive; they secured horses at General Johnston's headquarters; and, in a solemn frock coat, a stovepipe hat, Mr. Davis rode among his troops urging them to return to the front. They had, in reality, already been victorious.

Affairs in the deep South had not been so simple, so clearly drawn. The governor of Missouri, in the best oratorical manner of his day, responded definitely to Mr. Lincoln's call for volunteers. "Your requisition, in my judgment, is illegal, unconstitutional, and revolutionary in its object, inhuman and diabolical. Not one man will the State of Missouri furnish to carry on any such unholy crusade." In the face of this, Francis P. Blair junior, with the assistance of General Curtis, drove the Confederate General Van Dorn out of the state. The Northern victory at Pea Ridge, in Arkansas, held Missouri in the Union. The governor of Kentucky was in favor of secession, but the Legislature opposed it. Alabama had been one of the first group of states to withdraw; there was opposition to secession, led by Robert Toombs, in Georgia; and throughout the war Tennessee—Tennessee at first voted against secession and then joined herself to it—had two potential governments.

In the February of Eighteen-sixty-two General Grant had reduced Fort Henry on the Tennessee River and Fort Donelson on the Cumberland; this settled the question of Kentucky—the state issued a proclamation of neutrality—and brought about the fall of Nashville; the Union army advanced and practically cut Tennessee off from the South. In March Grant was on the Tennessee River, at Pittsburgh Landing. Beauregard—hurried south to support Albert Sidney Johnston—and Johnston were at Corinth with forty thousand men; and Johnston was insistent on an advance in force. Beauregard was very doubtful about attacking the Northern base; but battle, the Battle of Shiloh Church, was prepared. The armies then were so close together that General Beauregard, ordering the beating of a drum stopped, discovered that it was in the Union ranks.

Grant's forces lay between deep creeks, their backs to the river; only the full front was exposed and retreat was impossible. Johnston was joined by Braxton Bragg. The Right Reverend the Episcopal Bishop of Louisiana, Leonidas Polk, become a soldier, was with him . . . the troops of the North and South were practically equal. On Saturday, it was the fifth of April, the Confederates advanced in heavy rain; it grew worse and at midnight they stood at arms through a violent downpour. Sunday was very beautiful and Johnston was drinking his morning coffee, at a quarter past five, when the first cannon sounded. The Army of the North was completely unprepared for attack: sentinels were on ordinary beat, details for brigade guard and fatigue duty marching to their posts. Before eight o'clock Johnston carried the camp of the Sixth Union division—its colors and arms, stores and ammunition were abandoned.

The men's breakfasts stood on the tables, the officers' baggage and clothes were in their tents. Sherman's camp, then McClernand's, were taken; by ten o'clock all their supplies were captured.

At six o'clock Grant was engaged with breakfast at Pittsburgh Landing when artillery fire was reported and he took a steamboat for the field. He found his troops in complete disorder. Or, rather, it was almost complete—two brigades of Prentiss' division had established themselves in a wood thick with underbrush, and for six hours they resisted a massed and continuous attack. The Confederates called the Union position The Hornets' Nest. It was almost evening before Prentiss, with twenty-two hundred men, surrendered the Federal center. General Johnston, charging, was safe through the main affair, but a chance minié ball cut an artery in his leg and within fifteen minutes he was dead. His surgeon could have saved him, but Johnston had ordered him back to assist the wounded of both sides. Beauregard took command at Shiloh Church, where Sherman had slept the night before.

The Confederates, before the day was over, made a last effort to turn the Union left and reach Pittsburgh Landing. It was protected, however, by a battery of rifled guns on a hill and two Federal gunboats. The troops of the South had to cross a deep ravine and, under cannon and a terrific rifle fire, take a long steep rise. They advanced again and again, they fought until they had no cartridges at all, and then Beauregard ordered them to withdraw. There were fields at Shiloh so covered with dead that it was possible to walk over them, to walk on the bodies of soldiers, without touching the ground. Through the night the Union army was reënforced; at four o'clock, on Monday morning, the Confederates had moved back from Shiloh Church; the Federal advance rested on its arms and after eight hours' desperate fighting the Southern army was forced to retreat to Corinth.

It was a various and indecisive engagement: at the end of the first day the Union soldiers were falling back in a disordered rabble on Pittsburgh Landing; it was impossible to rally them; before the second day was over Beauregard was forced from the field. If he had not persisted in his attacks on The Hornets' Nest it is possible that General Beauregard would have routed the Union army; it was, in reality, practically routed through an afternoon; either he missed the opportunity for so much or he was unable to pursue it. Beauregard was without Grant's resources, his men were limited, his ammunition always insufficient.

The battles of the First Manassas and Shiloh were almost identical—they were both in essence Confederate victories, but at the end the completeness, the weight, of victory was lost. After Manassas the Union soldiers retreated from the Henry House plateau in utter disorder; they pressed through the fords of Bull Run and filled the Warrenton turnpike with an abject mass of fugitives; they refused to stand at Centerville or at Fairfax Court House, and were stopped only by the south bank of the Potomac River. Numbers of them ran over the Long Bridge into Washington itself. During this Mr. Davis and his generals occupied themselves with riding, in a serenity of moonlight, over the field of battle. At the end of the first day of Shiloh Beauregard rested on his arms.

The result was unhappy, nothing was decided, and when nothing, in a military sense, was decided Confederate victories were defeats. They could not wait for accumulations of men and events. Their fervor burned with a clear hot flame, but its fuel was scant: men killed, cartridges exploded, could not be replaced.

* * *

In September, Eighteen-sixty-two, Grant's army was marching toward Kentucky; General Price advanced to prevent this, but, before he could join forces with Van Dorn, he was repulsed. He escaped, however, and very soon afterward he was with Van Dorn. At the beginning of October they attacked the Federals at Corinth, but without success; the Union General Rosecrans, was relieved and General Pemberton, from Philadelphia, took command for the South. The winter that followed was, in the aqueous region of the Mississippi River, largely inactive: the Confederate battalions were spread out thinly over an immense country; the Union forces were concentrated under Grant in the formation of his campaign against Vicksburg. In the North, a year before, Jackson had been made major general and put in command of the Valley district at Winchester, Virginia. The Valley of the Shenandoah was connected with Richmond by two lines of railroad—the Manassas Gap Railway and the Virginia Central, running from Staunton; at the upper, in reality the south, end of the Valley the Shenandoah River flows in two forks, with the Blue Ridge between; they combine at Front Royal and from Strasburg north the Valley is simplified.

This topography was wholly familiar to General Jackson, he had been born in Clarksburg, westward of the Valley— a tall awkward man with enormous hands and feet, insensible to fatigue. At his father's death the family was literally penniless; his mother married again, but lived for only another year, and at seven Thomas Jackson was an orphan. He managed, against so much—or, perhaps, because of it— to get into West Point, where he was laborious and successful rather than distinguished; and in Eighteen-fifty-one he was appointed Professor of Artillery Tactics and Natural Philosophy at the Virginia Military Institute.

In the fall, then, of Eighteen-sixty-one, he was in command of the Confederate force at Winchester; where, with Ashby's cavalry, he had ten thousand men. General Banks, at Frederick City, had eighteen thousand Federal soldiers and the Union General Kelly had five thousand more at Romney. At the end of winter Jackson, however, commanded less than five thousand men. In March he retreated from the greatly superior force of General Shields; but, throughout a momentous period, he had prevented Northern troops from leaving the Valley; and General Lee reënforced Jackson with Ewell's division of fifteen thousand men. Against Jackson's twenty thousand the Union had available four thousand soldiers with Milroy at McDowell, a brigade of twenty-five hundred near Franklin, where twenty thousand more under Fremont were gathering; Banks had fortified Strasburg on the Valley turnpike and had twenty thousand men at Harrisonburg.

Jackson made a feint toward Richmond, he entrained near Charlottesville, but for Staunton, and on May eighth he fell upon Milroy and destroyed him. The broken Union ranks fled to Fremont, at Franklin; and, leaving Ashby's small command to cover his rear, Jackson returned to the Valley. On May the twenty-first General Jackson moved north over the main turnpike, he shifted rapidly to the left, to the Luray Valley; on the morning of the twenty-second he was marching down the Valley road; on the twenty-third he smashed the Union force at Front Royal. He withdrew with practically no losses, and Banks retreated from his fortifications at Strasburg to Winchester; more prudent still General Banks crossed the Potomac.

On May thirtieth a Federal army retook Front Royal and Jackson's position was absorbing: Fremont was on the Strasburg road, within eighteen miles of Winchester, with fifteen thousand men; Banks, at Jackson's rear, had fifteen thousand more; and Shields with ten thousand men and a second supporting ten thousand was immediately behind. There were fifty thousand troops opposed to Jackson's fifteen thousand; he had two thousand prisoners to move and a double row of wagons—laden with the spoils of Winchester in addition to his equipment and supplies—seven miles long. Well, he checked Fremont and his fifteen thousand men with Ashby's cavalry six miles west of Strasburg; Jackson with one little brigade kept Shields back; and on the last day of May his main army was bivouacked at Strasburg. Ewell's division relieved Ashby and held Fremont until Jackson's wagon train had passed; the next night his command was at Woodstock with Ashby guarding the rear. General Jackson retreated closely pursued by Shields and Fremont; the Confederates destroyed three bridges north of Port Republic; they held the bridge there against massed assault; they burned the bridge at North Fork and the Federal engineers required twenty-four hours to build a pontoon. On June the sixth Ashby was shot through the heart.

The seventh of June, at night, Shields' troops filled

twenty-five miles of the Luray Valley, and Fremont had reached Harrisonburg. General Jackson was near Port Republic and his escape was an established fact. That, however, did not sufficiently engage him—he preferred to hold Fremont back at Cross Keys with Ewell, smash Shields himself, and then overwhelm Fremont with his entire, his ridiculously small, command. On the eighth Fremont made a weak attack on Ewell and was thrown back in disorder, and early the following morning Jackson moved against Shields; he came upon two Federal brigades under Tyler in a strong position, but, after a hard engagement, he defeated them. By midnight his whole army was in camp at Brown's Gap. It remained there until the seventeenth and then left swiftly and secretly for Richmond.

The consequences of Jackson's Valley campaign were invaluable—by driving General Banks above the Potomac he prevented a Federal concentration on the Peninsula; the Confederate victories at Port Republic and Cross Keys led Mr. Lincoln into a disheartening mistake—McClellan was left unsupported. Jackson vanished; when he reappeared it was on the banks of the Chickahominy; but Banks and Fremont and McDowell were kept guarding the Valley approaches to Washington. An hundred and seventy-five thousand Union soldiers had been held inactive, totally useless, by Jackson's mobile command.

In May, with McClellan on the Chickahominy, Joseph Johnston entrenched his army before Richmond. Two Federal corps had crossed the river, and Johnston planned to destroy them before they could be reënforced. The Union soldiers were in rifle pits, they had a redoubt, near Seven Pines, a tavern on the Williamsburg stage road. There was a supporting division on the right and to the rear; a third corps had hardly moved from the river; and a violent storm prevented McClellan from crossing the Chickahominy in

THE DEEP SOUTH

force. Johnston had the advantage of battle. Longstreet was to attack at daybreak, but his orders were verbal and misunderstood; it was past noon before the Confederate advance was in motion and then D. H. Hill attacked alone. At five o'clock, near Fair Oaks, the South was repulsed; Johnston was twice wounded badly, the engagement lost and at two o'clock of the following afternoon General Lee appeared at Gustavus W. Smith's headquarters and, with orders from Mr. Davis, took command of the Confederate army.

Later of that June, it was the twenty-first, on Saturday, Lee summoned Jackson from Gordonsville for immediate orders. Jackson left on a freight train, but at midnight he deserted the train for an evangelical Sunday, attending two church services. Again midnight he started on horse for Richmond, fifty miles farther; and, in consequence of this, arrived at three o'clock Monday in place of Sunday morning. On march Jackson's brigades were constrained to observe the Sabbath; Jackson himself prayed continuously through battle.

* *
*

On the Fourth of July, Eighteen-sixty-three, the fortified city of Vicksburg fell. It was protected both by entrenchments and nature, for Vicksburg crowns a great bluff above the flood and bayous and alluvial swamps of the Mississippi River. At its foot impenetrable forests of cypress and wastes of water made it impossible for armies to operate; fortifications could not be erected. Below Vicksburg, as far south as Port Hudson, the Mississippi was commanded by the Confederacy; between Port Hudson and Vicksburg the Red River emptied into the Mississippi from the west, the sole means of communication between Richmond and Texas, Louisiana and Arkansas. A Confederate battery occupied

Haynes' Bluff, sweeping the river, twelve miles above the city; deep ravines guarded it against approach by land. Vicksburg was considered to be unassailable; for months Grant had proceeded against it by sapping and damming, with strings of bateaus and gunboats; but without any advancement of success.

Then the Union general—in defiance of all military probabilities and factors of safety—proceeded on one of the apparently mad courses that make brilliant the records of great commanders: Grant disembarked his army at Hard Times, below Vicksburg, ferried across to the east bank of the Mississippi; and, it was May, cut loose from his base of supplies. His men took two days' rations each, they lived on an enemy's country, and in nineteen days marched an hundred and eighty inconceivably difficult miles and won five separate engagements. On the third of June the Federal batteries were shelling Vicksburg, it surrendered, and the South sustained an irreparable damage. The trans-Mississippi States, the Mississippi River, were lost to it. After this, it had become September, General Rosecrans forced the Confederates out of middle Tennessee; he took Chattanooga without an engagement; but, following Bragg through the mountains, his troops were dangerously scattered. It was Rosecrans' idea that Bragg was in full retreat, but that fact was not present in the consciousness of Braxton Bragg. Rosecrans, with enormous difficulty, reassembled his men along Chickamauga Creek.

The Southern army in the West was greatly inferior to Lee's troops in Virginia; the Army of Virginia felt that it had never been defeated, but the Army of the West had seemingly never gained a victory; its arms, its equipment and organization were precarious. General Lee enjoyed the completest confidence, the affection, of the South; supports that Bragg was obliged to do without. Yet at the battle of

Chickamauga the Confederate fighting was so headlong, so determined, that over a quarter of the whole Southern troops engaged were killed or wounded.

Rosecrans, the Union forces, lay in the Valley of the Creek, on the west slope of Missionary Ridge; they were strongly entrenched; and Bragg, attacking before Longstreet arrived with supports, found his position awkward. All day of the nineteenth, September, he battled without appreciable result; and when General Longstreet arrived, at eleven o'clock at night, he immediately ordered a different formation and assault. It was to take place at a quarter before six on the following morning; but it was dangerously delayed; and General Thomas, holding the Federal right, had an opportunity to protect his position with a log fortification. General Thomas and his men exhibited once more the sheer ability of American soldiers, Northern or Southern, to fight: Thomas held his position all day. He repulsed assaults by Anderson, by Deas, by Manigault, by Gracie and Trigg and Kelley, Gregg and McNair and Fulton, he drove back Longstreet's five brigades, and defeated the efforts of Kershaw, Humphreys, Law, Robertson and Benning. The South fought the North with bayonets and clubbed muskets from two in the afternoon until six o'clock early evening.

At five o'clock Longstreet got eleven guns under Williams into position at the flank and rear of Thomas, but they were too far away, nine hundred yards, and their fire was ineffectual. At six Thomas successfully retreated to Rossville. Those were the heaviest losses of the Civil War. On the twenty-second, September, Thomas withdrew into Chattanooga. Braxton Bragg, following, established his lines on Missionary Ridge and Lookout Mountain; Hooker, in October, arrived to support Rosecrans; and Bragg ordered a night attack at Wauhatchie. There was a fitful moonlight, the engagement began with the shooting of a Union picket at ten o'clock, but in the confusion of shifting darkness nothing was accomplished. Morgan, with a force of Confederate sharp-shooters, was temporarily lost at the Federal rear; Law, for the Confederacy, fired successive and successful volleys from an ambush; Geary, with the Federals, charged and recharged Law; a column of two Union brigades, sent to support Geary, halted without orders for two hours and was overlooked; and as a result Law was able to withdraw comparatively safe.

General Grant then arrived to take command of the Federal army, he had sixty-five thousand infantrymen, together with artillery; Bragg's force had been reduced to less than forty thousand. With November nearly gone Grant attacked the Southern troops holding Missionary Ridge. Hooker and his men succeeded in climbing Lookout Mountain to the foot of its palisade—its sheer last precipice—and turned the Confederate left flank; at the extreme right Sherman, with masked pontoons, crossed Chickamauga Creek and got a foothold on the Ridge. At sunrise Hooker and Sherman attacked, Sherman again and again, but without success. At three o'clock Sherman was exhausted; the Confederates stood unbroken behind a half-finished breastworks. The Federals, then, formed in two great lines of battle over a front of two miles and a half, and there was an impressive momentary stillness interrupted only by a faint distant cannonading.

The Southern position was desperate, and a secret order had been issued for its troops to fall back to a second line of defense when the enemy was within two hundred yards; this was misunderstood and the result was a fatality of chaos—the heat was unsupportable, part of the Confederate forces moved back and part remained; soldiers reached the upper works utterly exhausted and breathless, they were lost in nausea or fainted on the steep slope. They rallied again, however, at a ridge five hundred feet higher still, where they held for a while the semblance of another magnificent lost victory. General Bragg, at his own request, was relieved of command; and the operations of Longstreet, moving against Burnside in eastern Tennessee, went forward to its tragic futility in the siege of Knoxville.

Longstreet advanced by rail, his artillery on trains of flat cars, the cannoneers pumping water into the engines and cutting up fence rails for their fuel, with Burnside in a skirmishing retreat. General Burnside withdrew, finally, into Knoxville past the middle of November and on the eighteenth Longstreet drove in the Union outposts and invested the city. An attack was ordered against Fort Sanders, a part of Knoxville, but the original plan was changed to another night engagement. A Confederate advance followed the signal guns of three batteries, and almost at once its column was hopelessly massed in a deep ditch protecting the face of the fort. Colonel Thomas, of the Sixteenth Georgia, was killed; Colonel McElroy was killed; Colonel Fizer's arm was shot away on the parapet; Colonel Ruff was slain on the counterscarp. After twenty minutes of hopeless struggle daylight began, and Longstreet, after a second advance, ordered retreat. A staff officer arrived with a telegram from Mr. Davis, announcing Bragg's defeat at Missionary Ridge, commanding Longstreet to join him at Dalton, and there was a truce until dark for the removal of the dead.

*   *
   *

The suspended victories and defeats of the Confederacy in the deep South were accompanied by irreparable loss— the last remnants of available resistance were engaged. No fresh divisions could be brought forward, ammunition and equipment were practically exhausted. Joseph E. Johnston's army, in Dalton, Georgia, was purely an army of defense. The South, the whole South, had reduced itself to utter poverty. The structure of its society, the form of its daily life, its property in ideas and ideas of property, were all destroyed. Even its code of honor, its sense of integrity, began to appear archaic. The deep South, in a word, with all that it signified, had come to an end. A certain ordered fineness of existence vanished. Only a naked and bitter pride, and cherished memories, remained.

A society cannot exist without its supporting forms, its setting—manners and dress and space and leisure. A minuet requires elegance. Dress and a manner are inseparable. There is a virtue inherent in polite circumstances—banks of tall wax candles and silver, jewelled buckles and sheer cambric, ruffled satin and pearls, powder and colognes. Women, charming women, and a cultivated society are synonymous; one can have literally no existence without the other; and poverty is fatal to both. But, before ruin overtook them, the American Civil War gave aristocratic and lovely women a last transcendent importance: they became the symbol of everything that was priceless in life. The perfection of delicate women was doubly perfected.

War, then, was still an aristocratic profession and affair; it had not entirely lost all the aspects of chivalry; its prerogative was commanded by kings and presidents. The lot of the common soldier, compared with the position, the rewards, of his officers, was insignificant. The great captains, the celebrated leaders, of the deep South were cavalry officers. Brilliant beings fired with inextinguishable bravery. They were part of the ideal pictorial conception of courage. Romantic. A word, I believe, that describes a complete agreement between reality and desire. The Confederate cavalry officers were supremely that. They were the extreme ideal come to earth of men cherished and adored by charming women. They appeared from the field, shining with valor, in Atlanta or at Savannah or Charleston, they married at dusk, and in the morning they were gone. Mostly forever.

Aristocratic women, lovely women—the women of the deep South—are not utilitarian at heart; they are not material. They are—at least they were—concerned only with their beauty and with love. Love and personal beauty! They were not, they could not be in that climate, perpetual and dry like straw-flowers, but bloomed quick and white and sweet; and what happened to them tomorrow was far from their apprehensions. They were glad to pay for the ecstasy of their supreme separate moments by a swift scattering of their petals. They did not, consciously, want the men they loved killed in battle; but the imminence of battle, the absence of tomorrow, gave their love a passionate intensity impossible to security and long peace.

Before the Civil War the fortunate women of the South lived in a great privacy: their public appearances were limited to formal watering places, to balls and to rigidly selected dinners. This was the result both of convention and the necessities of their situation, the distances that separated the plantations. It was, in essence, a masculine society: a masculine society is founded on the desirability, the actual charm, of women. In their rôle of women. After Eighteen-sixty-five, even in the deep South, society became commercial rather than masculine. The empire of charm largely departed. First extreme poverty assailed it, and then, as a result, economic necessity drove women into public knowledge. They left the plantation houses, the old peace of the living and of the dead, and went into cities; the isolation of plantations and little communities was broken by easy communication; the individual principalities of cotton were overthrown.

It could not be prevented, it couldn't even be condemned. In reality the South lasted for an amazing period in a world that had grown wholly different. It was a land almost totally foreign to the rest of America; it regarded what was different from it with disdain; the North and the West, for their parts, were increasingly impatient with its pretensions. Its ideas, as I have said, belong metaphorically to the heart rather than to the head; it was, like a beautiful woman, incurably personal. For the people who dominated it, it was paradise, and they fought for it with every particle of their possessions. They gave their silver and gold, their horses and food, and their lives. They went down in a glory peculiarly their own; they perished, as they would have chosen, with a final splendor.

The armies of the South, hopeless of replacement, charged the perpetually renewed armies of the North; it went into every engagement with fewer men than it had owned before; only its courage was not diminished. In lesser numbers it grew brighter. It was never, after the battle of Gettysburg, except in its women and a few fanatically devoted men, hopeful. The Confederacy, after Eighteen-sixty-two, fought with a desperation that was simply an obedience to its conceptions and its past. The Southern mind was not wholly innocent of mathematics; it realized, by the process of mathematics, that it was conquered; its body was killed and without body a spirit cannot remain on earth. The necessity not to disgrace its illusions kept it in the field until the superior humanity of General Lee insisted on surrender.

At the beginning, the first battle of Manassas, the Confederate ammunition was almost useless—it had been obliged to use the Archer projectile in cannon, and it would not fly point first, it tumbled and had no range. Throughout that impressive engagement the South owned only four six-pound guns, three three-inch iron rifles made in Richmond, and a six-pound brass cannon that at once became worthless. Its men had antiquated 69. calibre muskets with smooth bores, old long rifles of odd patterns, rifles that loaded at the muzzle. When the Confederacy wanted guns or supplies or mules it raided the fat armies of the North. The Stonewall brigade looked with gratitude on the Union General Banks as its sole commissary. That, however, had been in Virginia; conditions were harder in the deep South. When Johnston began his slow and successful retreat through Georgia his men could not renew or refresh themselves; they returned harassed and hungry through a land— their own land—starved and harassed.

A land stripped of its richness, the fields already choked with weeds, the houses, great and small, deserted. Windows broken, colonnades thrown down, chimneys fallen in piles of brick. The past obliterated in a sudden and complete disaster. General Johnston had less than forty thousand infantry and an hundred and twelve guns; Sherman had assembled an army of more than ninety-eight thousand, with two hundred and fifty-four guns; and Johnston, falling back from Dalton, established himself behind earthen parapets at Resaca; he retreated to Kenesaw, where he defeated the Union forces; he withdrew behind the Chattahoochee River, and again dug entrenchments. Then, in July, Johnston was relieved of his command and Hood fought in his place. Mr. Davis had a last thin dream of aggression, but the fate of Atlanta ended even that. The democracy conceived by Mr. Jefferson had finally—at the expense of Monticello—triumphed over the Federalistic, the aristocratic, precepts of General Washington. Mr. Lincoln, at a price, preserved the Union.

*   *
*

The greatest principle involved in government, individual liberty, had been ruinously fought for and, apparently, solved. The states were again, more firmly than ever, united. A bitter sectional difference was reduced to a political issue. That difference, once so deeply implanted in men's destinies, began, after Eighteen-sixty-five, to disappear. It was, in reality, the opposition of an aristocratic idea to a democratic conviction. The democratic conviction is not, at base, elaborate—it is the assertion that the dignity of the entire human race is implied and represented by every individual. That individual, then, in the interest of the whole, must be supported with a justice and privileges equal to those shared by all others. It is an abstract and perfect idea and, in spite of its simplicity, it is beyond the grasp of the generality of men. It is, for example, the exact reverse of a selfish interest. Nothing could be more impersonal.

The aristocratic principle—quite the reverse—believed that the dignity of the human race exclusively resided in a minority of especially situated, especially born and privileged, men. They, because of their superiority, were responsible for less fortunate individuals. Some men, a very few, had the affairs of life in their charge; the others, in the interest of all happiness and well being, were expected to live in the state and conditions society and God had called them to. That was the conviction supported by the deep South; it was not, perhaps, what they immediately fought for; but it lay behind their passionate refusal to subscribe to a Northern humanitarianism. At best the principle upheld by the South did create men with a singular impressive power of integrity, very great men indeed; at best it gave the relationship between master and slave a mutual acknowledgment of obligation and affection. At worst it bred an intolerable brutality. It placed an overwhelming responsibility in a few hands and relieved all others of participation in large events; but the others, discovered by France and Mr. Jefferson, increasing in power and mobility and ambition, swept the superior minority into oblivion. They obliterated the Alabama and Mississippi, the Louisiana and Georgia of Eighteen-sixty, destroying the good with the bad, what was ugly with most that was beautiful.

When General Lee surrendered to Grant he rode to meet him at Major Wilmer McLean's house in Appomattox; it was a plain structure, two stories of wood, with a wooden porch, set back from the street in a yard. It was Sunday, April ninth, Eighteen-sixty-five. Lee arrived first, accompanied only by his military secretary and a courier who held their horses; Grant appeared at half past one, with General Sheridan and General Ord and General Ingalls and nine members of his staff; and they met in Major McLean's parlor. General Lee sat at a small oval table, near a window, and Grant occupied a marble-topped table in the center of the room; for the most part the others stood. The Confederate commander wore a fine new grey uniform, immaculate with gilt, his spotless boots had burnished ornamental spurs; his long unstained sword was elaborate with jewels. A felt hat and buckskin gloves were on the table beside him.

Grant wore the common blouse of a private, dark blue flannel; only his shoulder straps showed his rank; his undistinguished trousers were thrust inside ordinary boots; he was without spurs or a sword; and his blouse, his trousers, his boots, were thickly splashed with mud. His hair and beard were brown, they hadn't a trace of time; but Lee's hair—he was sixteen years older than General Grant—was a pure silver. That moment perfectly illustrated the whole course of the Civil War—the South, the defeated past, and the triumphant North, the future. An aristocratic principle surrendered forever to democratic ranks.

Two things, however, were independently plain—first, that in a very few years the South itself would have freed its slaves; and second that, had it left the Union, it would, before long, have returned. For fifty years there had been a growing doubtfulness about the institution of slavery in the South; it was, in the most distinguished places, persistently condemned; a great number of slaves were voluntarily set free. The South, where slavery was concerned, had been trapped by its climate, by the spectacular rise in value of cotton. Cotton, of course, and slaves were synonymous. There had been, even throughout the deep South, a violent opposition to secession; its leaders did not believe it could be victorious; state after state fought against it. The Whigs, in the South, were powerful until the actual beginning of the Civil War. They were the heirs of the Federal party, the political descendants of General Washington, and they held bitterly to the principle of a strong central government.

The bravery of apparel, the visible fineness, of General Lee, making a last significant appearance, left a lingering regret and sense of irreparable loss. He represented so much that gave dignity and a beauty to life. Spurs were done and swords were soon to be thrown away. Marks and mementoes of chivalry, the old conduct of honor. The obligation of the most individual responsibility. What General Lee personified was definitely gone and human existence could not very well do without it. The power, the accomplishment, of General Grant were clear, but they weren't nearly handsome enough. Men required every possible detail of dignity; just as women needed tenderness and beauty. The deep South, the regretted South, was a land, a time, of bravery and grace. Democracy, like perfect Christianity, was a dream, but the old South, at once classic and romantic and pastoral, had been a reality.

The great plantation houses and the small lonely houses

had existed, the slave quarters for negroes who sang in the cotton fields, at the cotton press, labor and song. Men had proclaimed themselves to be higher than other men; women knew they were superior to others less lovely. Often this was true. It is, perhaps, more important to have valuable men than to value all men. Certainly beautiful women are more momentous than women who are plain. That is where democracy, the theory that all men and women are equal, is absurd. Ridiculous! The old South knew better. There are more plain women than beautiful, more undistinguished than distinguished men, and their vast multiplication overthrew a state which, naturally, they envied and condemned.

It is apparent, however, that, in spite of the importance of climate, more than climate was involved. The deep South, the heat, simply gave its children a burning intensity of feeling and mental indolence. No highly intellectual civilization, in that land, was possible. Intellectual men are disagreeable, they are the product of disagreeable weathers, of cold winters and pinched circumstances. Brilliant women, women with practical brilliancy, are not often visibly lovely. The qualities of the mind are polished by struggle, by enormous difficulty, and in the South struggle was not necessary, it was not possible. The long summers drove men into a continual siesta; they made women pale, delicate, in delicate pale muslins. It was a land, a society, that flowered in the evening, like the night-blooming cereus; it was lighted with a golden radiance and musical with fiddles; fiddles at night in the quiet, the peacefulness, of wide plantations. Night with no disturbance but the owls in the live oaks and the whip-poor-wills in the evergreens. Then the deep South went to war, the heavy sound of cannon drowned the fiddles. The music stopped.

THE PILLAR OF WORDS

THE PILLAR OF WORDS

THE South, like an older people, at a momentous time in its existence was led by a transcendent pillar; it was not, however, a pillar of smoke and of fire, but of words; and it did not serve as a guide to salvation. Quite the reverse. It is not probable that Mr. William Lowndes Yancey, by the sheer power of his speech, brought about the Civil War; but for a long while, and with singular persistence, with an unassailable courage of conviction, he talked to that end. Mr. Yancey was part of the great traditional Southern oratory that—in its day held to be the deathless voice of genius—quickly sank to a complete silence. It was, however, the characteristic, perhaps the only native, art of its section. The most dignified profession in the deep South before secession was statesmanship; not politics but statesmanship; and it was almost wholly founded on the power of oratory, the music and magic of a voice.

That was in a period and land when there was very little public and organized pleasure. The theatre, outside of New Orleans and Savannah and Charleston, practically had no existence; there was, broadly speaking, no music; except for casual horse racing there were no games or general spectacles. The people, with a universal need for the contacts and emotions of humanity, had little opportunity to meet in satisfactory numbers. They made, therefore, a pleasure out of their necessities, and went in masses to the county court days, to agricultural fairs and barbecues, and to great camp meetings. At such times and occasions their hunger for variety and excitement was met. Except then their lives were grave, often sombre—isolated on lonely self-existing plantations and in small communities hardly more elaborate than the original log forts and primitive forest stations.

There was almost no communication between house and house or way from place to place: the main roads, few in number, were impassable with freshets in the spring and with mud in winter; at all times they were difficult with stumps and deep ruts and bottomless quagmires; aside from them there were only dusty local reaches, traces over the mountains and insecure ways through the swamps. There were hardly any vehicles for transportation. Everyone rode horses who could ride; only the widely scattered rich owned carriages. The rich, at the beginning of summer, drove to the watering places or the cities where they spent the hottest and most malarial months; in the fall they drove home again; and that, with local visits, long precarious voyages to Europe, was the extent of their travel. The poor, except to migrate West or Southwest to new lands and hope, didn't travel at all. They couldn't.

In addition, everyone with the exception of the great planters lived at the price of an endless toil. Men and women got up before daybreak and worked, in the fields or house, until dark. They saw no one but the people working with them; they heard only the sounds, the voices, of utility and of Nature; they saw nothing but a circle of woods, the dark face of a river, rude walls. There were no books, no toys for children—the children knew tasks rather than play—even the churches were commonly without instruments of music; an elder led the singing with a tuning fork. There was literally no individual means of individual entertainment.

There were no means at all outside the court days, the barbecues and camp meetings for the generality of men;

THE PILLAR OF WORDS

and so men brought to them a passionate interest, a long accumulated intense excitement, that burned in dangerous personal and evangelical fires. Politics, in that existence, was bitterly absorbing. It was an outlet for a great many diverse emotions and needs. In addition it was, by the strictest necessity, purely personal, an affair of immediate human contacts. Of sight and the voice. It was always local. There was then, in the deep South, practically no national consciousness because there was almost no national intelligence: the states, the different sections of the country, like the individuals in Alabama or Mississippi, were very far apart. They were distant in the impassability of sheer miles and in the spirit bred by localities. A region isolated from the rest of America grew indifferent to all that happened, that existed, outside its own vicinity and knowledge. It was hardly conscious of what occurred beyond the range of its long smooth-bore rifles.

The rich, different from the poor, still suffered from the common situation—after the interests of the planter, cotton, there was practically nothing, except politics, to occupy men of position and intelligence and ambition. Politics and the law. One, the law, almost always led to politics; rather it was a marriage that gave birth to statesmen. A gentleman who was not by temperament a planter studied law in the North or in the South; he returned to his home, to his local courts; and there, with the community gathered about him, he argued his cases in the impassioned manner of the day. In other words he perfected himself in oratory. A more general occasion, a political issue, would rise and he'd try his power of speech, his command of classic allusion and invective, upon that. If it were successful his career as an orator, a statesman, had begun. He spoke, on such occasions, at the agricultural fairs, at secular intervals during the camp meetings, from courthouse steps and on the balconies of hotels. When he had acquired a reputation, when he had represented his locality at the state capital, or his state at Washington, immense crowds gathered to hear him. He lent his dignity, the power of his words, to the more inelegant barbecues. Literally thousands of people gathered for them; they commonly lasted for a week; for a week oratory filled the air with its grandiloquent images.

The orators were at once a source of emotion and the principal education of the deep South. They had incalculable power. The people as a whole were unlettered and violently impressionable; they had a very few generally shared simple conceptions; their minds were not troubled by new, by foreign, ideas. They were, as a people, hostile to outside influences and facts. When the orations came to an end, when the musical and adroit voices ceased, and they went back to the isolation of canebrakes, to the loneliness of a primitive soil, their minds for months were charmed and elated by ringing phrases charged with assurances of their own importance and the irresistible power of all they held to be dear.

This, then, was the state of existence that gave oratory its overwhelming but temporary influence. It was that existence which, at its best, brought statesmen—statesmen and not politicians—into being. The South declared that the lustre, the marvel, of oratory was imperishable; and at that moment, in a final ironical pillar of words, it was coming to an end. Mr. Yancey was the last to practice it in all its pride and sound and circumstance. Cannon stopped it forever; the cannon to which he, as much as any individual, laid the match blasted his round full periods, his high appeals, into nothingness. It could not have been more appropriately arranged—Mr. Yancey, with the traditional art of his section, of his time, had a part in the futile glory that brought his world to an end. He was not forgotten later—his importance faded before the Confederacy was realized; he was ignored, discarded, at the first sounds of the war he had given all his power to bring about. In an instant everything that he represented, that he strove to maintain, was destroyed. The mouth of oratory was stopped with earth.

* *
*

The politics, the political parties and principles, that William Lowndes Yancey knew were at once hopelessly involved and appallingly simple. They were simple in the overwhelming importance of the supreme issue of his time. The dangers, the disruption, of slavery had a faint but perceptible beginning in the Presidency of John Quincy Adams, in Eighteen-twenty-five: then the Democratic party was first divided in its attitude toward the Constitution. Adams was liberal in its construction, he supported a Federal or central power; and a reaction against that and him elected Andrew Jackson. President Jackson was a strict constructionist, and jealously protected the rights of the people, the individual states, against Federal aggression. At that time, however, both parties, the Federal and Democrat, were called Republican: Adams had led the Administration Republicans and Jackson the Opposition Republicans. The Adams party then became the National party and the Jacksonian principles were termed Democratic. The National party, of course—the Republicans of today—was at the same time Whig.

In Eighteen-thirty Andrew Jackson broke off all relationship with John C. Calhoun; Calhoun set about consolidating a purely Southern interest; and, as a result, his faction took no part in the Democratic Convention of Eighteen-thirty-six. The Democrats succeeded in electing Martin Van Buren, but their margin of victory was very slight, and the next President was William Henry Harrison, a Whig. That was the Hard Cider Campaign when the Democrats generally were called loco-focos. Southern leaders, then, loosely constructed the Constitution in their desire to add new slave states to the Union—they supported a Federal power to annex Texas. When that was accomplished, and there was a question of limiting slavery in new territories, the South completely reversed its position; it returned to the tightest construction of the rights of states it was possible to conceive.

President Harrison died almost at once after his election; Tyler became President; and, Southern in interest, he brought Calhoun back to Washington. He made him Secretary of State. It was John C. Calhoun who forced the annexation of Texas; and that act irrevocably split in two the Democratic party. The Democrats in the North became Whig in spirit; the Whigs in the South had to shift their allegiance to the Democrats. In other words, a Northern and a Southern party were formed. The old lines were lost in that one overwhelming division of interest.

There was not, however, an entire harmony in the South—the Whig tradition, the heritage of General Washington, was still strong. Maryland and North Carolina, Florida and Georgia and Louisiana, had large Whig majorities; they became Democratic only under the pressure of a last necessity. There was a very great opposition to secession throughout the South. There were, in reality, in the deep South, three parties—the Whigs, the Democrats and Extreme State Rights men. The planters were Whig, the people as a whole Democratic, the State Rights party was the creation of a new and fast-growing sectional consciousness. South Carolina, dominated by Mr. Calhoun, was a sole exception—it was the only state in which all classes were committed to individual liberty.

THE PILLAR OF WORDS

This, in the South, was a period of social and economic restlessness; there were continuous migrations of its people. Senator Clay alluded bitterly to the abandoned lands in the fertile valley of the Tennessee River. In actuality cotton, a crop that quickly exhausted the soil, was forcing a general movement westward. Bank systems were failing and the political situation became so unsettled that later, in Alabama alone, there were, in place of three parties, at least eight: Whig and Democrat, Bank men and Anti-Bank men, Unionists and Southern Rights Democrats, Know-Nothings and Anti-Know-Nothings. Mr. Yancey, for example, began his political career as the editor of a Union newspaper. He was an anti-nullification orator; he married a girl in South Carolina; she was rich and he became a slave owner; within a year he removed with his slaves to Alabama; and all traces of his former sentiments vanished. In Eighteen-forty he supported the Democratic party; the Hard Cider year saw him a complete advocate of State Rights. His success was instant:

At twenty-seven he was in the lower House of the Legislature of his state, at twenty-nine he was a state senator, at thirty a by-election sent him to the National Congress. His reputation as an orator was already so great that he was chosen to speak for his party upon the momentous question of annexing Texas. He replied to the attack of Clingman, who represented North Carolina; and his allusions were so acute, so personal—in the best style of the day—that Clingman demanded an explanation. He asked for the satisfaction usual among gentlemen. Mr. Yancey, who had already been one of the principals in a fatal affair, instantly agreed.

The meeting was bloodless, and—so secure was Yancey's position—the enemies of duelling in the government totally failed in their efforts to punish him: Preston King's resolution for an investigation was defeated in the House. The

Legislature of Alabama passed over the governor's veto an act relieving Mr. Yancey of the political disabilities he had automatically incurred. A religious paper, The Alabama Baptist, strongly condemned him, and Yancey's protest held stirring periods. "The laws of God, the laws of my own state, the solemn obligations due that young wife, the mother of my children, to whom you so feelingly and chastely allude, were all considered; but all yielded, as they have ever done from the earliest times to the present, to those laws which public feeling has framed, and which no one, however exalted his station, violates with impunity."

In Eighteen-forty-four he was returned to Congress; he had every encouragement for the realization of a brilliant public life; but at the end of that session he withdrew from Washington and joined himself to an active firm of Montgomery lawyers. Mr. Yancey made wholly clear his reason for this—he would never again, he said, accept a position under the government of the United States.

He continued, in the address which announced his political retirement to Alabama, with an unrestrained attack on Northern Democrats. He charged them with a blind sectional interest antagonistic to the South. "If principle," Mr. Yancey asserted, "is dearer than mere party association we will never again meet in common Democratic convention a large body of men who have vigorously opposed us." He was at last openly scornful of all compromise. With that speech the fundamental position of the South was established; the extreme possibility of its temper, secession from the Union, Mr. Yancey admitted in the controversy over the territory acquired from Mexico.

He was, in this, characteristic of his blood, of Alabama, of the qualities of his inheritance—words, oratory, were not oratory and words alone; they had the dignity, the force and danger, of expressing the exact state of his being. They

THE PILLAR OF WORDS

were not empty; rather they were charged with the gravest sincerity, the most headlong determination. The character of Mr. Yancey was both as ornate and bitter, and courageous, as his speech. He instantly sacrificed all his future in the government of the Union to go—to fly—to the support of his state. He upheld it in the South and in the North; he was indifferent to reverses and temporary neglect; he gave what was left of his life to the only course by which he considered the South might save its integrity. Its soul. To that great extent his oratory transcended sound; to that degree the elaborate graces of the South clothed a spirit of the simplest and most profound fortitude; the extravagant periods were changed into battle flags.

* *
*

William Lowndes Yancey's blood was Virginian, but his father, Benjamin C. Yancey, lived in South Carolina, where he lent brilliancy to the legal galaxy of the Palmetto State. He died, however, when William was three years old, and left little property. His son managed to secure for himself the brief advantage of a year at Williams College, then he was obliged to return to South Carolina, and at Greenville he began the study of law. Greenville lay at the foot of the Blue Ridge Mountains, where the high natural wall on the west merged into the wide prospect of the Carolina lowlands; it looked far over pastoral reaches to the Valleys of the Saluda and of the Tyger and the Catawba. It was beautiful, infinitely cooler than the coast, and rich planters with their families spent the summers there. Greenville dominated a region of sharp social, and political, contrasts—the spare habit of life and thought, the independent poverty, of the up-country met the slave-owning luxury of the cotton and indigo and rice fields.

The needs of small proprietary farms, of fractious Scotch-Irish farmers, were in constant debate with the interests of the great holders of land. The parents of Andrew Jackson came from the Catawba Valley; there were McLemores there and McCoys, Calhouns and Caldwells; and nearby, as different as possible, the politely born Earles and Perrys, the Hamptons and Butlers and Cunninghams. In Greenville the Union spirit of the mountains published its one paper, The Mountaineer.

Yancey began the study of law in the office of a Perry, but the signs of his actual concern, polemic oratory, were immediately apparent. Nullification of the Constitution was already cried aloud in South Carolina, a multiplication of meetings supported it, the state militia was practically disbanded. In opposition, the Union sentiment organized Washington Societies; they were military in form, and Yancey was captain in a mounted troop under his uncle, Robert Cunningham. His first oration was delivered at Lodi, where there was a celebration of the Declaration of Independence. He was constantly interrupted with the question, "Will you not fight for the land of your birth?" and he continually replied, "Where liberty is there is my country." If South Carolina became the advocate of anarchy, William Lowndes Yancey proceeded, he would not follow. He gazed at his audience, assembled in a meadow, and remarked the men around him, scarred and broken with age, who had been soldiers in the old war for independence. There was a prodigious supper spread under the trees, toasts were proposed and drained; Yancey rose and, in place of a conventional period, be begged to read a sentiment handed him by a lady.

"A happy and prosperous existence to our Federal Union; Union ladies wish and pray for its success; Union gentlemen should protect it and bring confusion to the councils of its enemies."

THE PILLAR OF WORDS

There was a long cheering and music; a meeting of Union men at the courthouse in Greenville made Yancey their secretary; but in the election that followed the State Rights party was victorious. It was then that Mr. H. O. Wells, proprietor of The Mountaineer, published a card. "Next week Mr. William L. Yancey will become editor of this paper. I am satisfied a large majority of subscribers will be gratified that a gentleman of Mr. Yancey's acknowledged ability, firmness, talents and attachment to our glorious Union is to occupy that relation to them." This attachment of Yancey's was, in reality, the mark of a passionate admiration for General Jackson, his love of the heroic and for heroics. He upheld it editorially and by speech with utter candor, a disregard of any possibilities to himself, with a fast-growing power of eloquence. As a result he gained the confidence and regard of the consequential men of his land.

In May, Eighteen-thirty-five, with political peace apparently restored to his state, Yancey resigned from The Mountaineer; he left, it was his belief, public life forever—at twenty-one he married Sarah Caroline, the fifth daughter of George Washington Earle and of his wife Elizabeth Robinson. The Earles were fine with pride, a handsome race of wide influence and properties in upper South Carolina, and young Yancey settled on a farm inherited by his wife, where he owned thirty-five slaves. He adopted with the ardor that was his fundamental virtue a pastoral and domestic life.

The year after his marriage, in the habit of his class, he bought cotton lands in Alabama; he spent the winters on his plantation there, with his family and slaves; but he returned to Greenville in summer. Yancey maintained a slight but continued interest in South Carolina affairs, and, early in the September of Eighteen-thirty-eight, he rode out twelve miles from Greenville to a muster of militia and political debate. A General Waddy Thompson and Judge Joseph N. Whitner were contesting an election to the lower House of Congress. The gentlemen, with the orations at an end, were gathered in coteries discussing the characters and prospects of the candidates, and a remark of Mr. Yancey's so displeased Elias Earle, a nephew of General Waddy Thompson's, that he replied with a deliberate rudeness. Elias Earle was seventeen and Yancey promptly boxed his ears. Youth, however, had no deterring effect on Elias, and he succeeded in hitting Mr. Yancey smartly and more than once with his whip. Earle was immediately restrained by the surrounding gentlemen, and Yancey spoke to him with studied moderation. He advised Elias—who was a cousin of Mrs. Yancey's—to explain all that had happened to his uncle the General. He said, "I did not intend to fight you, Elias, but only to chastise your impudence; I would rather give you Salvador than have a personal difficulty with you." Salvador was Mr. Yancey's especial and cherished saddle horse.

That was wholly satisfactory to all who had viewed the scene; General Waddy Thompson proceeded no farther with it; but Doctor Robinson M. Earle, the father of Elias and Yancey's uncle by marriage, at his first opportunity informed Mr. Yancey that in his opinion his son had acted with spirit. They were standing on the porch of a store in Greenville, and Doctor Earle proceeded to attack Yancey with part of the handle of a grain cradle. Yancey retreated step by step, facing Earle, and repeatedly warning him to guard himself. He finally arrived at the edge of the porch, the ground was three feet below him, his hat had been knocked off and his shirt ripped. There, at last, he took out a pistol and fired, hitting Doctor Earle in the left side and mortally wounding him. Dying, Robinson Earle, who was six feet high and weighed two hundred pounds, declared

THE PILLAR OF WORDS

that had Yancey not fired he could have whipped him easily.

This, when it developed that Doctor Earle was armed with both a knife and a bludgeon, did not seem improbable. Mr. Yancey was put on trial at the Circuit Court in Greenville; he remained completely calm during seventeen hours of argument. It was proved that Mr. Yancey had never before been in difficulty, that he was uniformly polite and quiet, and that he had a high sense of personal honor. The Judge, Josiah J. Evans, proceeded: "No one could believe that he had gone to that piazza with any hostile feeling toward Doctor Earle, or that he had carried there the pistol that was in his bosom for the purpose of shooting the unfortunate deceased. The court could impute to him no moral guilt. What happened seemed to be entirely accidental, and to be attributed to the angry and excited deportment of Doctor Earle." The Judge further explained that Mr. Yancey appeared to have kept the habit of wearing a pistol from his travels in the West. The verdict was manslaughter; a fine of fifteen hundred dollars was imposed together with twelve months in jail. Governor Patrick Noble remitted two-thirds of the fine and gave the prisoner his liberty.

*   *
   *

When, after his affair with Doctor Robinson Earle, Mr. Yancey returned permanently to Alabama, the Southwest was at the height of what was called the flush times. An extraordinary migration, not of the poor but of the rich, filled the roads leading out of Georgia—long trains of white-topped wagons followed by marching scores of slaves, black men and women and children. Their masters, the aristocratic proprietors of Virginia and South Carolina, rode at the heads of the processions. They established themselves again in a new and prodigally fertile land, a land watered with innumerable springs, where the hoofs of deer were dyed crimson with the wild strawberries covering the ground. Mr. Yancey had settled in Dallas County, near Cahawba, on the Alabama River; and his estate in slaves, his prospects, were at least equal to those of other young planters. His capital would produce a hundred bales of cotton and cotton was worth fifteen cents a pound.

Cahawba, lately the capital of the state, had recovered from a period of somnolent dejection. It had been built by fiat, at the juncture of the Alabama and Cahawba Rivers, and it was no sooner established than the error in its situation was plain—it lay directly on the Alabama River, it was largely enclosed by the Cahawba, and in seasons of high water its streets, the capital square, were flooded. It was, consequently, the reverse of salubrious, and it was temporarily deserted. The renewed traffic on the rivers, the new steamboats, revived it. Cahawba became the most important shipping point along the Alabama. Great warehouses and stores were built, the neglected residences repaired, countless others erected. It was the center of a rich and luxurious society; eminent men and their affairs made it the first town in Alabama.

It was, however, extremely simple—there was a single hotel of two stories, a long low colonnade; the lawyers had their offices under the roof of the courthouse; there were three bar rooms; the postoffice occupied the end of a store. The mail mainly arrived in the pockets of travellers and with the officers of the steamboats. The steamboats were a daily occurrence—the Tuscaloosa and Nashville and Wetumpka; the Lowndes—in honor of William Lowndes Yancey—and the Cherokee, named for Miss Cherokee Jemison; the Alice Vivian celebrated a famous belle; the Allen Glover and Sam Dale and the Pink Tony; the Morissette and Belle Creole and the Old Admiral. They were painted in white trimmed with gold. There were pianos and string bands of cabin boys. The cabin occupied the whole of a deck above the machinery and the cargoes of baled cotton.

The steamboats and plantation wagons—except for a railroad in the Valley of the Tennessee—were the only means of commercial transportation. The railroad was forty miles long and its cars were drawn by mules. The plantation wagons were drawn by six mules over roads solidly walled with impenetrable canebrakes. Hundreds of wagon loads of cotton came into Cahawba after the fall and winter harvest; endless stores of plantation supplies, family necessities, were loaded at the Bluff and driven into the back country. It was a peculiarity of the cotton trade that no money was locally involved—the planters consigned their bales to factors at Mobile or New Orleans; the planters themselves followed their crop to New Orleans or Mobile; and their pleasures and requirements were procured through the factors. Any credit they might have after that was turned into more slaves; they made, in their own phrase, more cotton. If a planter went into debt his factor carried the obligation, at a reasonable interest, until the next crop. It was a relationship of the utmost cordiality and confidence: the factors never lost a broad penny; the planters were safe.

That was the foundation of the society which established and surrounded Cahawba. The dwellings were spacious, they were built of squared cedar logs; the walls were papered; the floors covered with Turkey carpets; there were wide hearths of native grey limestone. Gardens were lovely in the spring with Mexican primroses and red and white Japonicas flowered through the winter. The roads were hung with Cherokee roses, starred with white Shasta daisies and yellow daisies; the fields were sweet with wild verbena and bright with ragged robins. There was both natural beauty and a cultivated luxury—no people on earth had more elaborate dinners or choicer wines, none was served by better servants or was more fashionably clothed, the world had never seen horses of a better blood—the descendants of Diomede and Glencoe and Margrave and Château Margaux. They were ridden and hunted and raced by the Goldsbys and Hunters and Spragues, the Witherses and Tayloes.

There was no hurry; time, except in its marking by the cotton crop, had no existence; there was no rigid and formal calendar of engagements and events. Visits were casual and unannounced in advance; a visit might last for a day or continue for a week; for a day or a week music and dancing and dinners and riding were uninterrupted. The planters generally were drawn from the dominant ranks of America; they were graduates of Yale and Harvard, the University of Virginia and of South Carolina College; and together they formed a bitterly proud, a truly haughty, class.

They permitted no trace, no taint, of commercialism to touch them; money had no acknowledged existence. Each plantation was complete within itself, it perfectly sustained the lives of all who depended upon it. The sale of a pound of butter, of a beef, was held to be incompatible with the hospitality of the whole region. Politics had no connection with material benefit. It was pursued with an absolute observance of personal integrity. To question the political correctness of a gentleman meant a willingness to meet him with pistols. The duel was universal; it was the staccato end to every disagreement; it alone, in Cahawba, maintained the local spirit of stainless honor. An ideal state, the perfection of human possibilities, for Mr. Yancey.

He addressed himself to his plantation with a vigorous practical mastery. Land had been high—the flush times—and he had rented his acres, but he showed every promise of solidity. When the Bank of the United States failed, with a consequent halt in industry, in addition to his planting he took editorial charge of the Cahawba Democrat and the Southern Democrat, two newspapers published in Cahawba. He had, it was apparent, given up politics, the rewards of a statesman and oratory. Mr. Yancey, however, in place of the summer visits to Greenville, had bought an hundred acres at Harrogate Spring near Wetumpka; he called his property Coosa Farm; and it was his intention to carry his family there to avoid the malaria of the freshly cleared forests about Cahawba. He was at Coosa Farm in preparation for this, the first summer of his purchase, when he was hurriedly called back to his cotton plantation.

A feud had secretly existed between his overseer and the overseer of a neighbor; the neighbor's man had poisoned the spring from which his overseer customarily drank; and Mr. Yancey's slaves, passing that way in a body, had filled their hot black skins with the fatal water. All the physicians available were called; Mr. Yancey spent hours at the bedsides of his negroes; he sent those who could recuperate to Harrogate Spring; they were disabled for a long period and the majority died. He was ruined. Yancey moved with his family to Wetumpka and took charge of the Weekly Argus; he studied law once more; the slaves that recovered he sold. He offered for sale, through the columns of the Argus, a thoroughbred mare and colt with a certified pedigree, an extra fine harness horse, and his parlor furniture. Mr. Yancey refused to take benefit of the bankrupt law; he disposed of all he possessed and completely met his various obligations.

* *
*

It was in Eighteen-forty, in February, that Mr. Yancey moved with his family to Wetumpka, and immediately following that change he was swept back into politics and the acrimonious Presidential campaign that nominated General Harrison—the Southern Whigs had battled for the nomination of Henry Clay, the Abolitionists demanded a candidate opposed to slavery; the General, and the North, were successful; and the defeat of Mr. Van Buren, a Democrat, followed. In July, after a silence of six years, Yancey spoke at a barbecue at Jackson's Grove; the following day he spoke in Autauga County; and on the third, at Drakes Cross Roads, he began his memorable series of debates—they lasted for twenty years—with Henry Washington Hilliard. Mr. Hilliard was a Whig and the leading political citizen of Montgomery, a gentleman of great learning and of the politest accomplishments—he had graduated under Doctor Thomas Cooper in South Carolina, studied law with William Campbell Preston, and then removed to Athens, Georgia. At twenty-three he was a professor at the University of Alabama; the following year he delivered an address before the General Assembly on the life of Charles Carroll of Carrollton; and in Eighteen-thirty-four he entered upon the practice of law in Montgomery. He took out, as well, license as an itinerant preacher of the Methodist Church. Mr. Hilliard spoke with great fluency and elegance; his periods were assisted by a tall and graceful and handsome person. His facts were beautifully grouped and his argument so logical that he was never forced to descend to the power of sarcasm which he was universally admitted to possess.

Mr. Yancey was not, in appearance, impressive; he was shorter than customary; his face was without striking features. His clothes were more remarkable for simplicity than for fit; his manner lacked animation and frequently showed the signs of a nervous exhaustion. He made no effort at ordinary conversation. When Yancey spoke he began with a mingled earnestness and solemnity; his exordium had an imposing slowness and formality; he proceeded, commonly, in a state of stoical suppression; but on the occasions when he gave full expression to his feeling the fury of his eloquence was memorable. Mr. Yancey, unlike Hilliard, indulged himself in a bitter vein of ridicule often intolerable to its victims. His manner, in short, except for ornate metaphor and gilded flights of fancy, was restrained. He was not, in the usual habit of his time, dramatic: McDuffie, speaking in the lower House of Congress, tore away both lapels of his blue broadcloth coat; William Mitchell Murphy, defending a client before the Marengo Circuit Court for murder, opened his case by conducting an imaginary conversation with the murdered man in hell, and, in order to hear more clearly the terrible reports of that unhappy individual—the unfortunate deceased—he laid his ear to the courtroom floor; the strained poses of Patrick Henry and the pictorial attitudes of Henry Clay were inseparable from their oratorical effects.

At the Drakes Cross Roads barbecue there was beef and mutton and poultry for the barbecue pits; there was a string band and horse racing and various sports; but at the Indian Springs barbecue in Georgia, where Mr. Yancey was invited to speak, ten thousand pounds of meats were consumed at a meal. The wagon loads of supplies extended for miles, the hills were literally covered with tents. At the tables every five hundred ladies enjoyed the company of a few soldiers from the Revolutionary War. The Democratic orations continued day and night, but with no success—on midnight the seventeenth of November the mail coach from the North brought to Montgomery the news of General Harrison's success.

In Eighteen-forty-one Mr. Yancey was elected to the lower House of the Alabama Legislature; in Eighteen-forty-two he formed the law firm of Harris and Yancey and sold the Argus. In the spring of Eighteen-forty-three he stood for the State Senate. There was a furious contest: the great Whig planters wanted an apportionment of votes based on a combined white and black census; the farmers of the hill counties wanted an unmixed white standard of count; Mr. Yancey represented the hills and he was elected by an enormous majority. In the term that followed he delivered an oratorical blast to a senator who calumniated General Jackson.

"Never, sir, was the soaring eagle in his pride of place hawked at and brought low by the mousing owl. In the heaven of his fame, bathed in the sun's glittering effulgence he still calmly makes his splendid gyrations, unscathed by the missiles of his impotent foes, and far, very far, above the reach of imbecile party malignity."

Mr. Polk, a Democrat, was elected to the Presidency of the United States; Henry Clay, nominated by the Whigs, was unsuccessful; and Yancey's political field widened. William King, a Whig and senator from Alabama, was sent by Mr. Tyler on a mission to France, and Dixon H. Lewis was appointed to fill the senatorial vacancy. Mr. Lewis was elevated from the lower House of Congress, and Mr. Yancey entered the contest for his seat. He would make, he announced, an hundred speeches—there was not a mile of railroad in the counties he was addressed to—and the opposition determined to crush him with an array of all the talent it could muster. At every meeting there were new, fresh, Whig orators; they counted on the physical difficulty of Yancey's task to defeat him; but in argument after argument he was triumphant.

He lived for months in the upper tier of Whig and Democratic counties without being put to a dollar of expense; he drank delicate sherry at the elaborate tables of planters and peach brandy with the hill farmers. Mr. Yancey was elected twice to Congress and his two canvasses didn't cost him five dollars. He was equally at ease in the luxury of the plantations and with the plainness of the up-country. However, one class then was as fortunate as the other— the hill farmers lived on great wooded commons, thick with grass for their cattle in summer and with mast in winter. There were water mills to grind the local wheat; at every fireplace there was a teck wheel to spin the warp and woof for the handloom in a back shed. Politics had no organization, no committees, paupers did not exist; the few jails were empty. The best men in debate won at the polls.

In Eighteen-forty-six, in his second term, Mr. Yancey, in the face of Northern aggression, resigned from Congress and moved to Montgomery. He returned to the practice of law, travelling the circuit on horseback, with saddle bags, thirty or forty miles from courthouse to courthouse. Each court continued through one or two weeks and all the lawyers stayed at the same available local tavern; six slept in a room and two occupied each bed. A few roads were good enough to permit driving, and Yancey became celebrated as a whip—it was his habit to proceed slowly until he was overtaken by an associate of the bar and then pass him with a stream of humorous comment at the expense of the other's slow progress. He invariably arrived at his destination, he had his papers in order, before the body of lawyers appeared.

He lived pleasantly in Montgomery, on Perry Street, where great trees, hackberries and live oaks and elms, met overhead and created a luminous green gloom. The houses on Perry Street were finely Georgian: large dwellings with wrought-iron balconies and railings; small houses of brick with classic porticoes. They were enclosed by tall wrought-iron fences and scrolled gates; and the wisteria, the honeysuckle, that grew on the verandas reached up and twined over the trees that lined the sidewalks. In spring the street was scattered with the petals of the wisteria. Mr. Yancey's place was kept in admirable order; he brought to it all that was possible of his country habit; he maintained—more for pleasure than profit—a public dairy; he was met at his gate by numbers of highly bred and carefully trained dogs.

* *
*

That year the Wilmot Proviso—actually prohibiting slavery in any of the territory acquired from Mexico—passed in the United States Congress and was carried to the Senate. This, in Eighteen-forty-six, was the actual, the formal, preliminary of war. In February, 1847, Mr. Calhoun presented his set of contrary resolutions to the Senate, the Proviso did not come up for vote there, and no action was taken upon them. In Alabama there were three conventions of protest between the May of Eighteen-forty-six and February in Eighteen-forty-seven. The first was nominally to elect a successor to Governor Martin. Mr. King had returned from his French mission and wished to return to the Senate; Dixon H. Lewis, completely delivered to Nullification, was a candidate for the same seat; Nicholas Davis was the Whig proposed for governor. Yancey supported Mr. Lewis and elected him; his selection for governor, Reuben Chapman, was successful.

During that campaign the War in Mexico—always regarded as a Democratic affair—gave the meetings and party cries a romantic excitement. The orators flung out like silk banners the names Churubusco and Vera Cruz and Resaca de la Palma. In July the friends of Mr. Hilliard arranged a monster barbecue in his honor at Mount Meigs—the Gibraltar of Whiggery in Alabama—and invited Mr. Yancey to be present. Mount Meigs was twelve miles from Mont-

THE PILLAR OF WORDS

gomery, a village built on a sandy plateau dividing the river swamp plantations and the prairie plantations, and the gathering was not only enormous but powerful and rich. Mr. Yancey, there, made the first of the great speeches that founded his approaching leadership.

A Whig Convention was planned for Montgomery early in Eighteen-forty-eight, but the Democrats assembled first, on the third of January, and Yancey wrote the Address to the Democracy of Alabama. At that time of year the roads were inconceivably bad, but forty-four of the fifty counties represented appeared in the persons of all their delegates. This, however, was only preliminary to the meeting of May. Then, following the development of a settled opposition to the Wilmot Proviso, Mr. Yancey presented the resolutions that became the Alabama Platform. At the evening session on the second day a set of resolutions was offered, but they ignored the question of squatter rights—the power of a territory itself to decide for or against slavery—and Yancey sent his written proposals to the Secretary's desk. They were read to the Convention, and Mr. Yancey, at his own request, read them again. He had scarcely begun when a Mr. Semple, who had offered an amendment to the first resolutions, interrupted him to withdraw his suggestion; within two minutes Mr. Cottrell, for the committee on resolutions, interrupted Mr. Yancey once more—the committee withdrew everything they had prepared.

That, I think, was the greatest triumph, it was the most impressive moment, of Mr. Yancey's life. The Capitol at Montgomery was filled to its whole capacity, the lobbies were solid with humanity, the galleries with perfumed and gala ladies were like parterres of flowers. The excitement, the applause, the flutter of handkerchiefs, held the immense company until after midnight. Yes, that was Mr. Yancey's supreme accomplishment; and it occurred, appropriately, in the official heart of Alabama. The capitol building was situated on a hill; its dome and portico of great columns were approached by tiers of marble steps and terraces of grass; the grounds were planted with magnolia and live oak trees; coral vines grew around the marble columns; there were honeysuckle and roses everywhere. Market Street, deep shaded with trees, swept down from the Capitol into Court Square, the center of Montgomery: the world of his people was at Mr. Yancey's feet.

It did not, however, remain there—Yancey immediately set out for the spring circuit of courts, and when he returned, in April, he found that the support, the confidence, of Democratic Alabama had fallen away from him. The State Gazette openly attacked him. It was discovered that the spirit, the eloquence, of a single valorous young man had carried Alabama far in advance of the other sections of the South. A Union sentiment, the dread of secession, rose in a troubled and indecisive opposition. Yancey entered into a period of public rebuke and private remonstrance. As the Democrats, however, became Whig in sentiment, he grew more open, more composed, upon the principle of state rights. At the Convention to nominate a President in Baltimore he persisted so far in his convictions that he withdrew, a solitary figure, discredited by his party.

The interest, the affection, with which he was viewed personally, and as an orator, showed little decline. It was proposed to hear him at a Cass meeting in Hayneville, the proposal was rejected, and word was circulated that he would speak under an oak on the square. The entire audience deserted its hall to hear him. Millard Fillmore was elected Vice-President of the United States; Congress passed a bill prohibiting slavery in California; a bill was presented to abolish the slave trade in the District of Columbia allowing both free and enslaved negroes to vote upon it; a Massachusetts resolution looked to the ending of all slavery in Washington. Mr. Yancey entered a bitter fight within his party over the election of a governor for Alabama. He was defeated and, declining a nomination for Congress, a James Lawrence Pugh was selected in his place to oppose Mr. Hilliard. A meeting of the candidates was prepared for at Mount Meigs, but Mr. Hilliard announced that he would not speak unless he could close the debate. He refused to entertain any of Mr. Pugh's counter suggestions. The next day Pugh renewed his offers without success. It was proposed, without result, to leave all arrangements to two Whigs. Then it was suggested that the candidates should not speak at all but leave the discussion for their friends. Mr. Hilliard, in his pride of oratory, objected to that. If Yancey spoke, Mr. Hilliard announced, he reserved the right of a final reply. Yancey then offered to debate with Hilliard provided neither of them referred to Pugh at all. Mr. Yancey, on these terms, agreed to limit himself to the Southern question. Hilliard would, it appeared, argue with Yancey, but he would not bind himself to refrain from the subject of Pugh. Mr. Hilliard, then, was willing to speak if each candidate had three supporters. That displeased Mr. Yancey; there was no debate; and Pugh lost the election.

The situation of the Union became darker. There was an agreement—the Compromise of Eighteen-fifty—under which Texas lost a parcel of land that was made into the Territory of New Mexico; New Mexico was to decide the question of slavery for herself and the Territory of Utah created with the same privilege. An act provided for the more scrupulous return of fugitive slaves; the slave trade in the District of Columbia was suppressed. That was all ratified by Alabama; and Yancey, now opposed to compromise of any color, organized the Southern Rights Associations; the Whigs bound themselves into Union Clubs;

and the following election was correspondingly bitter. Mr. Yancey again declined to stand for Congress; the proposal was from his associations; and they nominated John Cochran of Eufaula. Another long impassioned encounter with Hilliard began. The candidates spoke in the lower counties and Mr. Yancey and Mr. Hilliard disputed the region of the plantations. Hilliard, in agreeing to appear, had declined any joint debates; but, meeting Yancey at Union Springs, a discussion was arranged. It was to take place the following day, at Enon, and Mr. Hilliard, as customary, was to have the final word. This, however, Yancey's friends challenged, and the occasion was not realized. James Abercrombie, the Whig, was elected; the Union was still effective in Alabama; and Mr. Yancey retired for another short period of years into private life.

* *
*

The Whig influence—a Union sentiment—in Mr. Hilliard temporarily held Alabama firm against the representations of the Southern Rights party; Senator King insisted on moderation; Collier, Governor Watts and Houston, in surrounding states, were Union sympathizers; they kept the Nashville Convention from any motion of revolt and, in reality, defeated Yancey. Mr. Yancey was now the acknowledged leader of the extreme State Rights spirit. His power had once more declined but the extraordinary magic of his influence continued to grow. The political weight of Stephen A. Douglas, however, had momentarily increased. Mr. Douglas had succeeded to the leadership exercised by Henry Clay. He was the reverse of Yancey—full of bargaining and promises for the South; the doctrine of squatter sovereignty was his; the Kansas-Nebraska Bill, in Eighteen-fifty-four—the negation of all Yancey's efforts and belief—apparently accomplished what Douglas planned.

THE PILLAR OF WORDS

The Abolitionists, though, were forcing a state of Southern mind favorable to Mr. Yancey. They were helped, where Yancey was concerned, by the Free-soilers in Kansas. He devoted himself to the consummation of his hope—secession. In Eighteen-fifty-eight he wrote the communication celebrated as the scarlet letter. "No national party can save us. No sectional party can save us. If we could do as our fathers did . . . we shall fire the Southern heart, instruct the Southern mind, give confidence to each other, and at the proper moment, by one organized concerted action, we can precipitate the Cotton states into revolution." The Democrats of Alabama, now united on Mr. Yancey's Platform of Eighteen-forty-eight, sent him to the National Convention at Charleston. He had withdrawn, solitary and defeated, from the Baltimore Convention, but now the whole deep South was behind him. Douglas realized that his future was in Mr. Yancey's hands, he suggested compromise, but the delegates from the lower states would accept nothing less than the whole for which they contended. Yancey's oratory was exalted, his voice held a strange power over the assembly, and only a few votes kept his platform from acceptance. He left the hall not with the lonely follower of twelve years before but with the delegates of seven states at his heels.

He carried his speaking, his appeals, into the North, to Faneuil Hall in Boston, where he dominated a threatening uproar. "My countrymen," he said, "do not wreathe your arms around the pillars of our liberty, and, like a blind Samson, pull down that great temple on your heads as well as ours." From the moment, in return, that Mr. Yancey crossed the Ohio, his progress was an increasing triumph. He arrived in Montgomery, at home, on Monday, the fifth of November. Douglas was speaking in the city but he left that evening on the steamboat for Mobile. At dusk the people began to assemble at the Artesian Basin in the center of the city. Mr. Culp, Mr. Gaston, Mr. Phelan and Mr. Cheney, with others, formed the Committee of Arrangements. Captain Boyle, with a host of assistants, was Chief Marshal. Cannon were fired continuously; a procession with music formed, carrying transparencies of phrases from Yancey's speeches; and it moved up Perry Street to his residence. An especial committee waited on him and conducted him to a carriage drawn by four white horses. The people greeted him with a prodigious cheering.

The procession marched by a circuitous route—the city ringing with acclaim—to the corner of Perry and Market Streets; there it opened ranks and Mr. Yancey's carriage proceeded between walls of surcharged men to the new theatre. It was filled to the roof while twenty-five hundred people struggled at the doors. Justices of the Supreme Court sat on the stage, the Mayor was with them and Mr. Peachy Gilmore, Doctor Wilson, Doctor James Taylor and the Breckenridge and Lane Club. In an instant the floor of the stage was deep carpeted with the bouquets flung by ladies at Mr. Yancey. Three cheers were demanded for the greatest orator in the world. At the bank corner, in the city, the eloquent Mr. Gresham, together with others, spoke; the cannon at the Basin kept up their firing; windows and balconies were packed with spectators.

That, I am afraid, marked Mr. William Lowndes Yancey's end; he still had a part in what immediately followed: the Union spirit was not dead in northern Alabama and he fought it with an increasing arrogance of success; but, in that act, he was destroying the world he knew, the only world he could inhabit, the one that made and proclaimed his greatness. Cahawba, where he had first lived in Alabama, completely vanished—the ruin that fell upon the cotton trade brought back its old decrepitude, a flood in Eighteen-sixty-five further destroyed it, soon only a granite shaft marked where it had stood. A granite shaft where Cahawba had been ordered and a pillar of words that was Mr. Yancey. The spacious houses of squared cedar logs, the music and dancing, the blooded horses and high passions chastened with pistols, the aristocratic and extravagant, the happy, society of his youth, had reached an end. Like Mr. Yancey, like Cahawba, it would never again appear on earth. The injustice, the singing contentment and minor tragedies of slavery, was ended.

When the possibility of Mr. Lincoln's elevation to the Presidency was clear to Alabama, the Legislature decided, with scarcely a contrary vote, that it was the duty of Governor Moore to call a sovereign convention of the state within forty days. A committee of twenty-one gentlemen, secessionist in sentiment, waited upon the governor to learn his views, and he assured them that, if the Republican candidate were successful, he would summon the people of Alabama within two days. The Convention filled the hotels of Montgomery, and, while the delegates were still gathering, they learned that Governor Moore had seized the United States forts Morgan and Gaines and the Mount Vernon arsenal for the state. They heard, as well, that Associate Justice John A. Campbell of the Federal Supreme Court had personally denounced the governor's act as treason and asserted that he should be arrested.

The Convention began with extreme solemnity; the galleries and lobbies were crowded with the gentlemen and ladies of the old, the deep, South; and Mr. Yancey at once rose to move that on each day the session of the body should be opened with a prayer by Doctor Basil Manly. "Lord," Doctor Manly prayed, "of all the families of the earth, we appeal to Thee to protect us in the land Thou hast given us, the institutions Thou hast established, the rights Thou hast bestowed." Debate was opened by a resolution that would pledge Alabama not to submit or be a party to the inauguration of Abraham Lincoln as President and Hannibal Hamlin as Vice-President of the United States of America. Mr. Yancey, later, spoke for thirty minutes, his tone was violent and the Convention was thrown into a turmoil. Mr. Watts rebuked him. "This is no time for the exhibition of feeling or for the utterance of denunciation." Mr. Yancey, it was beginning to be evident, was already old-fashioned. His last triumphant journey was forgotten in the acclaim that met Mr. Davis, elected President of the Confederacy, through Chattanooga and Marietta and Atlanta to Montgomery. In February, Eighteen-sixty-one, it was Saturday, the President appeared on the balcony of the Exchange Hotel, supported by Mr. Yancey, and there Yancey, in a phrase of singular dignity and beauty, delivered his unrealized farewell to the people of Alabama. He said, turning to Mr. Davis:

"The hour and the man have met."

He died on a July afternoon, two years later, absolutely unnoticed in the general horror of death and war. Montgomery was intensely hot, the foliage was at its fullest green, but there was a breath of autumn in the air.

THE ROSE OF MISSISSIPPI

THE ROSE OF MISSISSIPPI

Varina Howell, for me she was the rose of Mississippi, was born in Natchez in the May of Eighteen-twenty-six. The Howells were Scots and Welsh and her grandmother had married an Irishman, James Kempe. The Kempes settled in Virginia before Sixteen-forty, but James removed with his young wife to the Mississippi Territory, and there he fought under Andrew Jackson. His third daughter, Margaret Louisa, married William Burr Howell—she was a great beauty and Howell was handsomely blond and tall in the tradition of his blood—and they settled in Natchez. Before his marriage, Joseph Davis, Jefferson Davis' elder brother, had tried to persuade Howell to buy land on the River forty miles below the town, in the rich alluvial bottom near The Hurricane, a Davis plantation, but William Howell preferred the lands near Natchez. His house was a large rambling dwelling, white on the high eroded Bluff, called The Briers—a tangle of Cherokee roses and bamboo bound together the magnolias and oak trees and pines that surrounded it. The Bluff was very high there; it fell away in almost perpendicular red walls to little valleys magnificent with uncut woods, bayous worn by floods sweeping far back into the low tablelands east of the Mississippi River.

William Howell was not a provident planter; but then neither was he above the help of houses, of families, intimate to him; and he lived in a region and times of extraordinary plenty. His first child was a son, Joseph; a trip into the North was undertaken in the interest of the infant's health; and the Howells visited Jefferson Davis at West Point. Jefferson was then eighteen, a cadet at the Military Academy, and he was impressed by Mrs. Howell's charm. It was after that Varina, Varina Anne Banks Howell, was born, and a black slave held her—her long white embroidered robe reached to the floor—for christening in the Old Trinity Episcopal Church. She became a vivid and strong little girl and played freely with Joseph, and subsequent smaller brothers and sisters, in the dry bayous near the River. She slid and rolled down steep declines smooth-carpeted with pine needles and magnolia leaves, and in the bottoms was engaged by robust games and ventures.

Varina's childhood—the influences and surroundings of her earliest impressionable years—was set in a vast and solemn land; the sombre immensity of the Mississippi River swept between sheer irregular bluffs and dark forests, impenetrable swamps, draped with Spanish moss. Natchez on the Bluff, tranquil and deep in trees on a wide green esplanade, was constantly filled with the carriages and horses of planters, ladies in rose-colored muslins and gentlemen in white à cheval, bearing themselves with a careless elegance. They dressed carelessly and lounged in an insolence of pride on the high Spanish pommels of their saddles. There were six streets leading from the Bluff, seven streets parallel to the River intercepted them, and the Mansion House, the principal blocks, were built of brick.

Varina's freedom of extreme youth was soon interrupted by education—she attended two terms at Madame Greenland's school for young ladies, in Philadelphia, and then came under the private instruction of a tutor, Judge George Winchester. In addition to such formal instruction her grandmother, Mrs. Kempe, repeated for her the heroic episodes of her grandfather's life in an earlier day, stories of General Jackson, and Thomas Hinds, who led Jackson's cavalry at the Battle of New Orleans. Mrs. Kempe, as well, made Varina familiar with the traditions of her family in Virginia, in Prince William County. Her time then—she was perhaps sixteen—was filled with study and a companionship appropriate to the daughter of the dominating planter class. Judge Winchester, who had come to the deep South from Salem, Massachusetts, was a learned jurist; and in his charge, Varina wrote, she studied hard to finish a course in the classics before her seventeenth year. At that age, in that society, she was considered old enough to put on long dresses and do up her hair, to appear at balls and supper parties.

She went, when she was seventeen, to a long party at the Davis plantation, The Hurricane. Varina was, at that time, mature in appearance, a seductive girl with the dark coloring of the Kempes. Her skin was ivory, pale like a tea rose, her eyes were dark and her features softly curved, she had full vividly red lips and beautiful teeth. She was vigorously graceful: already she owned the bearing that later grew into what was currently described as a haughtiness of manner. However, she was highly animated, Varina laughed a great deal and delicate flushes of color rose easily into the paleness of her cheeks. She followed with intense interest the elaborate preparations for her visit to The Hurricane—a number of seamstresses, hired for the occasion, were active in the sewing-room, a multiplication of maids was kept busy.

She went, finally, under the care of Judge Winchester, on the steamboat Magnolia, one of the most palatial boats of the era. The steamboats of that time, she found, were literally floating palaces of ease and luxury. They were larger than now and she had never seen any hotel where food was so exquisitely prepared. Fresh fruits and most beautiful flowers were sent to the captain at almost every stopping place, by the planters, to whom the boat meant ice, new books, all the luxuries New Orleans could afford. This fell at Christmas time, Varina stopped first at Diamond Place, Mrs. David McCaleb's plantation, thirteen miles north of The Hurricane, and the house was green with great clusters of holly and mistletoe gathered from the trees along the River. Mrs. McCaleb was the eldest daughter of Joseph E. Davis; the day after their arrival Judge Winchester returned to Natchez. He left her reluctantly—Winchester was unmarried—and with the caution that she was not to fall in love.

There rose, for the moment, a question of Varina's remaining at Diamond Place for the holiday season; and, while this was being discussed, a handsome and distinguished-appearing gentleman arrived on horse. He was, Varina was informed, Jefferson Davis, Mr. Joseph Davis' younger brother, and he bore a message that nothing must be allowed to stop her journey to The Hurricane. In addition she learned that he was hurrying to a political meeting at Vicksburg. Jefferson, Mr. McCaleb assured Varina, was a man of highly elevated qualities. She wrote to her mother:

"Today Uncle Joe sent by his younger brother—did you know that he had one?—an urgent invitation for me to go at once to The Hurricane. I do not know whether this Mr. Jefferson Davis is old or young. He looks both at times; but I believe he is old for from what I hear he is only two years younger than you are. He impresses me as a remarkable kind of man but of uncertain temper and has a way of taking for granted everybody agrees with him when he expresses an opinion that offends me, yet he is most agreeable and has a peculiarly sweet voice and a winning manner of asserting himself. In fact he is the kind of person I should expect to rescue me from a mad dog at any risk but to insist upon a stoical indifference to fright afterward. I do not think I shall ever like him as I do his brother Joe. Would you believe it, he is refined and cultivated and yet he is a Democrat."

The day following a Miss Mary Bradford, with a man servant, rode up to Diamond Place to conduct Varina to The Hurricane plantation. The servant led a noble horse— one of the finest in the celebrated Davis stables—with a side saddle and complete riding habit; there was a family carriage drawn by a pair of bays to fetch Varina's bags; and "all in blue unclouded weather," she remembered, "we rode over the rustling leaves through the thick trees to The Hurricane." She rode gay and free through the whispering leaves, under the shade of massive trees, calling in a young clear voice to Miss Bradford, accompanied by the carriage bearing her virginal finery, her crinolines and bracelets and ribbons and colognes.

* * *

It is difficult to dwell on Varina Howell's girlhood, in reality it is impossible to consider any stage of her active being, aside from politics. Fortunately the politics that so closely surrounded and influenced her was far more vital and engaging, intensely more personal, than what later it became. When Varina wrote amazed to her mother that Jefferson Davis, who was refined and cultivated, was yet a Democrat she simply expressed the feeling of the whole Whig aristocracy of planters. There was, then, no actual intimation of the War for Secession, no general consciousness in the deep South of the approaching attempt at separation from the Union; the planters, quite differently, after long and practically unbroken control of the government, regarded themselves, their interests and lands, as preponderant, the major part of the United States. They would not have believed that the nation could continue without them. With practically no exception the planters of Mississippi were Whigs; their paper, the National Intelligencer, was edited by a Mr. Gale and Mr. Seton, both strong Federalists—the earlier Federal party had become Whig—and only the poor and the inconsiderable upheld Mr. Jefferson's principles. Varina had heard nothing but a violent denunciation of Martin Van Buren and his rabble; the general opinions of Andrew Jackson she was familiar with were hardly more complimentary.

The Democrats were wholly abhorrent to the ladies of Mississippi; even at the height of General Jackson's popularity in the district of Natchez, after his triumph at New Orleans, feminine opinion and the leadership of Judge Winchester and of the brilliant young Mr. Prentiss kept the Whigs firm in command. The further truth was that Virginia, the ideals of Thomas Jefferson, had lost their power over the South; the feeling that slavery would, at some future time, be ended, had changed to the realization that slaves were grown too valuable for surrender. The Whigs, the traditionally aristocratic party, still, in Varina's eyes, supported that self-evident fact. But Jefferson Davis, practically alone in his class, had foreseen that ultimately the Democrats must represent his necessities and beliefs and he had attached himself to the increasing political eminence of John C. Calhoun.

Mr. Davis had already, before Varina Howell knew him, been defeated for the State Legislature. The Whigs, recognizing his inherent ability, his resemblance to Calhoun, put forward against him their most effective speakers. He had, however, equalled even Sargeant Prentiss in the grace and manner of his bearing; Jefferson Davis, it was admitted, had surpassed him in the logic and depth of his argument. Mr. Davis' democratic logic had little connection with the beginnings, the fundamental spirit, of that doctrine. It was, now, local to the lower cotton states, Georgia and Alabama, Louisiana and Mississippi. It fashioned Davis' ideas precisely as it had bred Mr. Calhoun and William Lowndes Yancey. Back of it lay the dramatic change, the improved machinery, of cotton spinning—in one period of twelve years the export of cotton had risen from two hundred thousand pounds to forty million pounds. The deep South had grown immensely rich. The result of this was evident to Varina, but, blinded by prejudice and education, she was unable to see what was clear to Mr. Davis.

Varina thought of him, however, with the very great deference then offered to any superiority of years. She thought about him, in reality, very often indeed. He was a romantic personage—after the death of his first wife, Sara Knox Taylor, he had lived in almost complete seclusion for eight years on his plantation, Brierfield; he had confined himself to the company of his brother and to his books. Then Jefferson had emerged from his retirement to take his astonishing stand with the vile Democrats. Everyone bows down before the younger brother, she told herself after a few days at The Hurricane. She had, it was plain, a great confidence in her own opinions. Varina was, in reality, unusual—a combination of personal charm and beauty with an acute intelligence. Her education had gone further than was common for young ladies of birth. Judge Winchester had early discovered that she thought for herself. Jefferson Davis was astonished when, reading aloud to Joseph and himself, she adequately translated Latin phrases into English.

She would, Joseph Davis asserted, take high rank in the world of femininity when she blossomed out and came thoroughly to herself. Jefferson, to whom he was speaking, made no reply and the elder added, "By Jove, she is as beautiful as Venus!" After a long pause Jefferson Davis said quietly, "Yes, she is beautiful and has a fine mind." Joseph liked to walk with her through his beautifully planted grounds. They picked scarlet camellias—throughout her life Varina, whenever it was possible, wore a scarlet camellia low in her hair—and he teased her about her friends the Whigs. She was never slow, never at a loss, to reply. There were other things in the National Intelligencer besides attacks on Martin Van Buren. Varina gave him the benefit of her views of the Duke of Wellington, on Lord Brougham, on London, she had command of a score of wordly topics.

Joseph Davis, an old man, was delighted with her, walking lightly by his side, dressed in a "rose-colored marino made with a corded waist and a full skirt." It was a style that set off her strong, graceful body wonderfully well. They explored everything in the plantation—the general store room, filled with boxes and bridles, saddles and guns. The guns, Varina commented, made the room like the Arsenal at Natchez. There were blankets and osenburgs, shoes and calico and pocket knives for the negroes. He pointed out to her all the aspects of his place: the heavy roof of the great house glittered in the sun with dormers; it stood in deep lawns cool with the shadow of immense forest trees brought, many of them, from Europe; the dwelling had an air of isolated and sombre grandeur. Part of it had been swept away by storms, by "the hurricane," and numerous rambling additions gave it a strange air of appropriateness to the rank luxury of vegetation that enclosed it. There were long rose gardens and arbors, peach and apple orchards, and, beyond the heavily constructed stables and cribs, green streets of white-washed cabins.

He showed her the house from the heavy and turbulent, the yellow, waters of the River; from the River the plantation was as wide and various and inhabited as a little town. They walked in the drawing-room, the tea room, and through the high-arched music room where portraits filled the walls. He showed her a painting of a thin-faced handsome man of sixty. "My father," he said. "Samuel Davis. He was a good soldier—none better, a good citizen, a good master to his negroes and the best rider in the country—looked like one of Charles' Cavaliers on horseback, like one would imagine Peveril of the Peak looked—Jefferson reminds me of him at times so much that it startles me." From the music room, Varina continues, they walked through high-panelled glass doors into the garden. Her world was thick with the golden light of late afternoon, and into it Jefferson Davis suddenly, romantically, rode. When she saw him then, she admits, she instantly thought of Wallace and Glendower and Bruce and like heroes of history.

Jefferson Davis remained at Brierfield and Varina walked with him in place of his elder brother. They rode the winding country lanes and through groves of magnolias grey with moss, by live oaks and cottonwood and gum trees. They saw the Mississippi River shining through clearings in the forest; sweeping down in an irresistible flood of great sullen waves; quiet in smoky crimson sunsets; immense and leaden and ineffably sad. Varina knew and related all the legends of the River; Jefferson Davis repeated miraculous passages from Virgil. She wore, on horseback, a long dark blue habit and a small hat with a curled plume. She managed her bay horse, selected for her with great particularity by Jefferson, with a perfection of ease. He rode Grey Medley, the horse that Federal soldiers were later to steal and present to General Grant.

* *
*

The evenings were filled by a light elegance of conversation and dialogues and reading in a more classic form. There was a great deal of rhetorical Latin. Ladies, in the widest crinolines imaginable and with towers of ornamented hair, exhibited their adroitness with French turns of speech and showed a pleasant taste in poetry. That, usually, together with the domestic engagement, made up the whole polite feminine world. But men of superior accomplishments demanded more—they required a not inconsiderable political understanding, some apprehension of philosophical systems, in addition to an indispensable charm.

Jefferson Davis was a highly-organized, a rigid and sensitive man; he was, even then, morbidly intense; and his requirements were peculiarly difficult. It was clear, however, at least to his brother Joseph, that Varina perfectly fulfilled them. Her good looks and mind, he asserted, fit her for any sphere that the man whom she married might well feel proud to reach. On the day before her departure from The Hurricane she sat through the late afternoon with Jefferson Davis in the music room. There was a fire of hickory logs on heavy brass andirons. Close beside her Davis saw that Varina had not put on what she called her sub-treasury brooch, an emblem of her Whig sympathies. That, commonly, had been the subject of humorous comment at The Hurricane, a Democratic house, but there was no politics in Jefferson Davis' sudden discovery of its absence. It was the sign of Varina's surrender to him. They became—if Jefferson secured the approval of her family—engaged. They stayed with their heads close together, lost in their planned happiness, until the sun had withdrawn from the room and dusk enveloped them.

The Howell family, Varina quickly found, not only approved of Jefferson Davis, it was delighted with him. Her mother remembered him, a handsome youth, from the long passed visit to West Point; her father, Whig and vestryman of Old Trinity Church, declared that the whole state was comparing Jefferson with Sargeant S. Prentiss. What, he rather surprisingly asked, did political parties amount to anyhow? It was the man after all. Yes, he reiterated—the complete parent—it was the man after all. Both the elder Howells now insisted that Jefferson Davis' politics was not a cause for concern. The truth was, William Howell intimated, that the Democratic party was growing daily stronger. The Whigs, he thought, but not too loudly, might not quite understand the new and rising power of the deep South. It is doubtful if Mrs. Howell ventured so far—the Whig spirit was last supported by the feminine world; it was attended with genealogical research, gilded with the identification of coats of arms; it served to distinguish the ladies of superior pretensions from what they universally called the common herd.

Varina herself went quickly through a political transformation: at first she had determined to ignore Jefferson's beliefs because she loved him; then she decided that, since his beliefs were his, she should meet them with affectionate regard; and then she adopted them, she adopted all of him, for her own. Varina, at first, was a little fearful of the opinion of her world; she was anxious to discover Judge Winchester's attitude toward Mr. Davis' convictions. But almost at once her vigorous mind and determined character, the power of love in her, killed all her questioning and doubt. From that moment until the end of her life she knew that Mr. Davis was right. The people who disagreed with him were wholly wrong. Her passionate loyalty, her absorption in the man she married, was characteristic both of Varina and of her times.

Women, then, thought themselves well lost in the men they loved and married; they made every effort to sink themselves in their husbands' personality; his necessity was theirs; his breath was their breath. In that way only, it appeared to Varina, could she be happy and justified, fulfilled.

She didn't lose her spirit, her individuality, but found it. She became, in a very real sense, one with Jefferson Davis. There was no subserviency in this; she willingly and freely accepted Jefferson's ideas; the quality of her love made that not only possible but imperative. The quality of her love, of course, was at once passionate and ordered; it was love safely contained in the formal necessities of religion and a social system. Varina's society, her world, was primarily masculine; it was founded on the agreement that men, in the abstract, were superior in strength and in mentality to women; the superiority of women was totally different— it lay in purity and fidelity, beauty and all the domestic virtues. That—at least it seemed so then—was the ideal of happiness and marriage. There was no direct competition of duties, of responsibility, and so there was no implied or actual inferiority. A man and a woman were different; singly they were incomplete; together, married, they accomplished the perfection of human relationship.

It was, then, unthinkable that Varina should continue to be a Whig when Jefferson Davis was an active Democrat. He was, through the period of their engagement, more active than ever before. He came very often to The Briers in the spring and summer of Eighteen-forty-four, he was campaigning for the nomination of elector for Polk, and his struggle against Prentiss, who represented Henry Clay, lasted into the fall. A very short while ago, indeed, Varina had regarded Mr. Clay as the noblest figure in the country! Her interest now was all Mr. Calhoun's, all Jefferson's, and she addressed herself to the problems, the growing difficulties, of Democratic power and management. Her sheer youth, her lightness of talk and spirit, left her; she grew thin, worn and intent; a grim determination—well recognized and dreaded in Southern women—settled upon her mouth.

THE ROSE OF MISSISSIPPI

Varina's love for Jefferson Davis, her anxiety in his political situation, finally overcame her, and she fell ill of a fever. When the month arrived for her wedding she was far too exhausted for that supernal ceremony. It was February, spring again; the gardens of Natchez were bright with the scarlet camellias Varina kept in her hair. Davis arrived and it was noticed in the family that at once she was better. She was almost gay. He returned soon upon that, she was almost recovered, and the date for their marriage was settled. The Reverend David Page, rector of Old Trinity Church, married them on the twenty-sixth day of February, in Eighteen-forty-five, with the simplest ceremony that could be devised. Varina was wedded at home, only a few people were present, and there was no breakfast. That caused a very wide comment and speculation in Whig society—could it have been because the Davis family were Baptists? Why, in addition, had practically no one seen Varina's trousseau?

Jefferson, on their wedding trip, took Varina to his sister's plantation in Louisiana, Locust Grove, on the Bayou Sara. His first wife had died there, and it was conceivable that Varina might have felt some private resentment; but it was clear that she didn't. She was deeply, romantically, interested in her husband's early tragic loss. Varina wrote, "We carried flowers to her grave in the family burying ground down by the garden before we left." They went from Locust Grove to Rosemont, to see Jefferson's mother. Rosemont was a wide cotton plantation; the dwelling had the columned portico, the tangle of roses and jasmine, usual in that region. Varina found the elder Mrs. Davis still beautiful at eighty-five and of a poetic temperament. Her eyes were bright, her hair was a soft brown, and her complexion as clear and white as a child's. They continued then—the main affair of their trip—on to New Orleans.

They stayed, inevitably, at the St. Charles Hotel, where there was the most elaborate bridal suite in the country. A great many fashionable people, Varina commented, but one she remembered most clearly was Mr. Wilde, the poet, whose sonnet, My Life is Like a Summer Rose, had made quite a local success. He was the uncle, she thought, of the poet and æsthete Oscar Wilde. General Gaines, at the request of some lady friends, was in full uniform. He had stern blue eyes and carried himself proudly. General Gaines indulged himself in a caustic comment at the expense of General Scott's System of Tactics. After six weeks she returned with Jefferson to Brierfield.

* *
*

Jefferson Davis had planned and built the dwelling at Brierfield, in the great tract known as Davis Bend, a simply constructed house with cat-and-clayed walls set in a grove of live oaks with the elaborate strangeness of a fig tree at each gable end. The slave quarters were nearer the plantation house than was common; Davis and John Pemberton, his body servant, had put the land into a high state of cultivation. Varina was an extraordinarily pure example of her day and situation and education—a child, in reality, who had devoted almost all her time to formal and classic books. She now entered into the domestic obligations of her existence, and they were difficult and continuous—she was, in effect, the sole mistress, the controlling moral and spiritual force, of a complete village. The very number of servants, of slaves, at once made her duties light and her responsibility serious.

Brierfield, except for the plantations beside it, was isolated from the resources, the immediate supplies, of cities—its only doctor was Jefferson, assisted by Varina, its principal nurse was Varina herself. Negroes, under slavery, were absolutely dependent on their masters; they bore, for the most part, no trace of any responsibility. They were, outside the performance of their simple unvaried tasks, helpless. Varina, in all that had to do with the house, in everything that touched the personal life of the negroes, had to depend on her own wisdom and patience and tact. Jefferson's concern was with the fields and field hands, with justice and discipline. He rode in the morning over his land, conferring with Pemberton and overseeing the planting and harvest. Varina was busy supervising the affairs of her primitive kitchen, directing the maids who washed her delicate tea china and the boys polishing her silver and cleaning the brasses.

The rooms she described to be of fair size and opening out on a paved brick gallery surrounded by latticework. It was her husband's first experience as an architect. "As he carried me over the house," she continued, "he dwelt specially on the great doors as most desirable for admitting plenty of cool air. However, when they were opened the side of the house seemed taken down. The fireplaces were very deep and looked as though they might have been built in Queen Elizabeth's time to roast a whole sheep. It was a cool house, comfortably furnished, and we passed many happy days there, enlivened by daily rides in which we indulged in many races when the road was smooth. The game was more abundant than chickens now. There were wild geese in great flocks made fat by the waste corn in the fields; and white and blue cranes adorned almost every slough, standing on one leg among the immense lily pads that yet covered the low places with lemon-colored flowers as large as coffee cups."

Great flocks of wild geese and blue cranes, immense lily pads and lemon-colored flowers! Varina had a deep affection for flowers, for plants and trees; she constantly rode over the plantation with Jefferson; and she came to know almost every individual tree and lilac bush. That was a time of happy and pastoral tranquillity; it was serene with a perfection of companionship and passionate with love. The negroes surrounded her with affectionate pride; old slaves confused her with their earlier mistress, Jefferson's first wife. It did not last. Spring was lost in summer; the crops were laid by; myrtle and star jasmine were in flower; and a renewed insistent political pressure was brought upon Jefferson Davis.

A widening recognition of his powers forced him to stand for election to the Twenty-ninth Congress, and at once there was a sharp change in the contentment of Varina's life. I could easily take the sense of her own words and make it comprehensible, simplify quotation out of existence; but, aside from all exactness, there is an acute beauty in her formal phrases, a living breath of sweetness, that it would be a fault to lose. "Then," she admitted, "I began to know the bitterness of being a politician's wife, that it meant long absences, pecuniary depletion and ruinous absenteeism, illness from exposure, misconceptions, defamation of character, everything which darkens the sunlight and contracts the happy sphere of home."

She made, however, no effort to restrain Jefferson—his life, his success, were entirely hers. Varina was a very proud girl; she became a woman proud to the point of difficulty; when the serenity of her earliest married life was over she clothed her spirit in a determination as fine as the muslins that adorned her body. Mr. Davis went to Vicksburg to introduce John C. Calhoun to a political gathering, Varina accompanied him, and her first view of Mr. Calhoun completed her allegiance to the Democratic party. The speaker was late and the audience restless. Then she saw Jefferson, tall and thin, beside Mr. Calhoun. She had never heard her husband speak publicly before; they had written his speech together and she made a fair copy of it, and they both were profoundly moved. He had asked her not to look at him, so she listened tensely to his voice: Davis proceeded slowly, insecurely; it was evidently difficult for him to remember his words; and they never formally prepared another. Dates and some names were noted on a minute square of paper. After the meeting she talked for a long while to John C. Calhoun, and a deep mutual regard began that lasted throughout their lives. The statesman sent Varina tremendous communications on government in which it was evident he felt no necessity to mitigate the difficulty of the subject for her comprehension.

Jefferson Davis had been elected to Congress and, with Varina, he continued journeying north from Vicksburg: they proceeded toward Washington by the Mississippi and Ohio Rivers to Wheeling, from Wheeling they went in a stage coach sixty-six miles over the turnpike to Pittsburgh; they left Pittsburgh by steamboat for Brownsville; and, again by stage, accomplished the seventy-two miles that lay between them and Cumberland. They took up their journey at Cumberland on a steam railroad and finally reached Baltimore; the last forty miles required near three hours by rail. It was a very rough and various trip. On the Ohio the river was filled with ice, the boat was frozen into a solid expanse, and they were forced to wait for a thaw. This was Varina's first actual contact with democracy—the common herd— and, the change in her had been so absolute, she responded to it with a gay good humor. A pilot's wife, who had been indignant at Varina's superiority, ended by giving her a paper of apricot seeds. She planted them, at Brierfield, and an apricot tree grew that Varina called The Pilot's Wife.

In Washington she was very alert; her mind, her curiosity,

was as active as her movements in society. Varina was a success at once: she carefully noted Mrs. Gaines, not then, she added, ankle deep in her great suit; the lovely Mrs. Ashleigh who afterward was Mrs. John J. Crittenden; Appollonia Jagello—a Polish heroine with a moustache and bass voice; Mrs. James Gordon Bennett; Mr. Calhoun and his family, newly moved into a house on Missouri Avenue. Mr. McDuffie, from South Carolina, Varina saw, closely resembled Mr. Calhoun but "bearing aloft a Cavalier's head, and who, like Launcelot, was not averse to dalliance for a while with pleasures of society." She doubtfully considered Judge Douglas, from the West, but Judge Woodbury of the Supreme Court impressed her immensely. He had brilliant eyes and gentle manners, and a beautiful daughter who became Mrs. Montgomery Blair. Mrs. Woodbury was well-preserved, a handsome and elegant woman, and a most amiable and charitable creature. A sentence and opinion of inexplicable feminine texture. Mr. Bedisco was the Russian Minister; he had married a school girl in Washington; and she, although scarcely more than a child, was equally admired by men and women.

*   *
*

Mr. Lincoln, Varina heard, was a member of that session of Congress. A Mr. Seddon was accompanied by his handsome bride. Colonel Dix, he became a general, was a senator from New York and one of the few members of government who possessed a house. Mr. Slidell passed through Washington on his way to Mexico; the Davises called, and the beauty of Mrs. Slidell—which was of the best Creole type—impressed them agreeably. The French empressement of her manner had an effect on Varina that was never effaced. Mr. Slidell, years older than his wife, owned features that were regularly handsome. Mr. Buchanan, then Secretary of State, came to see Varina Davis—he was tall and of fine presence and always wore a wide and immaculate white cravat, faultlessly tied. He was fair and delicate in color, his eyes, one had been seriously injured, were blue. A difficulty existed, however, in the nervous jerking of his head. His unwilling footsteps then were just upon the boundary of middle age, and a more charming man could hardly be imagined.

Varina's success swiftly increased; Washington society—except for a few individuals who resented the superiority of her bearing and the quickness of her wit—accepted her wholly. Her eyes, it was generally agreed, were her best feature, but her face had pride and beauty; it was charming with the freshness of youth. She talked for an evening with Robert Walker, the Secretary of the Treasury, Charles Ingersoll and George Dallas. No young men of this or any other day, Varina asserted, equalled them. Together they explored Byron and Wordsworth, Dante and Virgil. She knew Sam Houston and declared that he had a noble figure and handsome face. He had, in addition, a catamount skin waistcoat and ostentatiously left open his coat to show it. It was alternated with a waistcoat of scarlet. His manner was swelling and formal. When he was presented to a woman he took one step forward, bowed very low, and said, "Lady, I salute you." If she chanced to please him he took from his pocket a small snakeskin pouch and produced a wooden heart the size of a twenty-five cent piece. "Lady," he would continue, "let me give you my heart." He spent days in the Senate whittling out these hearts and he had a jeweller put rings in them.

Congress was stirred by the agitation over Texas and Jefferson Davis—who had a solid knowledge of the West—took a brilliant part in the consequent discussions. The War with Mexico became a reality, Davis was notified by Colonel James Roach, who bore the message from Vicksburg, that he had been elected to the command of the First Mississippi Regiment, and he immediately accepted that change of employment and responsibility. Jefferson and Varina Davis left Washington in June, they retraced their former passage, but the weather, the countryside, were now ideal. The rattle of the stage coach was lost in a heavy rumbling of artillery wagons. Jefferson was quick to inquire about it, and Varina had a sudden overwhelming premonition of loneliness. It was, he informed her, Duncan's Battery going down to Mexico. Jefferson was constantly preoccupied with a small book of military tactics, and, in a sudden irrepressible unhappiness—she felt quite unnecessary to him —Varina rebelled. She recovered almost at once and became part of his enthusiasm in the formations and maneuvering of soldiers. When he left Brierfield for the War, on an Arabian horse named Tartar, with a mounted body servant, Varina felt that it was like death.

She removed, while Jefferson was away, to The Hurricane, but on every day that it was possible she rode home, caring for her flowers and shrubs, watching every detail of the plantation. She began to worry about a fatality to her husband—she would never, then, have the children that were imperative to her. Varina grew thin with sharp shoulders, and eyes melancholy in large dark circles; her complexion lost its freshness; she was sallow, no longer beautiful. She imagined that she was the mother of a miraculously beautiful child, a boy. He would grow up to exactly resemble Jefferson. Varina wrote nothing of that to Mexico, fearful of distressing Mr. Davis, but her condition grew steadily worse and she was obliged to leave The Hurricane and return to Natchez and her parents. Jefferson Davis finally learned this, and, after the Battle of Monterey, where his services were distinguished, he obtained a sixty days' leave of absence—that, in the difficulties of travel, allowed him two weeks at home—and came back to Mississippi.

When he was forced to leave her again Varina was far steadier in spirit; she was fired by his stories of border warfare. His letters stayed for days warm in the bosom of her dress. Then he wrote that he had been wounded. She had a note from Thomas Crittenden praising Jefferson's valor at Buena Vista. Varina began to realize that he belonged to the nation as well as to herself. It might even be that the nation came first. She would, then, have to give him up. The world was a masculine world and her part, with all her spiritual and physical closeness to Jefferson Davis, was principally acquiescent. The last of her sheer youth, her untroubled gaiety, was gone.

When Mexico was defeated and Davis returned he was welcomed in New Orleans by Prentiss, his Whig opponent, with a speech of boundless eulogy; Jefferson Davis replied eloquently; the balconies of the city were crowded with women who threw down armfuls of yellow roses on the soldiers. Varina waited for him in Natchez, he arrived on a special boat, and a throng of people swept forward ahead of her. The crowd parted and he came forward, thin and pallid and on crutches. He was, actually, extremely ill; although, in the complete peace of Brierfield, his wound healed he was never well again. When he was once more comparatively active the governor of Mississippi, Brown, appointed Davis to fill the vacancy in the Senate created by the death of Jesse Speight. He continued to be weak; Varina was constantly troubled about him; she was far from well but she ignored that in her concern for Jefferson Davis.

He was, immediately, a conspicuous figure in the Senate; their position in Washington was now highly important. Varina brought her brother Beckett North and placed him in a school at Alexandria; her younger sister Maggie was constantly with her. National events were charged by a dangerous and explosive excitement, and Varina was intimately occupied by the public and social affairs that surrounded her. She began to assert her personality and opinions more decidedly; she dressed with an increased expensiveness. Men were drawn to her. She was, however, deeply religious; never tactful beyond the point of insincerity. Her supreme talent lay in the conduct of her marriage with Mr. Davis. They lived next to the United States Hotel; a bridge connected them with the dining room of that famous establishment. They had, appropriate to their time and position, a mess that always dined together. Governor McWillie and Mr. and Mrs. Burt of South Carolina belonged to it. The Toombses from Georgia were often present. Mr. Robert Toombs was very tall, he was very broad, he had very long black hair; and, when he was speaking, he contrived to toss it about in the manner of Danton. Varina was devoted to Alexander H. Stephens. A question rose of Jefferson's going to Cuba; General Lopez had come from Havana to beg his assistance; he conferred with Robert E. Lee, who asserted that such a venture would not be consistent with his obligations to the United States, and Lopez's representations came to nothing. That was the first meeting of Lee and Jefferson Davis and Varina. The controversies of the Thirty-first Congress increased in sectional bitterness, and when it adjourned Davis returned to the deep South for debate with the Whigs. He was, however, defeated in the next election, and he again occupied himself with the pastoral affairs of his plantation. Even in retirement the political and social fame of the Davises continued to grow; their prestige spread throughout the state. Varina, at last, was going to have a child. * *

*

Samuel Emory Davis was born at Brierfield on the last day of June, Eighteen-fifty-three, the slaves brought him their customary gifts of hens and eggs and yams, and, in the interest of their baby, Varina tried to persuade Jefferson to stay quietly on his plantation. Instead he went to the inaugural ceremonies of Franklin Pierce at Washington and accepted an invitation from the new President to become a member of his cabinet. Jefferson Davis was made Secretary of War. His family left Davis Bend again in a great stir; Pemberton had died and the plantation was put under a white overseer. They took a furnished house on Thirteenth Street, and Varina brought Beckett and Maggie again North with her. Her life in Washington was even more impressive than before; her child grew finely; she spent many placid evenings in the company of Mrs. Franklin Pierce. Varina read French and Latin, she practiced new fugues, and dominated the formal and official activities of society.

The brilliant human pattern in the kaleidoscope of Washington had changed since Jefferson Davis was in the Senate. Captain McClellan, commissioned to study warfare in the Crimea, looked even younger than he was; he blushed deeply when unexpectedly addressed and appeared to be a modest and gentle and sensible young man. Mrs. Pierce—a broken-hearted woman—was continually sick and encountered strangers with difficulty. Franklin Pierce, in Varina's opinion, combined a flawless courtesy with a gravely sincere and plain habit of speech. Professor John Le Comte impressed her favorably. He had an exquisitely beautiful wife. Varina conversed with Professor Agassiz and Doctor Pearce. She saw a little of General Scott—a grandiose man. "General Totten was an exceedingly elegant man in his deportment, and most kind-hearted and observant of all the courtesies of life, being a soldier in the scientific sense of the word." Mr. Charles Sumner was handsome and displeasing; his brilliancy, Varina Davis felt, was studied; his deference obeyed nothing better than a social policy.

The Davis house proved uncomfortable and they moved to another a few blocks away. Samuel, their son, died after a brief painful illness. For weeks Davis lost himself in work through the day and walked in bitterness of grief at night. The cries of children in the street were unsupportable to him. Varina was quiet. Soon her second child, Margaret, was born. Buchanan was elected President and the sectional difficulties were revived in Congress. Jefferson Davis was again elected to the Senate; he resigned from the cabinet in the March of Eighteen-fifty-seven and took his seat together with Douglas and Crittenden and Robert Toombs. The national tension fast increased; in the winter of Eighteen-fifty-eight party differences were so acute that they were reflected in social relationships. Varina managed to keep a cordial air in drawing-rooms of many different political colors, but it grew daily more difficult. Generally, the ordinary courtesies were wholly cast aside, public and private gatherings were rent with controversy. Jefferson was ill and Varina was again worried about him.

She developed, for the necessities of her situation, an apparently light attitude and humorous comment; she declined, it seemed, to take the declarations of either party entirely seriously. Davis contracted laryngitis, in addition, for the time, he was practically blind—he lay for two months in a darkened room, unable to speak, writing almost illegible communications on a slate. He needed, his doctors insisted, a long rest and change, and with Varina he went North for the summer; they proceeded by steamer from Baltimore to Boston, and from there to Portland in a packet boat. Varina had had a third child, Jefferson, and she was splendidly well. The faint blue circles around her eyes gave her beauty a deepened romantic interest. The Fourth of July fell when they were on shipboard, and Davis made a speech supporting the Constitutional Union; they found Portland charming; and, returning to Washington at the end of summer, Varina remained there while Jefferson Davis went on to his plantation. Varina, apparently occupied with the social calendars of her younger sister and brothers, actually was wholly delivered to the gravity of her husband's political position.

The situation in Washington became steadily worse, the deep South was torn in bitter disagreement, and Davis was caught in the local struggle. His letters to Varina were the reverse of optimistic, and when she again saw the sombre pallor of his face she knew they were confronted by an imminent and perilous dilemma. She continued, however, to attend dinners and balls; Mr. Seward, who was opposing every Democratic movement, kept up a habit of calling upon her. Varina went with Mr. Davis to the Democratic Convention at Charleston; it was Eighteen-sixty, and no one there followed its strategy with a more detailed interest or greater understanding: she watched with a cold enmity—Varina was now passionately partisan—the persistence of the Douglas faction; she was concerned at the diffuse organization, the poets and scholars, the lawyers and country gentlemen, behind Rhett and the South Carolina extremists; she was openly scornful of the failure of the Northern delegates to understand the spirit of the South.

Varina was, as usual, engaged by the stir and excitement of the crowds and events. A Mississippi delegate assured her that she was all that made the funereal Convention endurable. It entertained her when a Southern Free-soiler told her that the Convention was pied, very much pied, and not very much of anything else. When it became evident that the Douglas squatter sovereignty was lost her delight was unconcealed. John C. Breckenridge, upon his nomination, realized her ideal of a high chivalry. He said to her, "I trust I have the courage to lead a forlorn hope." He led the forlorn hope to preliminary defeat in his person, and Varina was inconsolable; she sent Breckenridge letters of bitter regret stained with her tears. Something more of her serenity departed; for the first time in her memory she found herself disliking, even actively hating, people. Her pleasure in Mr. Seward evaporated. The President, Buchanan, was pointedly indifferent to Jefferson Davis, and this served to stiffen Varina's pride of bearing; she dressed with an increasing carefulness; her manner was absolute in correctness. Beneath a mere appearance, however, her nerves were strained. She expressed her love for Davis with small emotional restraint; Varina was never, if it could be avoided, away from him. Their marriage reached a new perfection.

The Congressional representatives of Mississippi and Alabama and Florida gathered in grave consultation, and Varina was in a state of unbearable suspense. There was an enormous crowd in the Senate Chamber for the last day of that session and Varina sent a servant to hold two places; Jefferson's condition was again precarious and it was doubtful if he'd be able to speak. He did speak and, although there were many tears at his eloquence, Varina left with a sense of accumulating heavy trouble. The long suspense was over, the South was free, but she was an utterly hopeless and miserable woman. "We left Washington," she wrote, "exceedingly sorrowful and took our little children with us."

Their journey to Mississippi was turbulent; the people everywhere demanded to see Jefferson Davis, to hear him speak; and Varina was fanatical in her efforts to prevent him from overexertion. In the Alabama hills there was a scent of violets. The city of Jackson received them with a universal enthusiasm, and they proceeded immediately to Brierfield. A sense of tragedy, of loneliness, settled over Varina. The negroes crowded about the door asking for little Samuel, forgetful that he was dead. The plantation was invested with an air of neglect; the Cherokee roses had spread in a wild and unattended tangle. Jefferson Davis and Varina were in the garden, pruning a rose bush, a Glory of France, when a messenger arrived on horse from Montgomery—Mr. Davis had been elected President of the Confederate States of America.

*   *
   *

Varina knew that Jefferson Davis belonged in the military and not the civil branch of government, but she was overwhelmed by the honor that had come to him: standing later on the gallery of the plantation house she cried, "Holy, Holy, Holy, Lord God of Hosts!" Jefferson left, it was arranged for her to meet him in Montgomery, and she was swept into another hurried activity of departure. She unpacked and packed again ball dresses; the sewing-room was filled with seamstresses. Varina's love for the South grew more intense; her heart, she thought, would break with it. On her way to Montgomery she stopped at New Orleans, to see her parents. Captain Dreux, at the head of his battalion, serenaded her, but she couldn't command her voice to speak to him when he came up on her balcony. He brought her immense bouquets from his men. Her journey up the Alabama River depressed her; the Exchange Hotel, the President's temporary residence in Montgomery, was no more encouraging—their rooms were crowded with men seeking preferment, with statesmen and lawyers, congressmen and planters and merchants. There was a confusion of contrary pressures and interests and individuals—the

Honorable William C. Rives of Virginia, Pierce Butler, Butler King, William Lowndes Yancey, James M. Mason, John Preston, Steven Mallory and James Chestnut.

They moved to a house at the corner of Bibb and Lee Streets; it was filled, together with politicians, with hampers of roses. Davis went to his office at nine in the morning and returned at six completely exhausted. He slept but little. He ate practically nothing. His first Presidential message closed with the solemn protestation that the South desired peace at any sacrifice save that of honor. When the government was removed to Richmond, Davis, sick from labor and anxiety, was carried on a bed. Varina was forced to see him go without her; when, a week later, she followed, the country was filled with soldiers in butternut trousers and grey homespun coats with epaulets of yellow cotton fringe.

Richmond was an armed camp; the Spottswood Hotel—they were again in temporary quarters—was no more relieving than the Exchange in Montgomery. After the battle of the First Manassas, Varina was distraught by the growing antagonism to the President. The question of cotton, the paramount question of finance, came up and found no solutions. Davis' physical condition had improved little if at all; he was unable to eat under any excitement; and Varina gave up all entertainment except formal receptions and the most informal breakfasts. In the evening Mr. Davis could bear to see no one. The Provisional government came to an end and in February, Eighteen-sixty-two, Davis was elected President of the Confederacy. It was a morose day with a pall of cloud, pouring rains; Mr. Davis stood under an insufficient awning in the public square but the gathered and cheering people were unprotected from the weather. The President, dedicating himself to the service of the South, was so pale and emaciated that he seemed to Varina a willing victim going to his funeral pyre; she was so affected by emotion that she was obliged to offer some excuse and leave the ceremony.

The mainly passive activities of women in a state of war began—they made clothing for the soldiers and sewed together the silks of battle flags, they fed families in poverty and supported orphans, they played guitars, sang, for the wounded in tobacco warehouses turned into hospitals. The cause of the South became worse; it rapidly grew desperate. Women, like Varina, bred in an aristocratic and luxurious pride covered their worn out shoes with pieces of satin from old boxes; old faded scraps of silk were cut in strips and picked to pieces, they were carded and spun into thread, and stockings knitted from them. The only dyes were barks and copperas. Guinea wings decorated palmetto hats; goose feathers were transformed into camellias for trimmings; antique velvet jackets made their unabashed appearance; black silks, more often than not, were the remainders of old umbrella coverings. The buttons from soldiers' uniforms decorated dresses everywhere. Raspberry leaves were used for tea; persimmons and black pepper, with hickory nuts and walnuts, were put in fruit cake. The coffee was groundnuts and parched okra, often sweet potatoes. For figs there were persimmons in brown sugar. The sad little pretenses and courageous delicacies of privation.

The brief hopes raised by the Confederate successes in Eighteen-sixty-two collapsed in Eighteen-sixty-three. The victory at Fredericksburg was the only light that, for a little, stayed the advancing shadows of ruin. Shiloh was lost, Vicksburg and New Orleans fell, Gettysburg turned General Lee back from the richness, the promise, of Northern conquest. Disaster became universal; and when, in the spring of Eighteen-sixty-five, it was clear that Richmond would be invested, Jefferson Davis begged Varina to go into the deeper South. She protested bitterly against leaving him, but she obeyed his desire. Varina sold everything she could not take; Davis, who still had a little gold, reserved a five-dollar piece for himself and gave her the rest. Mr. Burton N. Harrison, President Davis' secretary, accompanied her to Charlotte, North Carolina. Rumors of fresh defeats reached Varina there: when the treasure train of the Confederacy and of the Richmond banks, escorted by Captain Parker and her brother, Jefferson Davis Howell, arrived at Charlotte, she decided to continue on with it.

At Chester, where the tracks were destroyed and further progress impossible, Varina was met by General Preston, General Hood and General Chestnut. Preston said, "We of this day have no future. Anything that a man can do I will do for you or the President." An ambulance was secured for Varina, it was overloaded, her maid was too weak for any effort, and Varina, with a cheerful baby in her arms, walked through the darkness and mud five miles into Abbeville. She reached the little church that was her destination for the night, past one o'clock; others were before her, but they were sleeping on the floor; the communion table had been kept for Varina. From there she proceeded to Washington in Georgia.

Jefferson overtook her beyond Washington; he travelled with his family for three days; then left it for the care of state papers. Near Macon he was surrounded by Union troops, secured, and taken to the Macon hotel where General Wilson had his headquarters. Davis, who thought his family would be permitted to accompany him, asked to be sent North by the greater safety of water. This was agreed to, but he was denied Varina's support. A tug boat came up to the ship in which they were confined and bore off Varina's brother; a second tug went away with Mr. Stephens, General Wheeler and Davis' private secretary; the following day a third appeared with a detachment of German soldiers.

Jefferson Davis conferred with their officer and returned to Varina. "It is true," he told her, "I must go at once." He begged her not to gratify their enemies with any signs of grief, and she said goodby to him quietly. They parted in silence. Varina watched him as he was carried away from her, standing erect and bare-headed between files of foreign soldiers, and Jefferson seemed to her a man of another and higher race.

A provost guard, with female detectives, came on the ship and searched her baggage; Varina asked permission to debark at Charleston where her sister was ill; this was refused and they left for Savannah in a half gale. Soldiers broke open and robbed her trunks. Mr. Davis, again in a precarious condition, was confined to Fortress Monroe, and Varina, with great difficulty, got a permit to see him. He was so sick it didn't seem possible to her he would live through the month. She then labored ceaselessly for the release that was later granted him. Their money was gone, the plantations at Davis Bend wasted or seized; but Varina, at last, had Jefferson Davis for her own; for the remainder of his life he was wholly in her tender and immaculate hands. She wrote, "I watch over him ceaselessly . . . twenty years difference asserts itself . . . I am in terror whenever he leaves me."

MILITARY FIGURE IN BRONZE

MILITARY FIGURE IN BRONZE

THE actuality of war between the North and South began in a totally unnecessary and blundering engagement—the reduction of Fort Sumter. The attack was skillfully planned, the Confederate batteries accurately laid, Fort Sumter was fast battered into an honorable submission, but that end had not been officially provoked by the Union government in Washington or desired by the government of the South at Montgomery. This success mocked by futility was characteristic of the whole military career of General Pierre Gustave Toutant Beauregard, newly put in command of the state troops of South Carolina.

At the end of December, Eighteen-sixty, Major Robert Anderson, commanding two companies of United States artillery at Fort Moultrie, moved his gunners into the greater security of Fort Sumter, and immediately Charleston put itself in a state of war. In January a transport steamer, the Star of the West, attempted to bring arms and supplies and reënforcements to Anderson, but the battery on Morris Island made a landing impossible. The Star of the West was driven out to sea. General Scott, for the Union, wanted to withdraw the troops from Fort Sumter. Four members of Mr. Lincoln's cabinet agreed with Mr. Seward in assuring the President that the fort could not be provisioned. Major Anderson sent word that he would require twenty thousand men for a successful defense. The full strength of the United States army was seventeen thousand. Then Washington—at that time with no will to fire the first or any other gun

— decided to ship provisions to Fort Sumter; Mr. Lincoln sent word of this to the governor of South Carolina; and General Beauregard telegraphed the formal notice to the Confederate Secretary of War.

On the tenth of April, Beauregard was ordered to demand the surrender of Sumter; if that was refused he was to proceed with its reduction by force. Major Anderson declined to withdraw, and at the same time admitted to the aides bearing Beauregard's note that if the Confederates didn't batter the fort to pieces he would be starved out in a very few days. This admission General Beauregard repeated to his government, and he was advised that the South did not desire needlessly to bombard Fort Sumter. If Major Anderson would state the time at which he would leave, Beauregard was authorized to avoid the effusion of blood. Anderson was informed of this further offer, but he felt obliged to maintain a saving condition in his reply. He would withdraw at noon of the fifteenth provided he received no supplies or further instructions from his government. This was not held to be satisfactory and at half past four, on the morning of April twelfth, Fort Johnson fired the first shell.

It was quickly followed by another from Cumming's Point; and then the circle of batteries, a ring of fire, opened upon Sumter. At seven o'clock, after a breakfast of pork and defective rice, Fort Sumter replied. It was all extravagantly useless. The actual firing had not been ordered by General Beauregard; his aides, South Carolinians, assumed that responsibility. Probably Beauregard would again have transmitted Anderson's reply to Montgomery; in no more than another day the South could have peacefully occupied Fort Sumter. Peace, however, even the slightest delay, was obnoxious to the spirit, the determination, of Charleston. South Carolina had utterly seceded from the Union. The Battery, the wharves, the balconies that overlooked the bay, the housetops, were crowded with spectators. In the generality of men and women watching the flight and explosion of shells there was a passionate enthusiasm, the sense of a too long delayed and priceless freedom; they were not only willing but eager to assume the responsibility of war; but there was a shadow and a weight on the hearts of the more thoughtful and the better informed.

General Beauregard, however, who owned a very vivid and dramatic imagination, saw in any proposed relief to Fort Sumter the menace of a naval descent on the coast of South Carolina. A number of merchant vessels, standing off the bar, waiting the result of the bombardment, took the shape of a United States fleet. Beauregard was certain that four large steamers were plainly in view. Six men-of-war were reported in the offing. The United States ship Baltic, commanding the expedition of relief, arrived off Charleston an hour and a half after the action began; she found only one warship present; another came up at seven; and the Powhatan, carrying the actual necessities of the expedition, Mr. Seward, for reasons of his own, had diverted to Florida.

All day the bombardment continued, but in the early afternoon the firing from Fort Sumter diminished; at dark it stopped completely; but through the night—it was extraordinarily thick and stormy—the Southern mortars discharged occasional shells. In the morning, Saturday, all the Confederate batteries went into action, and Sumter returned a fire directed especially upon Fort Moultrie. Soon, however, Fort Sumter was seen to be on fire—forty rounds of hot shot had been thrown into it from an eight-inch columbiad gun served by a detachment of Company B under Lieutenant Alfred Rhett. At one o'clock the Union flagstaff was shot away, but it was immediately replaced in a smoke bright with flames. That was marked by cheers from the Confederate parapets; the Southern troops cheered Major Anderson when the shots of Sumter were successful; they hooted and jeered at the United States ships of war inactive outside.

General Beauregard dispatched three aides with an offer of assistance to Anderson; he refused help; but immediately afterward a white flag was flown from Fort Sumter. The terms of surrender were honorable. "I marched out of the fort," Major Anderson reported, "Sunday afternoon the 14th instant, with colors flying and drums beating, bringing away company and private property, and saluting my flag with fifty guns." There were salutes from all the surrounding batteries; the palmetto and Confederate flags were raised simultaneously over the damaged walls of Sumter. General Beauregard, during that ceremony, did not appear—he had no wish to contribute to the embarrassment of Anderson, who, at West Point, had been his professor and his friend.

Fort Sumter was occupied, and the triumph of Confederate arms, a victory without the loss of a man on either side, celebrated in the churches of Charleston; a Te Deum was sung in the Cathedral. General Beauregard, in the orders of the day, congratulated his troops on the brilliant success which had crowned their gallantry. He proceeded with great energy in the rebuilding of Sumter: the embrasures on the upper casements were filled with fresh brick masonry and showed only narrow loopholes; a large traverse of concrete and brick was constructed to protect the barbette guns of the right face from ships; two casement howitzers were mounted at the sally-port for the defense of the quay and the pier; a telegraph connection with the city was strung by way of James Island. A system of cranks and cog wheels was invented that permitted the guns to keep their aim on moving objects and the hot shot furnaces were restored. The fort was supplied with a gas works, a bakery, a forge, a fire engine, a shoe factory, a machine for converting salt water into fresh. Beauregard organized the troops created by the State of South Carolina; at the request of Governor Pickens he made a complete reconnaissance of the coast. Jefferson Davis telegraphed him, "Thanks for your achievement and for your courtesy to the garrison of Sumter. If occasion offers tender my friendly remembrance to Major Anderson." South Carolina, by an act of legislature, gave Beauregard the privilege of educating two pupils at the military schools of the state. The Confederate Congress memorialized his skill and fortitude and courage.

* *
*

General Beauregard's family had been distinguished in a military sense for six hundred years. An ancestor, Tidor, who was called the Young, led a revolt of Welshmen against Edward the First, in Twelve hundred and ninety. It failed and Tidor escaped to France, where he was cordially received by Philip Fourth, and became part of the Court. He married Mademoiselle de Lafayette, a maid of honor to Marguerite, Philip's sister. Jacques Toutant-Beauregard, in command of a flotilla under Louis Fourteenth, decorated with the Cross of St. Louis, was the first of his blood to come to Louisiana; he remained there and married Madeleine Cartier. They had three sons, and one of them, Louis, wedded Victorine Ducros. Louis and Victorine, for their part, had a daughter and two sons; the younger married Helen Judith de Reggio, a descendant of the dukes of Reggio and Modena and the house of Este. Pierre Gustave Toutant-Beauregard was their third child.

Pierre Beauregard was born in the Parish of St. Bernard, near New Orleans, in the May of Eighteen-eighteen. He went to a primary school for politely born boys kept by

V. Debouchel—he was eight years old and had a passion for military affairs—and was then taken to New York and placed under the instruction of the Messieurs Peugnet. The Messieurs Peugnet were retired officers of the French army who had served under the magnificent Napoleon, one a captain of cavalry and the other captain in the engineers, and Pierre Beauregard's military taste was confirmed. He learned, in addition, to speak English. At sixteen he entered the Military Academy at West Point and graduated second in the Class of Eighteen-thirty-eight. The July of that year he was appointed Second Lieutenant of the corps of Engineers.

His marriages, there were two, long separated, were no less brilliant than those of his ancestors. Marie Laure Villeré, his first wife, was the daughter of Jules Villeré of Magnolia Plantations, and Perle Olivier, daughter of Colonel Charles Olivier. A Villeré, Étienne, had accompanied Iberville and de Bienville to America in Sixteen-ninety-nine. His descendant was that Governor Villeré who succeeded Claiborne in Eighteen-sixteen. Beauregard's second wife was Caroline Deslondes, one of four very lovely daughters of a celebrated Creole family.

Immediately after his early marriage the War with Mexico began, and at once Beauregard entered upon the art to which his being was addressed—together with Captain Bernard of the United States Engineers he fortified the city of Tampico. In March, Eighteen-forty-seven, he joined the expedition under Major General Scott against Mexico City. Beauregard distinguished himself at the siege of Vera Cruz, in bold tours of hazardous duty in the mountain passes of Cerro Gordo, and throughout the engagements in the Valley of Mexico. His plan for the attack of Mexico City, at first rejected by older officers, was finally adopted and resulted in victory. He was promoted to a captaincy for gallant conduct in the battles of Contreras and Churubusco, August, Eighteen-forty-seven. His bravery at the heights of Chapultepec, in September, brought him a majority.

The later difficulties and failures of his commands under the Confederacy were not due to any military fault in Beauregard, but to the circumstances of his personality and surroundings: Louisiana—forgetful of the Spanish occupation—remained French in spirit until it was finally absorbed into the United States. It was bound to the Confederacy by situation and sentiment; but its Latin traditions, its formal civilization, were foreign to the nationality and laws and temper of Missouri and Alabama, Georgia and Mississippi. Pierre Beauregard, principally French in blood, was reared upon French institutions and habits of thought and ideals. His conception of perfect glory was Napoleon. He was, accordingly, sustained with an insensate pride, a fantastic serious vanity. He regarded his birth and position and talents without an atom of compensating humor.

The deep South, a landed and slave-owning society, was at the same time peculiarly American; it had acquired its freedom too lately, Thomas Jefferson had not been long enough dead, for it to have become aristocratic at heart. A feeling of equality, of the integrity of the individual, was still strong. The American character, especially American humor, was fundamentally realistic; it was sceptical; hard circumstance colored it rather than dreams. General Washington in nothing resembled the Emperor Napoleon. Pierre Gustave Toutant Beauregard had a spirit different from the actualities around him; he never, it was clear, understood them; he remained to the end, as handsome as possible, a soldier in bronze. This was not evident in his contact with the men under him; he was—a good general—always careful of their needs; his democracy where they were concerned was easy and complete.

His difficulties were created by his attitude toward equals, toward his superiors. It was not invariably plain to his equals that he held them in equality; his superiors were permitted to doubt his allowance of their superiority. Beauregard spoke and wrote valiantly, his words had the ring of metal, the touch of formal greatness that was in him. He wrote and spoke, because of this, with frequency and with zest—he was forever addressing his troops and the Confederate Congress and Jefferson Davis. He was full of visions and elaborate plans for the immediate ending of the war, the complete destruction of the North. They were all dramatic, remarkable, and none was quite possible.

The Congress at Richmond and Mr. Davis, in return, met him with an increasing coldness; they rapidly lost confidence in him and the President's feeling, characteristically, advanced to an acute dislike. A soldier in the mould and form of the First Napoleon, in bronze, had little place in the harassed consciousness of the Confederate government. His courage and devotion were admitted, but his ability—even his proved skill in military engineering—was worse than questioned. He was, incontestably, treated very badly: at first regarded as the appropriate leader of all the Southern forces, he was ordered from command to command, from post to post, with no attention paid his dignity, his rank, or to his possibilities. Beauregard behaved, under the circumstances, remarkably well; his whole career was a struggle between his enormous pride and a conception of duty. In practically every case duty won. He went wherever he was directed, he did what he could with the material and opportunities offered him, he never failed to gild even the smallest actions with the glamour of his intense and bravely romantic visions.

In action General Beauregard was wholly calm; defeat was powerless to shake him; he undertook difficult measures

MILITARY FIGURE IN BRONZE

and issued momentous orders with a prompt clarity of mind. He led his charging troops with a brilliant bearing that swept every soldier forward with him. Beauregard, at critical moments, could even forget rhetoric; he wrote Van Dorn, who had asked for arms, "I regret I have none . . . but we will take more. Come on." His dispatches, as I have intimated, were not always so admirably restrained:

"About dark on the first calm night," he addressed a subordinate officer, "the sooner the better, I would rendezvous all my boats at the mouth of the creek in rear of Cumming's Point, Morris Island. Then I would await the proper time of night, which should not be too early nor too late, in order to take advantage of the present condition of the moon; then I would coast quietly along the beach of Morris Island to a point nearest the enemy's position where General Ripley shall station a picquet to communicate with you and show proper lights immediately after your attack to guide the return of your boats."

He was frugal, Spartan, in habit; he ate sparely—a small piece of biscuit and glass of water at supper; he completely abstained from drink in societies and at a time when drinking was universal; General Beauregard's courtesy, his correctness toward women, was as absolute as all the traditions of chivalry descended in him.

* *
*

Soon after the fall of Sumter, when Beauregard was beginning to bring South Carolina into a military order, Mr. Davis summoned him to Montgomery, and the long futile interference of government commenced. The President wished General Beauregard to support Braxton Bragg at Pensacola. He replied carefully that Bragg would resent what must appear to him as no better than interference. In addition, it was Beauregard's opinion that Fort Pickens was totally unimportant. A deputation from New Orleans begged to have General Beauregard returned to Louisiana, and, in reply, Mr. Davis sent him back to Charleston. When the government had been moved from Alabama to Richmond Beauregard was ordered to Richmond. All the stations were thronged with people waiting for the train fetching him—the hero of Fort Sumter—north; Attorney General Benjamin, and Governor Manning, of South Carolina, a volunteer aide, made addresses. At Richmond there was great enthusiasm, the carriage and four horses inevitable, it seemed, to the pomp of the Confederacy were waiting for him; but Beauregard preferred an ordinary vehicle, and proceeded with his officers directly to the Spottswood Hotel.

General Beauregard advocated a concentration of troops in northern Virginia, he sent a plan of this to Mr. Davis, and it was ignored. He suggested a junction with General Holmes and this was declined. He succeeded Bonham in command of the Southern forces at Manassas, the first of June, Eighteen-sixty-one. There was no parade of flags or music upon his arrival, he was without an imposing staff. The troops took small notice of a quiet-appearing man in an old blue uniform coat of the United States army almost entirely bare of insignia. Some soldiers from South Carolina said, "Old Bory's come." Often, on an unimpressive horse, he was seen motionless in the middle of the plains gazing in the direction of Bull Run. In clear relief at evening against the sky. He spoke to picquets briefly but easily and passed at a rapid gallop along the line, a nervous intent figure with a swift brightness of comprehension in the black eyes beneath the straight brim of a Zouave cap.

Before the battle of Manassas the South had twenty thousand volunteers under Beauregard; General Joseph E.

MILITARY FIGURE IN BRONZE

Johnston had eleven thousand more near Winchester; there were three thousand men with General Holmes at Aquia Creek; and the entire force was under the military direction of Jefferson Davis. Beauregard, through his spies in Washington, learned that the Union advance had started, he telegraphed Mr. Davis, and Johnston and Holmes were at once ordered to Manassas. General Johnston arrived on the nineteenth July, and automatically, because of his superior rank, took command, but he left the actual conduct of battle to Beauregard. An order to Ewell to advance was lost; all Sunday morning Johnston and Beauregard waited on a hill by Mitchell's Ford for the attack; they realized, finally, that it had strayed and, as a result, the Confederate left flank was in acute danger of annihilation.

General Jackson, with less than three thousand bayonets and a few companies of General Lee's disorganized command, held the South firm. General Johnston and Beauregard reached the engaged troops; Johnston, taking the colors of an Alabama regiment, called upon his men to follow him. Beauregard at a full gallop re-formed the line under furious fire. His sallow Creole face was filled with blood; his voice sounded clear and imperative above the firing.

His expression, except in battle, was composed, set; at other times it didn't, but for a slightly deepened color, exhibit any signs of emotion. He was quiet, sombre; he seemed to be waiting calmly for some expected momentous event. When he smiled—it was rare—his eyes sparkled with a sudden life, his firm muscles moved slowly, and his brilliant white teeth showed with a startling and dramatic effect under a heavy black moustache. Aside from that his face was gaunt, metallic, in a shadow of melancholy. It bore a constant dusky pallor of care and sharp responsibility and endless watching. His eyes were at once inflamed and somnolent.

He did, however, laugh at the report in Northern journals that at Manassas he continued to ride his horse after the animal's head had been blown off. "My horse was killed," he admitted, "but his head was not carried off. He was struck by a shell, which exploded at the moment when it passed under him. A splinter struck my boot, and another cut one of the arteries in the animal's body. The blood gushed out and after going fifty yards he fell dead. I then mounted a prisoner's horse—there was a map of the country in a saddle pocket—and I remember it was a small dingy horse with a white face." He was, in such things, excessively modest.

As the war progressed, and fatality and defeat multiplied, General Beauregard's face was grimmer, the muscles were drawn in a hard tension, his eyes sank more and more deeply in a slumberous waiting. His moustache, which had been so resolutely black, became grizzled like his beard, silver like his hair. It was reported, not without malice, that later in the war he was unable to procure a black dye imported from France.

At Manassas—the tributes of South Carolina repeated—Beauregard was enormously popular. His dignity mitigated an invariable reticence—no individual knew his plans, the movement of a regiment, until they were put into execution, and then the colonels alone received an explanation. His headquarters was at a small farmhouse on the Alexandria road, it had two lower rooms—the front was filled with desks, with clerks and orderlies and dispatch riders, the back room was a kitchen and place for stores. The general's room above was hung with maps of the state and surrounding country. There was a plain pine table with neatly folded dockets, a pervading air of order and coolness, of exact calculation. Hour upon hour Beauregard sat solitary over his maps and specifications and projections. In Charleston, the correspondent of the London Times remembered, the maps and plans were supported by two vases of flowers and for paper weight a little bouquet of roses, geraniums and sweet scented flowers lay on an incompleted letter.

His relations with Jefferson Davis grew steadily more difficult. The fact that at one time he allowed himself to be mentioned as a candidate for the Presidency did nothing to relieve them. Mr. Davis became extremely disagreeable. He was patronizing. He said to General Beauregard, who had complained of an improper rebuke from Benjamin, "Now, my dear sir, let me entreat you to dismiss this small matter from your mind. In the hostile masses before you, you have a subject more worthy of your contemplation." The President could be sharper. "You surely did not mean to inform me that you or your army are outside the limits of the laws." Beauregard's proposals continued to be ignored by the Confederate government: if he asked for more troops they were denied him, he was told he had enough; if he retreated he had executed that movement too soon or too late, or unskilfully. If he was absent through illness—his throat was a continual source of weakness—others were immediately given his commands.

In return he was possessed by a not unnatural but unfortunate sense of animosity. He compared Mr. Davis' policy with his own, "the passive defense of an intellect timid of risk and not at home in war, and the active defense reaching for success through enterprise and boldness." The government, he inferred, was envious of him. "Kemper quickly obtained for me some two hundred good wagons, to which number I had limited him so as not to arouse again the jealousy of the President's staff." In his biography General Beauregard was even more specific. "The President of the Confederacy, by thus persisting in these lamentable errors, lost the South her independence." He was handsomer in the smoke of Manassas. "I salute the Eighth Georgia with my hat off! History shall never forget you," he shouted.

*　　*

*

Beauregard was commissioned general on the twenty-first of July, Eighteen-sixty-one, and he immediately addressed himself to the problems of the enemy on every front. He advised coast defenses at New Orleans, Mobile, Galveston and Berwick Bay; he called attention to the exposure of Port Royal; he offered his councils to General Lovell about the river obstructions between Fort Philip and Fort Jackson. This resulted in little more than an unamiable correspondence with the War Department, and Beauregard, in the course of this, issued a challenge to the Secretary of War. He wrote The Richmond Whig directing attention to the difference between patriotism and office seeking. In November he distributed to his troops the new Confederate battle flag—a red field with a diagonal blue cross edged with white bearing white stars—from the design he had invented. Debate about the conduct of the battle of Manassas, the actions of Mr. Davis and of Beauregard, was still active in the Richmond Congress in January, Eighteen-sixty-two.

General Beauregard was concerned with the disbanding of the twelve-month volunteers; that, he reflected, would leave nothing but the rawest recruits to oppose comparative veterans of greater numbers and superior supplies of war; and he sent a detailed proposal to the Honorable Roger A. Pryor, of the Confederate House of Representatives—the governors of the states, called upon by the Secession government, were to bring the regiments in the field up to their full apportionment, reserves were to be supplied by draft.

No notice of this was taken; probably it wasn't submitted to Congress. Instead, Colonel Pryor, of the Military Committee, visited Beauregard at Centreville and proposed his removal to the Department of the West. He didn't want to be separated from the Army of the Potomac—he had organized and disciplined the greater part of it—his throat was again precarious following an operation, his friends urged him not to accept the change, but he finally fell in with the representations of necessity.

The journey to Bowling Green was a continuation of his triumphant procession through the countryside, the railroad stations were thronged, the officials of Tennessee detained him a day at Nashville for presentation to the State Legislature. Beauregard, on arrival, had an interview with General Albert Sidney Johnston; he made an effort to return to his men in Virginia; but Johnston persuaded him to remain in the West. Beauregard then recommended a concentration of troops at Fort Henry and Fort Donelson, a battle forced upon General Grant; but Johnston, unwilling to risk so much, followed the course of his own planning. Fort Henry fell and Beauregard was kept in Bowling Green by a violent inflammation of his throat, a severe cold and persistent fever. However, he telegraphed Colonel Pryor to meet him at Nashville for the purpose of reporting to the Military Committee the precise state of affairs in the West. Pryor left Richmond but, discouraged by reports of broken communications, he turned back. General Beauregard, not yet recovered, met Johnston for a conference at Edgefield; Fort Donelson surrendered; the position of the South was notably harmed.

Beauregard was settled in his conviction that the reverses to the Confederate army were the result of its passive attitude; there must, he asserted, be a resolute offensive; and he insisted on calling upon the States of Mississippi and

Alabama, Louisiana and Tennessee, for whatever men and supplies they could furnish. He would accept enlistments for ninety or even sixty days. The confused results, the tragic disappointments, of the battle of Shiloh followed. On the seventh of April, Eighteen-sixty-two, past noon, the Union left was strongly reënforced, and Braxton Bragg called for supports. Beauregard, bearing the battle flag of the Eighteenth Louisiana, led the relief in person. Colonel Augustin, an aide, protested against such exposure. "The order now," Beauregard told him, "must be follow, not go." He left the Louisiana companies with Bragg and returned to bring up a Tennessee regiment. Its flag was heavy, Beauregard was weak from illness, and he was obliged to hand it to Colonel H. E. Peyton of Virginia.

The enemy were engaged in overwhelming numbers and General Beauregard conducted a difficult and successful retreat. He carried away twenty-six stands of Union flags and colors and thirty guns; yet, although he had accomplished a variety of victory, the War Department was dissatisfied. Mr. Davis sent interrogations. Beauregard removed to Tupelo; he planned defensive works about Vicksburg; he made Forrest commander of cavalry in middle Tennessee; and then his condition again forced him to rest. He gave temporary charge of his department to Bragg, but Jefferson Davis made Bragg's position permanent. General Beauregard was removed. Braxton Bragg telegraphed him, "I have a dispatch, from the President direct, to relieve you permanently in command of this department. I envy you and am almost in despair." In July Bragg wrote to Beauregard, asking his advice; he received it in—as usual—full; Bragg didn't however, follow it; and his campaigns in Tennessee and Kentucky were disastrous.

In the restless leisure of his recuperation Beauregard followed the movements of the war with an anxious attention; he composed another elaborate plan for the immediate success of the South and sent it to the War Department; that met with the silence of inattention and, in August, he reported again for duty in the field. The usual difficulty of finding him an adequate command followed and he was at last reassigned to the defense of South Carolina and Georgia. General Beauregard arrived in Charleston on the fifteenth of September, there was a demonstration of pleasure at his return, and he assumed command on the twenty-fourth. Beauregard made an extended tour of inspection in his department and found, to his great dissatisfaction, that the exterior system of coast defenses had been abandoned. The interior lines were little better. He took up again the armament of forts and established fortifications, anchored a boom in the main channel of Charleston Harbor and changed the position of commanding heavy guns; he obstructed the mouths of the Cooper and Ashley Rivers, and established a system of flag stations along the coast that communicated with railroad substations, it was served by carriers, and provided a daily intelligence of the movement of enemy ships.

Men and materials were dangerously scarce—General Beauregard made estimates of possible batteries, of the labor required to protect the river obstructions, he made requisition for negro labor upon the earthworks about Charleston. The Secretary of War had promised to send Beauregard guns, he withdrew the order and Beauregard, in hot indignation, requested a suspension of his decision. The Secretary persisted in his refusal; the Ordnance Department declined to pay for banding the cannon. Mr. Davis added his negation, and a battery of seven-inch guns went to Mobile instead. There was every indication of an attack on Charleston, and Beauregard recalled troops from North Carolina, he improved arrangements for the concentration of men by rail. He was, in his customary inclusive manner, convinced of the usefulness of iron-clad ships, and Commodore Ingraham, Beauregard asserted, proceeded upon his suggestions. A Confederate ram disabled the Mercedita and gave chase to two Union steamboats; the Chicora set fire to the Northern Quaker City and disabled the Keystone State. The United States fleet outside Charleston retired— the blockade, for a space, was undoubtedly raised. Colonel Joseph A. Yates, from the shore, overcame the Isaac P. Smith, a Union gunboat, and added her to the Confederate defenses. General Beauregard appealed to the authorities and citizens of Charleston and Savannah:

"It has become my solemn duty to inform the authorities and citizens of Charleston and Savannah, that the movements of the enemy's fleet indicate an early land and naval attack on one or both cities, and to urge that persons unable to take active part in the struggle shall retire. Carolinians and Georgians! The hour is at hand to prove your country's cause. Let all able-bodied men, from the seaboard to the mountains, rush to arms. Be not too exacting in the choice of weapons. Pikes and scythes will do for exterminating your enemies, spades and shovels for protecting your firesides. To arms, fellow citizens! Come to share with us our danger, our brilliant success, our glorious death."

*　　　*

*

The city of Charleston occupies a point of land made by the flowing together of the Ashley and Cooper Rivers. The rivers combine and, forming Charleston Harbor, protect the city from the sea; on the north the harbor shore is the mainland and James Island bounds it on the south. The actual southern limit of the harbor is Morris Island, at Cumming's Point; Sullivan's Island, near Fort Moultrie, marks its exact northern bound. These specific islands determine the seaward entrance; they are two thousand, seven hundred yards apart; and Fort Sumter, built on a shoal, is a little inside the entrance and almost at its center. The water between Fort Sumter and Morris and James Islands is shallow, unfit for navigation; the main channel passes to the north of the fort; it is very deep there and turns south along the shore of Morris Island where it turns again, sharp to the east, and reaches the sea with eighteen feet of water on the bar.

On Sunday morning, the fifth of April Eighteen-sixty-three, Union iron-clad vessels, gunboats and transports began to arrive off Charleston for the attack General Beauregard had foreseen. They were clearly visible from Fort Sumter and could be made out by watchers on the city steeples. There was a salute and hoisting of flags in the fort. On Monday morning Rear Admiral Du Pont displayed his flag on the New Ironsides, and the armored fleet crossed the bar, prepared for an advance; it was, however, hazy, uncertain, and the day was spent sounding and marking the channel off Morris Island; the squadron lay at anchor four and a half miles south and east of Sumter. Tuesday was clear and sweet. The Confederate forts in the harbor were prepared for conflict, but Beauregard was not confident—he was facing an entirely new condition, an absolutely untried form of battle. Union troops had been landed south of James Island; his lines there were very weak; and the Stono River, below the island, commanded Charleston at the rear.

Du Pont's plan, it soon developed, was to pass the batteries on Morris Island without engaging them, and take his stations on the north and west of Fort Sumter. He waited for high water, at twenty minutes after ten, but it was not until shortly past noon that his pilots advised moving. The Weehawken, then, fouled an anchor chain on a raft attached to her bow—a guard against obstructions and torpedoes—and there was a further delay of an hour and a half. The Passaic, standing next, signalled for permission to steam ahead, but the Weehawken was clear, and the attack moved slowly forward meeting the ebb tide. It was seen, at Fort Sumter, that there was time for dinner: at half past two the long roll was sounded; the garrison, in the uniforms of dress parade, took their posts; discipline suppressed a universal cheering. The Confederate garrison flag streamed from the principal staff on the northern salient; the flag of the State of South Carolina, a blue field with a white crescent and palmetto, stood at the western angle of the gorge ramparts; the colors of the First Regiment were at the east angle. Colonel Rhett ordered a salute of thirteen guns and the regimental band played on the ramparts within hearing of the enemy. Rhett took his position on a parapet where, calmly watching the advancing fleet, he was visible from all parts of the fort.

A complete hush of nature and of expectancy enveloped the harbor; the glassy water, blue under the serene blue sky, showed only a faint swell. Behind the inner obstructions the Chicora and the Palmetto State, the Confederate ironclads, steamed deliberately up and down; the Promenade Battery, the wharves, every place of advantage on the water, were again thronged and crowded by citizens of South Carolina and soldiers intent upon the fate of Fort Sumter. The leading monitor was almost abreast of Sumter when a small cloud of white smoke rolled up from Fort Moultrie; the stillness was broken by the loud sudden report of the first gun. The range was too great for a columbiad, a smoothbored cannon; one gun from the Passaic, holding her position second of the line, was fired in reply; and then the Weehawken opened upon Sumter. The east barbette guns of the fort answered by battery at precisely three o'clock. All the guns that could be brought to bear—from Fort Moultrie, Beauregard Battery on Sullivan's Island and Bee Battery, Gregg Battery at Cumming's Point—joined with the fire of Fort Sumter.

The flag ship, New Ironsides, leading the second division of the squadron, was soon observed to hang without way in the ebb. Her bow swung dangerously from point to point; she seemed, rather than held by the tide, to be unmanageable through a lack of steam. That created a great confusion in the fleet. The line, in addition, had already been disarranged by the backing of the Weehawken and Passaic: the Weehawken had concluded not to experiment with her raft and the obstructions dead ahead. It was expected, however, that the armored frigate would move forward and bring into action her powerful broadside of seven XI-inch guns; and when, instead, she halted a mile distant and drifted still further away no one was secure in his orders or position. The New Ironsides was, actually, squarely over a large boiler torpedo anchored off Wagner Battery and connected by electric wire; Langdon Cheves, in charge of that post, tried in vain to ignite it; it would not fire but the flag ship ran into both the Catskill and the Nantucket. At twenty minutes past three she was obliged to signal the squadron to disregard her subsequent movements.

Within Fort Sumter the sound of the cannonading was terrific. A shot from the Weehawken passed over the men serving the barbette guns of the right flank and cut an exact hole in the regimental flag; another threw down a shower of bricks on the heads of men at the east angle; a third, piercing a scarp wall, set fire to the straw bedding in the soldiers quarters; still another, exploding at the water's edge, sent up a column of sea water that ruined the new uniform of Adjutant Boylston. It filled the crown of his scarlet cap. The fire in the barracks was perilous—it threatened the service of guns overhead; there were powder magazines close by. It was extinguished, though, without harm by the fire engine and hose General Beauregard had installed, served by the officer of the day, Lieutenant Charles Inglesby.

At first the firing of the fort was rapid, by battery, but as it proceeded it grew deliberate, accurate and highly effective. Where the Union fleet was concerned both the maneuvering and gunnery were defective—the defensive advantage of iron plates resulted in a loss of offensive power; the guns of the monitors, controlled by machinery, could be discharged only when the turrets revolved; often the turrets jammed and there was no possibility of fire at urgently necessary moments. The Weehawken and Patapsco were each hit more than once a minute and together they were not able to discharge that many shots through twenty minutes of intense engagement. The four vessels of the second squadron, without the flag ship, came up; the Catskill went into action followed, at ten minutes of four, by the Nantucket; the next in line, the Nahant, at four o'clock, was hotly involved with both Fort Sumter and Fort Moultrie. The Keokuk, steaming ahead of her division to a station close under the walls of Sumter, opened fire ten minutes later. The whole squadron was engaged. More than a hundred heavy cannon were in continuous fire. A smoke bright with sunlight enveloped the iron-clads. A light wind disturbed it and showed the water about the vessels torn with shot and falling in glittering fountains following the explosion of mortar shells beneath the surface. Great columns of water were rent by the flashes of Fort Sumter's fire.

*　　*

*

The monitors of the first division were quickly involved in difficulties—the Passaic was taken out of action by Captain Drayton, anchored to the eastward, for an inspection of damages; the Weehawken, with her raft, was holding back from the bars to navigation; the Patapsco ran aground, she got off, but not before she was subjected to an exact fire from the Confederate batteries. The Catskill, passing the disabled first division, lost her XV-inch gun at the third discharge. Commander John Downes took the Nahant into the hottest sector of the fight, but he fired only fifteen times before three solid shots jammed his turret and made his steering gear useless. The Nahant drifted helplessly in on the flood tide, she was at the point of destruction, when the steering gear was repaired, and Downes was able to bring her off. Her guns were useless and he was obliged to come to anchor. It was even worse on board the Keokuk —Commander Rhind knew there were serious defects in his ship's construction, but that did not prevent him from bringing her bow on to Fort Sumter, hardly more than five hundred yards distant. He received the concentrated fire of all the guns that could be brought to bear from the fort and Sullivan Island; his monitor was struck ninety times; nineteen shots pierced her hull at and below the water line; the turrets were riddled by rifle-bolts and ten-inch shot. Rhind was obliged to withdraw after thirty minutes; his escape, in his ship's condition, was miraculous; she sank at her anchorage off Morris Island early the following morning. At half past four Rear Admiral Du Pont gave the order to withdraw from action. The squadron stayed passively at their anchorage south of Morris Island for five days and then steamed slowly out to sea.

Immediately after the victory of General Beauregard's forces the Secretary of War ordered five thousand of his men to proceed to Vicksburg. Beauregard protested, explaining the imminent danger of a renewed attack; but, by way of reply, he was directed to proceed to Mobile with still another part of his troops. That, he explained, would directly invite fatality. Beauregard continued with the improvement of the Charleston defenses, he placed additional guns in Wagner Battery, on Morris Island, since the Federals, after the repulse of the iron-clads, had continued to occupy Folly Island, close by; they did more than occupy it—they built a strong fortification and a military road from the island's end to end. The Confederate mortars threw an occasional and accurate shell into the Union activities, but that was all; they didn't, the truth was, realize the importance of the operations within a thousand yards of them. The Federal engineers had secretly constructed batteries for forty-seven guns.

During this General Beauregard's forces were steadily decreased by orders from Richmond; on the seventh of April he commanded thirty thousand and forty men; on the tenth of July, Eighteen-sixty-three, he had fifteen thousand three hundred and eighteen. He had, he reported, but fifty-eight hundred and sixty-one men of all arms in the First Military District guarding the fortifications around Charleston. He protested again, with the greatest justice, against the persistent reduction of his power. When, on the tenth July, the Union masked batteries opened fire from Little Folly Island there were only nine hundred and twenty-seven men defending Morris Island. On James Island there were but twenty-nine hundred and six more.

The morning of July tenth was sultry, thick with heat; the Confederates had expected an attack, but they were overwhelmed by the weight and fury of a cannonading that lasted for three hours. The Southern guns were disabled; the casualties were heavy. The damaged batteries, however, kept up a determined fire against the flotilla advancing against them; the infantry, under Major G. W. McIver, moved forward to meet the attack at the water's edge. It was seven in the morning. The Union boats, using howitzers and supported by battery fire, landed a division led by four Connecticut companies, the Sixth Connecticut Division, and a main column with New York, Maine, New Hampshire and Pennsylvania troops. The Confederate batteries were fought to the last shot, but the smallness of their force made a retreat necessary through three miles of deep sand, under an insensate sun, to the protection of Fort Wagner. They were harassed along the beach by four monitors into the shadow of Wagner's walls.

At dawn, July eleventh, the first assault on Fort Wagner was made. It was short, desperate, and resulted in a total repulse of the Union troops. Four Federal batteries, mounting twenty-seven rifle guns, were then erected for the purpose of battering Fort Wagner before the next assault. They were supported by the floating fire of the armored squadron. In Fort Wagner, Colonel R. T. Graham was relieved by Brigadier General William B. Taliaferro, a Virginian who had served brilliantly in the campaigns of General Jackson, and moved to the First Military District of South Carolina at his own request. Taliaferro at once ordered a successful sortie. On the eighteenth, following a land and naval bombardment of extraordinary severity, lasting eleven hours, the Union made the second assault. It was stubbornly attempted but resulted in complete and disastrous failure:

A colored regiment, under Shaw, came forward on the double quick, but, meeting a streaming fire of lead at the fort ditch, it broke and fled in utter disorder, leaving its colonel dead on the parapet. Strong's advancing brigade, caught in the narrows of Morris Island, was thrown into a helpless disorder by the demoralized negroes. Maine and Pennsylvania regiments were corrupted by the panic; Strong had only the Sixth Connecticut and Forty-eighth New York regiments capable of fighting. General Strong and Colonel Chatfield, of the Sixth Connecticut, were both mortally wounded. About a hundred men of Putnam's brigade, with their leader, gained the southeast salient of the fort, and, within the shelter of a bastion, held it for more than an hour. Colonel Putnam was killed on the parapet. General Seymour, coming up to his relief, was badly wounded by grape shot. The battle lasted with a fluctuating violence for near three hours; the Union losses of men were two thousand.

On the twentieth of July a light fire from 30-pound Parrott rifles was directed upon Fort Sumter. A preliminary fire of heavier guns took place at the beginning of August. Jefferson Davis, before this, had again demanded reënforcements for other departments; Beauregard was hampered by a lack of transports; the negro labor furnished him was inadequate. At five o'clock, the morning of the seventeenth August, the first of the great Union bombardments of Fort Sumter began from Morris Island. It was extraordinarily accurate and severe. By eleven morning five hundred shots had been discharged. The fire slackened between one and two, but it was vigorously resumed and continued until dark. It was seen by Beauregard that the ruin of Sumter, a fort of brick, was assured. That night a large quantity of stores and ammunition was removed to Sullivan's Island. The second day the Union firing was heavier, the outer walls were cracked and demolished, inside the destruction was appalling. On the third day of assault the cannonading was worse still—two hundred and forty-one shots struck within the fort. Three new heavy guns were added to the Federal batteries on the fourth day; the débris of brick was fifteen feet high. The fifth day broke down the eastern scarp, great craters were opened under the traverses, parapets were demolished. At dusk General Beauregard visited and inspected the fort. On the sixth day, immediately after the opening bombardment only four guns could be worked in Fort Sumter. There was an attack by the Union iron-clads that night.

* * *

At three o'clock—the early morning was foggy in addition to the dark—five monitors under Dahlgren anchored within eight hundred yards of Fort Sumter and opened fire. The first shell struck and killed a sentinel on the west wall, and his sudden screams were audible on board the iron-clads. There was a severe bombardment, fifty shots and shells; three were placed with great accuracy close to a powder magazine; another burst above an ordnance storeroom where there were three hundred loaded shells, and Colonel Rhett ordered them to be rolled down into the water. Lieutenant Iredell Jones and Lieutenant Grimball accomplished this. The surrounding Confederate forts fired at the monitors; Sumter could manage only six shots from two guns—a XI-inch Dahlgren recovered from the sunken Keokuk and a ten-inch columbiad. They were the last fired in battle from the destroyed fort.

The bombardment from the land batteries was resumed before dawn on the seventh day of attack. At two o'clock in the afternoon a shell threw down a mass of brick and mortar on the officers' mess, and Colonel Rhett's knife was broken in his hand. An adjutant was badly hurt, some lieutenants, an ordnance officer and an orderly entering the room were wounded. The firing stopped early in the evening. The night was spent in the labor of shipping more powder and stores to a safer place.

On the night of August twenty-first fire opened on the

city of Charleston, from the Marsh Battery, nearly five miles distant, with the 8-inch Parrott gun the Confederates came quickly to recognize and called the Swamp Angel.

The first massed attack on Fort Sumter reached a pause the twenty-third of August. The second period, beginning on the morning of the twenty-fourth, lasted nine days. A 300-pound Parrott rifle that threw fifteen thousand pounds of metal had been added to the breaching batteries. One shot from it equalled in destruction two or three days' firing by the hundred and two hundred pound rifles. A conference, ordered by General Beauregard, was held in the fort with Colonel Gilmer, chief engineer of bureau, and Lieutenant Colonel Harris and the junior commanding officers of Sumter. The engineers, on their return, advised Beauregard that it should be held to the last extremity. "There are," they continued, "many elements of defense within the fort in its present shattered condition which if properly used may enable a resolute garrison to hold it for many days."

The garrison as well as the working force labored at night in the removal of stores of war. It was, under fire, with the treacherous ruined footings of the fort, as arduous as it was dangerous, but more than fifty-six thousand pounds of powder, and great stores of loaded and unloaded shells, were transferred to more secure points. General Beauregard made inquiry about the dismounted and inoperative guns—they were buried in fallen masonry, in the splintered wood of the carriages, in the iron of the platforms; but John Fraser Mathewes, assistant engineer, with a number of picked men at night, managed to get down from the parapet to a bed of sand bags on the water's edge two of the heaviest guns in the fort. They were floated away the following night. For six months Mathewes successfully removed great rifles and mortars through crumbling débris, over walls of ruins with a sheer drop of forty feet to the rafts rising and falling on the tide, against the slippery rock, below.

The strain of sixteen days' continuous bombardment, without any hope of reply, brought the garrison of Fort Sumter to an exhaustion that demanded relief. Colonel Rhett and the first regiment of South Carolina artillery were slowly withdrawn; the fort was converted into an infantry post. Major Stephen Elliott was put in command. "You are," Beauregard addressed him, "to be sent to a fort deprived of all offensive capacity, and having but one gun, a thirty-two pounder, with which to salute its flag, morning and evening. But that fort is Fort Sumter, the key to the entrance to this harbor. It must be held to the bitter end; not with artillery, as heretofore, but with infantry alone; and there can be no hope of reënforcements. Are you willing to take the command upon such terms?" Major Elliott said:

"Issue the order, General. I will obey it."

Following this Jefferson Davis visited Savannah and then Charleston. He made no mention whatever of the officers in charge of the Charleston works. He gave them no praise.

On September fifth a terrific cannon fire was opened on the Confederate Fort Wagner; the fort was soon reduced to a dazed silence—four thousand rifle projectiles and mortar and naval shells fell upon it—and its nine hundred men were crowded into the limited suffocating space of the bombproof and behind low sand hills. A Federal boat attack, at night, at the rear of Fort Wagner, was repulsed. A second attempt upon Cumming's Point advanced in twenty barges. Captain Lesesne calmly waited until they were within a hundred yards of shore and then opened fire with a ten-inch gun and howitzers. The enemy replied with boat-howitzers and muskets; a few succeeded in landing but they were immediately driven back. A great calcium light was directed upon Fort Wagner to prevent repairs to the walls at night. Union sappers pushed forward to the flank of the fort's eastern side, they entered the ditch at ten o'clock the night of September sixth, and it was at once realized that Fort Wagner must be abandoned. Served only by a few depleted companies of men, it had withstood a massed attack from land and sea for fifty-eight days. The Federal forces gained an empty island and a useless victory.

Beauregard's decision to hold Fort Sumter, even if it were no better than an infantry post, was received with acclaim by South Carolina. Major Elliott had made his attitude clear; and, after the retreat from Morris Island, when Rear Admiral Dahlgren sent a flag of truce and demand for the surrender of Sumter, he was equally firm:

"Inform Admiral Dahlgren that he may have Fort Sumter when he can take it and hold it."

An attack, Elliott was convinced, was in preparation on the eighth September, and he ordered from the city a full complement of hand-grenades and fire-balls. He placed Captain Hopkins with forty-three men in the ruined gorge, protecting a slope from the water; Captain Lord, with forty-two men, was stationed in the southwest angle; Lieutenant Saltus with a small detachment lay in support; Lieutenant Harris with twenty-five men was placed at the left of the sea-face. An hour past midnight a sentinel showed Elliott, who was on lookout, two lines of barges advancing upon the northeast and southeast angles of the fort. Elliott ordered the sentinels not to fire. His men under Captain Hopkins waited along the broken parapet. A division of boats came smartly forward and they were landing sailors when the Confederates opened the engagement with rifles and hand-grenades. Marines in the outer barges replied; the sailors, shooting ineffectively with revolvers, were driven to refuge in the breaches and débris at the foot of the wall. They were dislodged by grenades and fire-balls and bricks thrown from the parapet. The Southern batteries on James and Sullivan's Islands, the iron-clad Chicora, guided by the rim of fire on the seaward face of Fort Sumter, filled the water there with shot, grape, canister and shell, and the assaulting force withdrew in confusion. None of the defenders of Fort Sumter was wounded; six of the assaulting force were killed, two officers and seventeen men wounded, ten officers and ninety-two men, and five launches, were captured and sent into Charleston.

* * *

There was no cessation in the attack upon Fort Sumter until December, Eighteen-sixty-three. On the sixth—the first time for forty-one days—no shots were fired against it. There had been a second great bombardment, and a third. After a defense of incorruptible faithfulness and courage, of almost utter exhaustion, General Beauregard was forced to withdraw the Southern forces on the eighteenth of February, Eighteen-sixty-four; Charleston was never conquered; but his difficulties with the War Department continued. He could scarcely secure the men absolutely needed for the defense of Florida; while he was at Camp Milton his cavalry were withdrawn from South Carolina and Georgia and he was forced to return hastily to Charleston. There he received the announcement of his wife's death in New Orleans; and, when he returned from Louisiana, in reply to a telegram asking for leave of absence —he was again ill—he was requested to assist Lee in the defense of Richmond.

At Drury's Bluff, close beside Richmond, Beauregard conceived another plan—this was to make possible the crushing of Grant's and Butler's armies; he submitted it to General Bragg; Bragg approved it but required Mr. Davis' consent before moving. This, Jefferson Davis, after a visit to Drury's Bluff, refused. But Beauregard in the battle that followed was victorious; Butler's army was driven back and surrounded. The Confederate success would have been brilliant, complete, if General Whiting had obeyed his orders. Whiting, General Wise reported, was drunk—his request to be relieved of his command was allowed. A confusion of misunderstandings, wilful or singularly unfortunate, followed: General Beauregard, in command at Petersburg, repulsed the assault of three Federal corps; at that time, the first general commissioned by the Confederate government, there were only two divisions, less than ten thousand men, under him; Lee arrived, he became familiar with his position, and again Beauregard was returned to an inferior activity.

He was ordered to Charleston to investigate a difficulty between General Ripley and General Jones; he had an interview with Mr. Davis at Augusta; and he was detailed to General Hood in the Department of the West. Nothing was accomplished there but disagreements with Hood—Hood was deliberate, Beauregard thought procrastinating, and Beauregard demanded swift advances, aggression, battle. After heavy Confederate losses before Franklin he struggled to secure reënforcements from the trans-Mississippi; he failed; and, in the December of Eighteen-sixty-four, Beauregard was once more in Charleston. He insisted on what, in all propriety, should be assigned to him, and—for the first time—he received it. He was given command of the West. Beauregard inspected the military works at Mobile, he left hurriedly for Augusta at the rumor of a Union advance, he moved from place to place in the vast field of his responsibility. February, Eighteen sixty-five he was again in the East, he advised concentration on Columbia, South Carolina, a retreat from the seacoast and outer cities.

He was obliged to withdraw from Columbia; he proceeded to Ridgeway, to White Oak, and then to Charlotte; it was impossible, with his few troops, to oppose the advance of Sherman. On the first of April, General Lee directed him to assume command of all western Virginia and North Carolina troops within reach. Jefferson Davis summoned him for conference at Danville, he was departing when he learned that Lee had surrendered. A telegram arrived from the government. "The President started for Greensboro at 10 h. this evening and would be glad to see you on his arrival. Please give me every information about raiders. Are Greensboro and road now safe?"

General Beauregard's movements were so diverse that he had established his headquarters in a box car; he had, in reality, three box cars—one was his office, bedroom and dining room, the second held the mobile part of his staff, the third stabled his horses. In Greensboro the cars were put on a side track, and, early of the morning, he was informed that the President's train, the cabinet and government officers, were close beside him. The President, the cabinet, were extraordinarily cordial; Mr. Davis, to Beauregard's amazement, had a visionary hope of continuing the struggle against the North. General Johnston and Beauregard, after the President's flight, assumed what burden remained; Johnston arranged with General Sherman terms of submission; Beauregard completed his last official duties and turned to his home on the last day of April.

He collected, at Greensboro, all the Louisiana soldiers on detached duty—there were about twenty—and they departed for New Orleans together. They travelled, with only a few small pieces of silver, by rail, by horseback, and on foot. Lieutenant Chisolm, who had an ingenious and resourceful mind, suggested that they commandeer a wagon, stock it with tobacco and nails, twine and thread, the necessities of country people, and give them in exchange for their own requirements on the road. They secured their supplies from a quartermaster who had been ordered to distribute whatever remained among the troops and moved slowly South. The journey—it was impossible to conceal the identity of Beauregard—was a triumphant progress. The wagon proceeded from Atlanta to West Point, from Montgomery to Mobile. General Beauregard took passage by steamboat for New Orleans and landed at the Pontchartrain end of the new canal on the shell road, five miles from the city. A great throng of people, he was informed, was waiting to see him; he tried to avoid them, to reach his dwelling by inconspicuous ways; but he was only partly successful: men and women and children surrounded his horse; they all reached up to shake his hand. He could say nothing and came into his house at sunset.

The Charleston that General Beauregard had faithfully and victoriously defended was empty and dark, the shutters of the houses were closed, the rooms overlooking the streets abandoned. The women of Charleston labored to give their dwellings, the mansions of the happy past, an appearance of dreariness and desertion, to save them from the rapacity of disorganization. This was not always successful: a negro company of Michigan troops, with a negro in command, smashed the locked gate of the Cunningham house, they tore up the flowers of the garden and, drunk with liquor and malice and power, streamed plundering through the rooms. It was noon and their bayonets glittered in the sunlight. Depressed and gaunt, war-spent, soldiers, returned cautiously to the city; window blinds on the streets were raised no more than an inch by watchful women; questions were asked and answered in muted tones.

On the night General Beauregard withdrew the defense of Charleston a gunboat burning at the head of Columbus Street, the burning bridge of the Savannah Railroad, struck the upper part of the city, the clouded sky, with a fitful and sullen red glow. At seven in the morning the last of the troops stationed at James Island departed with a firm and echoing tread. Only women were left—on their way to the commissary stores a terrific explosion shook the city and drove them into a blind panic. There was another and heavier explosion, its smoke darkened the sun—the Northeastern Railway depot had been blown up! The bodies of hungry women searching there for provisions were buried deep under the ruin. Old negroes became insane with fright. The steeples of Charleston were empty of their bells, the bells had been melted for General Beauregard's cannon.

THE LONELY STAR

THE LONELY STAR

THERE is no more immediate way to explain Albert Sidney Johnston than to say that, within the interrupted span of his being, his character and attainments were not inferior to those of General Lee. He lived, however, and he died under a lonely and dark star—the sign of an early harassed Texas which ultimately became its symbol in the United States. General Johnston, a rare combination, was both a sensitive and courageous man; a man of reflection and action; his life was continually troubled, broken into fragments without coherence or, to him, promise; he firmly met, as it occurred, each responsibility, each disappointment faintly colored by humiliation; but through long periods of inaction, of isolation, he submerged himself in sombre thought. His feelings were singularly warm and human; he was capable, as he was capable of fortitude, of deep attachments. His love, like his public life, lay in shadow: it too was overcome very early by death.

He was born in Kentucky, in Washington, Mason County, the February of Eighteen hundred and three. His father was a doctor, Doctor John Johnston, an early settler; his grandfather—descended from a Scots family of influence and property—was a native of Salisbury, Connecticut. John was educated at New Haven, he studied medicine in Litchfield, and began its practice in Connecticut. In Seventeen-eighty-three he married Mary Stoddard and they had three sons—Josiah, Darius and Orramel. They removed soon after their marriage to Kentucky, and in Seventeen-ninety-three Mary

Johnston died. The following year Doctor Johnston married Abigail Harris, the daughter of an older settler who had emigrated from Newburyport, Massachusetts. They had six children, John Harris, Lucius, Anna Maria, Clarissa, Albert Sidney and Eliza. Abigail Johnston died after twelve years of marriage, and the doctor wedded for the third time, to a Mrs. Byers, but without children. Doctor Johnston was blunt, energetic and independent; he gave all his children a proper education; he labored diligently at his profession but, redeeming debts for which he had become security, poverty made his old age difficult. Albert Sidney's mother, like a great many pioneer women, was quiet and gentle; she was remembered to have been handsome, with a naturally fine mind; but she died too soon to give her young family the support of her qualities and influence.

Albert Sidney was reared in the hard simplicity that marked the early years of so many contemporary notable men. He went to school to James Grant, a mile and a half from Washington; he did well enough in his classes; better than well at mathematics; his Saturdays he spent hunting in the Kentucky woods and beside the Kentucky rivers. The knowledge and resources of James Grant soon failed to satisfy him, and he persuaded his father to send him to a school in West Virginia. That turned out to be no improvement upon his earlier instruction; he stayed for only one session and then entered the drug store kept by a Thomas Dume. He went to Transylvania University, at Lexington, Kentucky, an institution of learning picturesquely situated at the edge of the Wilderness, and studied diligently; but he left there too at the end of his first session. He was restless from a desire to go into the navy:

The gallantry of the war on the sea with England, the daring of Stephen Decatur at Tripoli, made any civil life to appear unbearably dull. Two of his close friends were awarded warrants as midshipmen; but Albert Sidney's family objected to that especial form of glory; instead it was proposed for him to accompany a married sister who was journeying to Louisiana. He went with her—it was the fall of Eighteen-nineteen—to the Parish of Rapides; he visited his brother, Josiah, there; and Josiah managed to shift his interest from the sea to the land. As a result of this influence he returned to Transylvania University and remained for two years. His preference was still mathematics, he succeeded moderately well in the natural sciences, and, with hard study, became sufficiently acquainted with classic antiquities. His great desire now was to be a soldier; Josiah agreed with that ambition—he had become a member of Congress from Louisiana—and he procured an appointment for Albert Sidney to West Point.

He was, there, universally esteemed—Johnston was made sergeant major of cadets and afterward selected by the commandant for the position of adjutant, then the most coveted office in the corps. It was a highly romantic age—the struggles of South American republics for independence, the revolt in Greece against Turkish tyranny, the poetry of Byron and the eloquence of Henry Clay, were all reflected in the feelings and opinions of the young men at West Point. Albert Sidney Johnston was offered commands by the agents of revolutionary governments; they spread before him visions of honor peculiarly hard for him to resist; he did, however, resist them; and when he graduated, in Eighteen-twenty-six, his high rank entitled him to enter the arm of the service he preferred. There was then no cavalry corps, the artillery was stationary on the seaboard, and, since the infantry was in active employment on the frontier, he chose the infantry.

The years immediately following were without incident. He visited his brother Josiah—who had been elevated to the National Senate—at the capital. Josiah was a man of importance, he was at once intimate with Henry Clay and a supporter of the Adams' administration; he enjoyed the cordiality of both political worlds; and Albert Sidney Johnston entered a brilliant and intellectual society—he became familiar with Mr. Clay and Calhoun, Daniel Webster and Benton and Everett and Scott. His manner and appearance were equally agreeable; he was successful at the White House and the Clays' and in a gayer Washington life; but he didn't like society even at its best; he wanted only to return to active service. General Scott went so far as to offer to make him his aide-de-camp, a position that must be followed by swift promotion, but Lieutenant Johnston refused. Although, he said, much gratified to have been mentioned by General Scott, he felt that a life of inactivity in a large city did not accord with his views, that he preferred to be off to the far West and enter at once upon the duties of his profession. Josiah regretted his decision, but he did nothing to oppose it; Scott for a generation regarded Albert Sidney Johnston with a studied coldness.

He left Washington—it was thirty years before he returned to its self-seeking officialism—and proceeded directly to Sackett's Harbor on Lake Ontario. The President, John Adams, signed his commission in April, Eighteen-twenty-seven, attaching him to the Sixth Regiment of infantry, under Brevet Brigadier General Henry Atkinson. It was a celebrated command, stationed at Jefferson Barracks, nine miles below St. Louis on the Mississippi River, and Lieutenant Johnston reported there with great pleasure. Jefferson Barracks was important since it allowed a rapid transportation of troops to any position in the West, and in addition it was naturally beautiful—the barracks occupied land rising gradually to an impressive bluff above the river, and covered with oak and hickory trees set so far apart that, without underbrush, it was possible to ride on horseback in any direction. It was almost possible to conduct military maneuvers in the shade of the leaves.

The only event of the year Eighteen-twenty-seven was an expedition against the Winnebago Indians. They had put to death some white settlers; they seemed determined upon war, and a detachment of the Sixth regiment, accompanied by two companies of the Fifth and men from the Second regiment, under Major Whistler, forced the Winnebago tribe to deliver the leaders in the late outrages, Red Bird and Le Soleil and two others, to the United States. Back again from that enforcement of justice Lieutenant Johnston solaced his lonely hours at Jefferson Barracks with airs on the flute.

* * *

In Eighteen-twenty-eight General Atkinson appointed Johnston adjutant of the regiment. He possessed, Colonel Alexander said, in an extraordinary degree the confidence, esteem and admiration of the whole barracks. During the intervals of military life and playing on the flute Albert Sidney Johnston had a part in the society, at once innocent and gay, of St. Louis. St. Louis was still largely French in spirit, a place of pretty songs and informal dancing, of herb gardens and holiday cakes; Johnston was familiar with the Gratiots and Chouteaus, the Mullanphys and Bentons; and at a ball at Mr. Chouteau's he met Henrietta, the eldest daughter of Major William Preston. He had fought under Anthony Wayne and later left Virginia to settle in Louisville. Johnston and Henrietta Preston were remarkably alike, they were persistently mistaken for brother and sister; and when, after she returned home, Johnston was sent on recruiting service to Louisville, they soon became engaged.

They were married in January, Eighteen-twenty-nine. The

descriptions of her show a woman taller than common, with a full body, a brilliant color, clear hazel eyes and dark hair. Her features were irregular, and charming; she had a lovely voice. Their life was simple, happy and uneventful: they lived in plain quarters, with plain and limited furniture, at Jefferson Barracks; a few small pieces of cut glass represented elegance; they occasionally visited Henrietta's mother —the major was dead—in Louisville. In the January of Eighteen-thirty-one their first son was born; the tranquillity of their happiness continued until the Black Hawk War. The Sacs and Foxes had two contending war chiefs—Keokuk and Black Hawk; Keokuk was an amiable Indian, but Black Hawk, thirteen years his senior, who had suffered indignities from white aggression, was bitterly hostile to the United States. He refused, when his tribe moved by treaty to the west bank of the Mississippi, to accompany it; he stayed in his village, denying the validity of treaties made with other tribal chiefs; and Governor Reynolds of Illinois called out seven hundred militiamen to repel the invasion of the state.

Jefferson Davis, who was absent on furlough in Mississippi, immediately rejoined his company; Albert Sidney Johnston, Eaton, and Robert Anderson, all lieutenants, were commissioned colonels on the staff of the governor of Illinois; Abraham Lincoln, who had been a captain in Whiteside's command, reënlisted in a spy company. Black Hawk was overtaken in July, it was Eighteen-thirty-two, and successfully engaged at Wisconsin Heights. Only one white man but forty Indians were killed, the Indians were pursued until night, when Black Hawk made a gallant stand in order to get his women and children safely across the Mississippi River. He accomplished this and, with his remaining warriors, escaped in canoes in the dark.

While Johnston was away on active duty his eldest daughter, Henrietta Preston, was born; there was a second daughter, and Mrs. Johnston began to be ill. Her condition showed no signs of improvement—definite symptoms of lung fever developed soon afterward—and she asked her husband to resign from the army. This, for Albert Sidney Johnston, was an immeasurable calamity; his heart, his entire being, was military; but he agreed at once with his wife's desire. He took her first to New Orleans, then to Red Sulphur Springs, in the vain hope of recovery; at New Orleans he resigned his commission in the Army of the United States; Henrietta Johnston died near Louisville in Eighteen-thirty-five. He occupied a farm he had bought outside St. Louis and sank into the solitude of melancholy and a deep distress. Josiah, his favorite brother, had been blown to atoms in the explosion of the steamboat Lioness on the Red River. The darkness of Johnston's mind increased until even he saw that his present state must be brought to an end, and he determined to go West again. He planned to establish a colony in the Sioux lands, and applied to the government for support, but it was refused him, and he was persuaded by his wife's family to engage himself with business in Louisville.

He was, however, totally unfit for that existence; he had no taste for trade, and an increasing restlessness possessed him. This was his situation, his state of mind, when Stephen F. Austin, commissioner for Texas to the United States, arrived in Louisville and made a stirring speech on behalf of the republic south of the Sabine River. A Mr. Dangerfield, agent for Texas, engaged Johnston with stories of the heroic and embattled Texans; and Johnston, in return, gave them his instant sympathy and a not inconsiderable sum of money. He determined to give himself, to offer his sword, to the cause of Texan independence. Johnston proceeded at once by way of New Orleans to

Alexandria, Louisiana; from there he continued on horseback and crossed the Sabine the thirteenth of July, Eighteen-thirty-six. At Nacogdoches he met General Sam Houston; he went with Leonard Groce to his plantation on the River Brazos; and finally he arrived at the headquarters of the Texas army on the Coleto, near Goliad.

It was an amazing and wholly new body of troops, since the Mexican government had made its first grant of land to an American, Moses Austin, only fifteen years before. Moses Austin had died before he could take possession, the grant was continued to his son Stephen, and the impatient independent spirit of American settlers at once commenced an informal war on Mexican tradition and rights. The purpose of Mexico was far different—it had hoped, with the peculiar vanity of its Spanish blood, first to erect a barrier of colonies against the possible aggressions of the United States, and second to suppress the violence of the Indians who wasted the whole of a majestic country. It was the first belief, that American character could be bound to the alien institutions of Mexico, that led to revolt.

The Mexican government made a fatal mistake in forgetting the controversy over the southern limit of the Louisiana Purchase. It had been settled, finally, at the Sabine River; but a great number of Americans contended that the Rio Grande was the logical and proper boundary; they considered that the land south between the Sabine and the Rio Grande should have been and was part of the United States. The Northern settlers on the various grants that followed Austin's felt little sense of obligation or loyalty to Mexico City. They proceeded promptly and vigorously upon that supposition. The first American immigrants arrived in the future state of Texas the autumn of Eighteen-twenty-one; they reached the La Bahia crossing of the Brazos in December and camped on what they called New Year's

Creek. Within a few weeks Josiah H. Bell, from South Carolina, joined the settlement and located a headright grant of two leagues of land on the west bank of the Brazos.

In Eighteen-twenty-three Stephen Austin was directed to confer with the Mexican governor of Texas and locate a town central to the colonists as a seat of local government; the village of San Felipe de Austin was accordingly established; and the Baron de Bastrop was designated to issue titles to the settlers. They, for their part, solemnly agreed to become Roman Catholics. A criminal code was written by Austin: gambling was prohibited under a heavy fine; but horse racing, being calculated to improve the breed of horses, was not held to be gambling; it was a high misdemeanor for a man and woman to live together without marriage; five sections were devoted to offenses concerning slaves and slavery; the civil code fixed adequate terms of labor on the bodies of fraudulent debtors. Three hundred and seven separate Colonial grants of land were made under the decree securing Austin's rights; the only restriction prohibited Northern settlement within ten leagues of the Gulf coast; but even that protective area was soon surrendered.

* *
*

Almost at once the Fredonian Rebellion began—while Stephen Austin was in Mexico City, endeavoring to have his father's grant confirmed by successive and even different varieties of government, a Hayden Edwards was there moving toward a Texan settlement of his own. He occupied a house and entertained lavishly, and with roulette wheels, and, successful in his aim, he established himself at Nacogdoches. The opening of Texas to Northern immigration soon brought some very accomplished rascals to Nacogdoches, they combined with the lowest Mexican element present, and furnished the innocent settlers on the Edwards lands with an increasing and highly undesirable excitement. A Mexican, Sepulveda, and an American named Norris arranged to have Norris chosen alcalde, everything promptly became far worse, and Edwards informed the governor at San Antonio of the precarious state of local affairs. Governor Blanco, however, who had no talent for Americans, preferred any influence that might be Mexican, and replied by expelling Edwards and his colonists from their grant.

Hayden Edwards, with his brother Benjamin, had already spent a fortune in their land project, any interruption to it would mean ruin, and he determined to defy the Mexican authorities: Benjamin, on the sixteenth of December, Eighteen-twenty-six, rode into Nacogdoches and declared the establishment of the Republic of Fredonia. He bore its flag with him and promptly raised it in a violent Texas norther, a wind that tore the pine trees from the ground. This was largely bravado, the Edwards were in a difficult position, and they turned for assistance to the Cherokee Indians. An alliance was formed—after independence was secured the Fredonians and Cherokees were to divide equally the whole of eastern Texas. The arrangement in particular lay between the Edwards, an adroit citizen of the world named John Dunn Hunter, and Richard Fields, the Cherokee chief.

The Fredonian army of fifteen persons created an enormous disturbance in the Mexican government; the Fredonian Rebellion was looked upon as the first effort of the United States of the North to conquer Mexican territory; a large sum of money was voted for an expedition against the rebels. It was commanded by Colonel Ellis P. Bean, who had come down into Texas in Eighteen-twelve and become a naturalized Mexican citizen; a detachment of two hundred men joined Bean from Bexar; in January, it was Eighteen-twenty-seven, they were close to Nacogdoches. Before they could go into action, however, the alcalde, Norris, raised an army of sixty-seven loyal souls and marched against the Fredonian forces. Only twenty of them were available, eleven white men and nine Indians, but—one Fredonian was wounded—they surprised and totally defeated the Mexican government.

Colonel Bean, more penetrated by a local spirit, moved differently—he conducted an intrigue with the Cherokee tribe. At a council of war he persuaded the Cherokees to deny their agreement with Hayden Edwards and support the Mexican authorities. In proof of their better understanding they immediately killed Richard Fields, their chief, and the cosmopolitan John Dunn Hunter. After some useless skirmishing the Fredonians dissolved their republic.

Its effect, however, continued to trouble Mexico, rumors that the United States was planning to move its boundary from the Sabine to the Rio Grande persisted: Henry Clay, then Secretary of State in the cabinet of John Quincy Adams, felt that it was necessary to address an expression of regret to the Mexican minister Obregon. In April, Eighteen-thirty, Mexico passed the momentous decree forbidding further emigration to Texas from the North; but it had no effect on the American wave of settlement; thousands of colonists continued to arrive: there were a thousand American families in Texas in Eighteen-twenty-six; ten thousand Americans present in Eighteen-twenty-eight; four years later there were more than thirty thousand. Men of note were among them: R. M. Williamson from Georgia, who became known as Three-legged Willie and the Patrick Henry of the Revolution; Gail Borden, from New York; David G. Burnett of New Jersey; and the Whartons, John and William, from Tennessee.

Further difficulties were brought about by Colonel John

Davis Bradburn, who had been born in the United States but was in command of the Mexican garrison at Anahuac on the east end of Galveston Bay. He incarcerated two Americans, Travis and Jack, who had questioned his elevation of mind, and announced that he would transfer them to Vera Cruz for court-martial. A committee was sent to him from Brazoria, demanding the release of the prisoners; this was refused and a small force was raised to effect their freedom. Bradburn sent a company of cavalry against the expedition, it was repulsed with great ease, and William J. Russell shot and killed a Mexican sentinel. This was the first blood shed in the direct contention between Texas and the Mexican government.

The American force captured Anahuac, they allowed Bradburn an unreasonably short time in which to reach the Louisiana frontier, and they decided to extend their activities to Colonel Ugartechea, at Velasco. The volunteers for that affair made John Austin captain—he was from New England and not related to Stephen—and the attack was conducted by land and sea. The sea operation was carried on by a small schooner armed with two cannon and eighteen rifle-men. The action lasted for a day and a night, seven Texans were killed, the Mexican losses were forty-two dead and seventy wounded, and the terms of surrender sent Ugartechea south of the Rio Grande. Soon after Colonel Piedras, at Nacogdoches, commanding the only remaining Mexican garrison in Texas, agreed—when some forty of his men had been slain—that he too would benefit everyone by moving into a more Mexican atmosphere.

The charges Mexico made against the United States at the time of the Fredonian Rebellion were repeated with a greater animation, and, in July, Eighteen-thirty-six, Colonel Mejia, a supporter of Santa Anna in his revolt against the government, left Tampico with six ships and four hundred men to restore the sovereignty of Mexico in Texas. The Texans met that immediate difficulty by receiving the colonel with a great cordiality and proclaiming for Santa Anna; there was an impressive banquet at the plantation of William H. Wharton on Eagle Island, below Brazoria, with floods of rhetoric, music and champagne; and as a result of all this Mejia returned South convinced of the propriety of affairs in Texas. In August, however, Horatio Chrisman, first alcalde of San Felipe, with John Austin, the second alcalde, issued a call for a general convention of all the colonies of Texas. Fifty-six delegated from sixteen districts —the Mexican inhabitants of San Antonio could not be induced to join such an enterprise, assembled on the Brazos; and a memorial requesting separate statehood, Texas was one of the provinces of Coahuila—was presented to Mexico City. It accomplished nothing and a second convention met the following year. A period of formless local contentions led to General Sam Houston and the triumphant year Eighteen-thirty-six.

It began badly. The fourth convention of all Texas had no more than adopted its declaration of independence when the massacre at the Alamo occurred; a Doctor John Grant, who had taken it upon himself to invade Mexico with less than two hundred men, encountered a division of the Mexican army near San Patricio, and all but one of the Texans were killed or captured; a battle occurred at Coleto, and the northern force, without artillery or ammunition, surrendered to humane promises and reasonable terms. They were removed to Goliad where, with a command of men from Nashville, Tennessee, under Colonel Miller, captured at Copano, they were—three hundred and sixty-four souls —marched out and shot to death in a glimmering March dawn. *   *

*

General Houston, at Gonzales, had a few half-clad men without ammunition, and he was forced to sanction a general retreat. One wagon, drawn by four oxen, was reserved for his munitions of war, and all the rest were filled with women and children. Fresh recruits joined Houston; at the Colorado River he had five hundred men; but there was no artillery, they hadn't a cartridge. The news of the Alamo was followed by details of the losses, the outrage, at Goliad; a detachment of the Mexican army appeared on the south bank of the Colorado; but without ordnance Houston could not go into action. The American army, the population of Texas, fell back to the Brazos. The Brazos was swollen by April rains, the confusion there—the single ferry boat could carry but one wagon at a time—destroyed the last semblance of decent order. The crossing, however, was at last effected; and Santa Anna, with the best of his troops, followed over the river at Fort Bend.

He rode hard, with six hundred men, and reached Harrisburg on the fifteenth of April. Santa Anna sent a negro to Houston with the message that when he had cleaned out the land thieves—the Texas civil government—he'd pay his respects to him. That night General Houston slept on the ground, in wet clothes, with his saddle for a pillow. But Santa Anna, who had moved into Texas with nearly eight thousand men, wholly confident of an easy victory, had ridden far in advance of his supporting troops. Houston marched his absurd command to high ground on the San Jacinto River, and there, after consulting with his officers, late in the afternoon of April twenty-first, he decided to attack the Mexicans. He ordered Colonel John A. Wharton to form the army for an immediate offensive.

The destruction of the Mexican troops was complete: Santa Anna, Cos and General Almonte were captured; Castrillion, who had led the charge at the Alamo, was killed. Two Texans were killed and twenty-three wounded. The government, which had retreated to Galveston Island, returned to its affairs, and two treaties, one public and the other secret, were concluded with Santa Anna. In the second he bound himself to see that the cabinet of Mexico would receive a mission from the Texas government, settle all existing difficulties, and acknowledge the independence of the republic.

That was the position of Texas when, in the July of Eighteen-thirty-six, Albert Sidney Johnston joined Houston's army. It was, specifically, under the command of General Thomas J. Rusk, but it was more notable for desperate individuals than for discipline. The wide bounties of land offered to soldiers, the prospect of spoils, the sheer fact of war, had attracted all the wild youth of the Mississippi Valley. The army, in reality, threatened to become more dangerous to Texas than to its enemies. Johnston, who was so fortunate as to possess a horse, joined the few mounted men who composed the cavalry as a private.

In a portrait made at that time he has high cheek bones, an irregular nose, and a clear red and white color; his chin is delicate and handsome, his teeth white and regular, his mouth determined; brown hair falls across an impressive brow; his eyes are direct and steady and intensely blue. He was more than six feet high, with broad shoulders and a deep chest. His bearing was stiffly military, dignified rather than graceful. Johnston had no great skill with firearms, but he rode with perfect command of himself and his horse. His manner was vigorous and decisive; it was, at the same time, kindly and frank; he was pleasant, informal, with children, and rigorously formal in all his contacts with women.

General Rusk, soon after Johnston's arrival in Texas, offered him the post of adjutant general, explaining that he would have to defend it from other candidates, and Johnston promptly accepted both responsibilities. President Burnet appointed him colonel in the regular army; General Sam Houston commissioned him aide-de-camp with the rank of major. He was called to Columbia, where the Texas Congress was sitting, for affairs of the government, and then sent on a mission to New Orleans. While Johnston was in Louisiana, Rusk, unable to keep order among his troops, resigned his command to Felix Huston, a Kentuckian, who had emigrated to Texas by way of Mississippi politics. He was a large impressive-looking man of proved gallantry, his ambitions were greater than his knowledge of military science, but he announced that he would challenge any officer who attempted to supercede him. In the face of this President Burnet, who put a certain dependence on military ability, made Johnston brigadier general with command of the army, and reduced Felix Huston to junior brigadier. When Johnston arrived Huston's supporters in camp—they called him Old Leather-Breeches—were in a dangerous state of revolt. Huston met Johnston civilly and then addressed a letter to him:

"Headquarters. Camp Independence. Feb. 4, 1837.
"Sir: From the acquaintance I have had with you, and your high reputation, I wish to tender you my regards as a gentleman and soldier.
"Your assuming command of the army would have excited in me no feelings but those of respect and obedience to you, as my superior officer, were it not for the fact that your appointment was connected with a tissue of treachery and misrepresentation, which was intended to degrade me and blast my prospects in the Texian army.
"You, in assuming command under an appointment connected with the attempt to ruin my reputation and inflict

a stigma on my character of course stand in an attitude of opposition to myself.

"This situation might not in ordinary cases lead to serious results. But as I have not made up my mind to leave the service, and cannot consistently with honor submit to humiliating circumstances, I prefer taking a plain and direct course, to one which would lead to a similar result from the mere force of circumstances.

"I do this, as I really esteem your character and know that you must be sensible to the delicacy of my situation.

"I therefore propose a meeting between us, in as short a period as you can make convenient. My friend Major Ross has authority to make all necessary arrangements. Reiterating my respects and regards, I am

"Your most obedient, humble servant,
Felix Huston."

In a brief reply Albert Sidney Johnston accepted the challenge. There were, it was discovered, no duelling pistols available, and it was proposed to use Huston's horse pistols, crook-handled and twelve inches in the barrel. Johnston agreed to this; although—Huston was a celebrated shot—he could have chosen rapiers; and, while Felix Huston closely buttoned his coat, presenting as inconspicuous a mark as possible, Johnston laid his coat aside, binding his sash about his waist, and exposed his body in a white shirt. This Huston, but with an angry impatience, was forced by pride to copy.

Johnston, who was fully aware of his disadvantage, had determined on a course that required an absolute command of head and steady nerves—the pistols had hair triggers, and he planned, by shooting first, to cause an involuntary contraction of Huston's finger and draw his fire. This he was successful in doing at the first encounter—he missed

Huston and Huston missed him. Johnston successfully repeated his endeavor. He did it a third, a fourth, and then for the fifth time. Felix Huston was increasingly exasperated; but his superior ability, in the sixth exchange of shots, overcame Johnston, and he fell with a ball in his hip. Huston asked leave to approach him and express his regret; a surgeon declared the wound to be so dangerous as to allow little hope for recovery; and Felix Huston, riding pale and agitated back to camp, waved aside the throng of men that hurried forward to greet and congratulate him. His influence sharply declined and he returned discredited to the United States.

*   *
*

Johnston's wound was first thought to be fatal, it was then dismissed as slight, but in reality it was extremely severe, it was the source of constant pain and lameness throughout his life. He was obliged, because of it, to turn the command of the Texas army over to Colonel Rogers. This was in May, Eighteen-thirty-seven, and he spent the summer and fall in Kentucky. A profound depression settled upon him, he tried to resign his Texas obligations but President Burnet would not release him. He returned South, Mirabeau B. Lamar was elected President, David Burnet Vice-President, and in Eighteen-thirty-eight Johnston was appointed Secretary of War. He had, in the service of Texas, first suffered from malaria and the exposure of frontier life, and later, neglecting private affairs, his material possessions were greatly reduced. At the beginning of Eighteen-forty he felt obliged to address General Houston formally:

"City of Austin, Jan. 5, 1840

"Sir: I have just been informed that on last evening, and also on this morning, you thought it necessary to use the most vituperative language with regard to me, for what cause I know not. In doing so you bore in mind the responsibility you incurred, and you will not be surprised that I inform you that immediately after the termination of the present session of Congress I will hold you accountable.

A. Sidney Johnston."

General Houston immediately disclaimed all intention of speaking except in the highest terms of Johnston. Before that Johnston had written in a far different mood to George Hancock. "I would be pleased to hear that you will settle here. Standing alone without a relative in the country, I feel like an exile. What more could a man desire than the countenance of kind and devoted friends to sustain him? These are mine, in the finest climate and most beautiful and lovely country that the blazing eye of the sun looks upon in his journey from the east to the west. Yet I am not contented. I sometimes fancy myself most miserable. I stand alone. But here I have cast my lot; and here, come weal or woe, I shall, unless fate has otherwise decreed, spin out the thread of life. I hope you will make up your mind to come to this fine country. In a gallop over the hills this morning, I frequently noticed the beauty of the flowers. Here you will live ten years longer, which is a consideration with most persons. For myself, I look to the end with more concern than to the length of life. I feel that I can encounter the grim monster unflinchingly wherever he may present himself."

He resigned from the government of Texas in February, Eighteen-forty, and again returned to Kentucky—he had become deeply attached to a Miss Eliza Griffin, a cousin of his first wife's, and they were married near Shelbyville in the autumn of Eighteen-forty-three. He had bought China Grove Plantation, in Brazoria County, Texas; it held fifteen hundred acres of cotton land and over four thousand acres of deep prairie; but he had given sixteen thousand dollars for it; and that price Johnston found to be oppressive. His properties in Kentucky were sacrificed to maintain China Grove, Johnston was at the point of leaving again for Texas to administer it personally when the War with Mexico began. He was appointed inspector general of field division of volunteers under Major General Butler; the American army was concentrated at Ceralvo, and Johnston moved forward upon Monterey with the First Ohio regiment. He met Jefferson Davis in the converging fire of the Mexican salients; his horse was wounded three times; all the other officers about him were dismounted or disabled; but Johnston was obliged to stay, a conspicuous mark, in the saddle, since his efficiency was limited on foot.

He went back to Texas, to Galveston, where he was received with a clamorous applause, but he was again depressed in spirit—he had no fixed rank recognized by the government of the United States; it was the fashion to give military commands to consequential politicians, party leaders were transformed into generals and became the centers of factions and heroes of the press; and no attention was paid to Johnston's very great abilities. His children now required education, and, in their interest, he surrendered all the property he had inherited from his wife Henrietta. Johnston had very little money left; he lived, at China Grove, in a double log cabin covered with clapboards with a wide rude porch; his household kept the primitive simplicity of pioneer existence—pine tables and hickory chairs, the utensils and supplies, the stock and farm implements, that were absolutely essential.

Four hundred acres of China Grove had been cleared, the forest covered a thousand more; to the south and east there was a square league of prairie; the thick belt of woods was filled with a wild life. There were jungles, and a swamp that, in the spring overflow, rose to the threshold of Johnston's house. From the porch the prospect reached over a grassy plain beyond sight; in early spring the grass was bright with blue lupin, there were crimson phlox and fragrant mimosa; herds of brown deer were scattered through the herds of longhorn cattle; great flights of birds settled in the pools left by the winter rains—cranes, heron, wild geese, brant, ducks and sea birds, gulls and curlews. In summer the deep grass turned golden. The winter was a season of long driving rains, of violent northers. A grove of China trees shaded the house; the yard held live oaks, tall pecans, beautiful native forest trees closed in by a hedge of Cherokee roses.

Johnston's family was composed of his wife and an infant son, a negro with his wife, two negro boys and a girl. He intended to stay on his plantation only until it could be sold but continual disappointment mocked his design. He raised a crop of Indian corn for bread—food for his family and animals—he made cotton and a small crop of sugar cane for the purchase of supplies, he grew vegetables and worked, through the evening, in his flower garden. A single shot brought down a dinner of rice birds. Johnston hit an eagle at very long range, its wing was broken, and it lived chained to a log. He played chess and was a slow but persistent reader—Shakespeare and Dickens and Gil Blas, but he preferred Mrs. Somerville and Sir Charles Lyell. His great literary accomplishment was the slow translation of Herodotus.

He was at once melancholy, regretful of lost activities and events, and happy; his marriage was successful—after five years he wrote that no single unpleasant word had passed between his wife and himself—and he was delighted with two children, both sons, born on the plantation. The monotony of his existence, however, increased his inherent sense of depression; fever followed the floods to his doorstep. The family at China Grove became sallow and gaunt, ague-stricken in appearance. Johnston was, he felt, alien to his surroundings and occupation; nothing he accomplished was what he had wished for, nothing about him was appropriate to his abilities. In mind and spirit he was a soldier. The small inconquerable happenings of life, the firmness of his character, had combined to keep him from his different desire.

When General Zachary Taylor was made President, Johnston's friends labored to secure an adequate appointment for him, and Taylor offered him the semi-military post of paymaster. He accepted this, hoping to be transferred to active service, at the end of Eighteen-forty-nine, and resolutely fulfilled his minor duties. Pierce became President, Jefferson Davis was Secretary of War, and Albert Sidney Johnston was at last recognized: he was made colonel of the Second Regiment of cavalry and ordered for immediate service in Texas. He was, it is conceivable, a radiantly happy man, leading a regiment of United States regulars, near eight hundred strong, down the road to Fort Mason.

* * *

In Eighteen-fifty-seven Colonel Johnston was put in command of the expedition against the Mormons. He arrived at Fort Leavenworth the first part of September, completed in a week all necessary arrangements for the undertaking, and marched with an escort of forty dragoons, over incredibly bad roads deep with mud, nine hundred and twenty miles in twenty-seven days. At South Pass he organized a military force, he prohibited all communication with the Mormons, and decided to change his base for the winter to

Fort Bridger. It was November and his troops encountered an early winter storm of furious violence. The oxen, the mules and horses, already half starved, died literally by hundreds. They progressed only thirty-five miles in fifteen days. Before retreating the Mormons burned and destroyed Fort Bridger and spoiled the crops there—Johnston found only the ruins of a trading post. He fortified it, constructing two lunettes, and went into winter quarters at Camp Scott.

During a winter of extreme hardship, of innumerable difficulties met and conquered or turned to his advantage, Johnston was still followed by the old animosity of General Sam Houston. The General was in the United States Senate, and indulged himself in a bitter criticism of Albert Johnston.

Commissioners from President Buchanan arrived, it was June, Eighteen-fifty-eight, they accepted Brigham Young's submission to the United States, and issued the President's proclamation of pardon. Johnston moved his command to Cedar Valley, Camp Floyd, midway between Salt Lake City and Provo, where he assisted the civil authorities in the establishment and execution of law. There was nothing further for him to do, he asked to be relieved of duty in the far west, and, in February, Eighteen-fifty-nine, he returned to New York by way of San Francisco and the sea. Through the summer that followed Texas men of influence urged the government to give Johnston command of the Department of the Southwest. In November the adjutant general made that appointment; but, because of the increasing difficulties between the South and the United States, Johnston asked to be sent to California instead. He sailed from New York with his family, by the Isthmus of Panama, on the twenty-first of December.

The swift approach of the War of the Rebellion gave him a new source of trouble—he was an officer in the Army of the United States, but his deepest allegiance was to Texas.

He, too, occupied the impossible position of believing that the Southern States were justified in leaving the Union without approving of the method they adopted. Johnston hoped war might be unnecessary. Nevertheless, he presented his resignation; a successor to his command arrived from Washington. Johnston's position was increasingly precarious—soldiers had been placed in Los Angeles to watch his movements; he was, virtually, a prisoner in what had been his own department; his only way of escape, of return to Texas, lay across the desert.

He left Los Angeles with his negro servant Randolph on the twenty-fifth of June, Eighteen-sixty, and went to Chino ranch and then to Warner's ranch; on the thirtieth of June he was at Vallecito. He left Vallecito that Sunday night, and rode eighteen miles to Carrizo Wells. He left Carrizo Wells three o'clock on the afternoon of July first, and reached Indian Springs, thirty-seven miles distant, leaving the next day for Alamo Springs. It was twenty-eight miles, he went on at once—this was the third of July—thirty miles to Cook's Wells, and on the Fourth he continued to Fort Yuma. Johnston left Yeager's Ferry, at Fort Yuma, on the seventh, and followed the Gila River, and thence two hundred and seventy miles to Tucson. He reached there on the eighteenth, departed on the twenty-second and rode thirty miles. On the twenty-third he rode forty miles to arrive at the bitter disappointment of a dry desert camp. The twenty-fourth saw him first at Dragoon Springs, fifteen miles farther, and then to Apache Pass, another fifty miles distant. He travelled from Apache Pass to the Rio Grande, an hundred and sixty miles, in three days; and he arrived at Mesilla on the twenty-eighth of July.

His journey lay through one of the hottest lands in the world; the thermometer often reached to an hundred and twenty degrees in the shade; Johnston was surrounded by swarms of flies, dense masses of mosquitoes, stifling clouds of dust. Most of the water, where he had water to drink, was brackish. The Colorado Desert is a depressed basin, treeless and arid, one hundred and thirty miles across. For sixty miles there is no trace of water or of any vegetable or animal life. The mules that accompanied Johnston's small party sank to their knees in dry sand; a hot wind lifted the fine loose metallic particles in pillars that fell and rose again like ashes. Marauding bands of Apaches and Navajos were a constant menace; between Tucson and Mesilla he encountered two wrecked stage coaches, the guards, drivers and passengers—fourteen persons—murdered. They held the attention, the meticulous care, of wheeling and falling buzzards. Travelling toward Carrizo Wells Johnston saw a brilliant and fateful-appearing comet.

Before he reached Richmond deputations to the Confederate capital had requested the assignment of Johnston to the command of the West. General Polk was present for no other end. Mr. Davis was in full agreement with this, and he was given charge of the Second Department—Tennessee and Arkansas, Mississippi west of the New Orleans, Jackson and Great Northern and Central Railroad, and of military operations in Kentucky. He was made a full general, the highest military rank in the Confederacy. Johnston proceeded at once upon his commission, and found himself, his army, in a position of immense difficulty: the Federal troops were in possession of nearly the whole of Missouri; their heavily massed forces at Cairo were an extreme menace to his left flank in Kentucky. Although General Johnston had practically imperial power he was forced to recruit his troops through the inadequate machinery of the states; he was never able to procure sufficient supplies of war.

His command included three armies—Buckner at the

center, about Bowling Green; Zollicoffer was on the right at Cumberland; Leonidas Polk extended at the left to Columbus. At the Battle of Belmont, Polk counted the Federal losses to be not less than fifteen hundred. There was six hours of tenacious fighting—honorable to both North and South—and after an hour's pause the broken and retreating Confederates formed again, and, with an irresistible charge, were finally victorious. At Woodsonville, Colonel Terry, commanding the Texas rangers, charged with seventy-five of his men on established Union nests; he led with six rangers, employing his revolver with extraordinary skill, a fatal effect; but he was killed by a ball in his brain. The Texans bore his body off from the field. The Rangers left Houston with eleven hundred and sixty men, five hundred more joined them in their term of service: when, at the war's end, they surrendered, two hundred and forty-four were left alive.

In Eighteen-sixty-two Fort Henry fell before the Union assaults, and the surrender of Fort Donelson soon followed. The Federal troops were assembling in the West in overwhelming numbers; and, with the destruction of Fort Donelson, almost half of the Confederate soldiers in Tennessee were killed, captured, or hopelessly scattered. Their positions at Bowling Green, Nashville and Columbus were all turned; the Valley of the Cumberland was lost. Johnston's line of retreat, however, was safe if his flanks were unbroken. He kept Bowling Green as long as it was humanly possible, and then silently prepared to withdraw. Nashville, filled with a disorganized mob, was in a panic, a rabble on the wharves robbed the army supply boats. It was indefensible, and General Johnston withdrew to Murfreesboro, determined to effect a junction with Beauregard near Corinth. His staff officers, Colonel Mackall and Colonel Gilmer, held that it was a sheer impossibility; but he collected an army of stragglers, moved through Shelbyville to Decatur, saved his provisions and stores, removed his depots and machine shops, obtained new arms; and, the end of March, Eighteen-sixty-two, with Beauregard at Corinth, he commanded fifty thousand men.

* * *

Some of Hardee's troops had arrived from Bowling Green; Leonidas Polk was present with part of his command from Columbus; men from Pensacola and Mobile and New Orleans were gathered under Braxton Bragg; there were additional new levees, hastily raised and badly equipped. It was an army with more enthusiasm than knowledge, more valor than discipline. There was an extraordinary variety of arms, rifles and smooth-bored and rifled muskets, percussion locks lately changed from flint and steel and original flint locks, shot guns of all calibres and patterns. Albert Sidney Johnston, who had brought a smaller number of men than Beauregard, offered him command, but General Beauregard refused to take Johnston's place. The plan of the battle of Shiloh, which immediately followed, was Johnston's, however, and not, as Beauregard later asserted, his. General Johnston's order for his army to advance silently was immediately disregarded—there were Rebel yells and calls and the discharge of guns. The presence, the weight, of the Southern army, had been entirely unsuspected by the Federal forces late Saturday night, the fifth of April, Eighteen-sixty-two; past midnight the Union bands were serenading at different headquarters.

Johnston slept badly; at half past five in the morning he was on horse, moving to the front with his staff. He continually sent an aide to ask Bragg why a division had not appeared. At half past twelve, with no report of the delayed men, he exclaimed, "This is perfectly puerile! This is not war! Let us have our horses!" He galloped to the rear and discovered the missing column. The Confederate army was drawn in three lines of battle late Saturday afternoon; after four o'clock the celebrated council of war on the issue of a battle at Shiloh was held. Johnston and Beauregard and Polk were present, with Gilmer and Breckinridge; General Hardee was not. Beauregard characteristically advised battle; Grant, he said, must certainly now be aware of their movements; General Johnston, in spite of confusion and noise and loss of time, still hoped to surprise the enemy. He ended, finally, all discussion:

"Gentlemen we shall attack at daylight tomorrow."

Saturday night, after storms of rain, was clear; Johnston slept quietly in an ambulance wagon. The morning was cool, with the pure freshness and scents of spring. As he mounted, General Johnston said confidentially to his officers, "Tonight we will water our horses in the Tennessee River." Sharp skirmishing began before he reached the front. He met Colonel Marmaduke—who had been with him in Utah —holding the center of the Confederate line. "My son," Johnston said, "we must this day conquer or perish." He cried, "Men of Arkansas, they say you boast of your prowess with the bowie knife. Today you wield a nobler weapon— the bayonet. Employ it well." He moved from position to position supported by men who loved, who adored, him: Leonidas Polk, his friend all through life; Hardee, for six years his major; Breckinridge, bound to him by old and indissoluble ties; Gilmer was his engineer. His staff followed him, surrounded him, with reverence—Preston and Brewster were part of it, Jack and O'Hara. Hardcastle and Bowen and Rich, a score of young officers, had been his pupils at war. Basil Duke followed him from civil life; Morgan and Colonel R. A. Johnson and Colonel Ben Anderson were sons of early friends; Gibson, many others, were allied to him by blood and marriage; Wharton and Ashbel Smith came with the Texans.

The lines of the Federal troops, under the flag of the Union, were in uniform blue; the Confederates wore every conceivable garb and color—grey and domestic butternut and blue in a Louisiana regiment that later became perilously confusing. Every Southern regiment advanced under a corps battle flag: Polk's was a white cross on a blue field; Braxton Bragg's had a blue cross on crimson; Hardee's charged a white medallion on a blue field; there were, in addition, state flags—the lone star of Texas and the pelican of Louisiana floated with the heroic bunting. At each wave of assault there was the shrill indomitable Rebel yell. The men from Kentucky advanced with a steady step singing, "Cheer up, boys, we'll march away to battle."

General Johnston rode slowly along the line, his hat was off and his sword was in its scabbard. In his right hand he held a little tin cup: earlier he had reprimanded an officer for plundering a Union tent, and then, regretting the severity of his tone, he had taken the cup, saying that was his part of the spoils. He rode easily, on a thoroughbred horse named Fire-eater. His voice was compelling. "Men," he cried, "they are stubborn. I must lead you." A sheet of fire burst from the Federal position along the crest of a ridge; the Confederate line sank in death through the dark valley; the Confederates went up to the crest of the hill; the Union troops fell back. Johnston's horse was shot in four places, his uniform was cut by bullets, his boot sole was torn by a minié ball, but he had escaped serious injury. Governor Harris rode up to him from the right; Johnston spoke to him, he sent him with an order for Colonel Stratham. Harris returned. The retreating Federal soldiers were shooting with an angry persistence, and a second minié ball struck General Johnston. Harris said, "General, your order is delivered and Colonel Stratham is in motion." Johnston reeled, and Harris put his left arm about his commander's shoulders; he grasped his collar, righting him in the saddle. He asked, "General, are you wounded?" Yes, he was told, it was feared seriously. Captain Wickham helped to lift him from his horse.

Governor Harris kneeled on the ground and demanded, "Johnston, do you know me?" Albert Johnston smiled at him. There was no other response. Harris untied his cravat, unbuttoned collar and vest and tore open his shirt, searching for a more serious wound than the swift bleeding in his right leg, but he was unsuccessful. He raised General Johnston's head and gave him a swallow of brandy; he gave him a second swallow but the brandy only gurgled with the breath in an inert throat. After a few moments breathing stopped. In addition to the wound that killed him Albert Sidney Johnston had been hit by a spent ball midway of his right thigh, a fragment of shell had cut him above the right hip, and he had been shot in the left foot. His surgeon, who could have saved him with little difficulty, Johnston had dispatched to establish a hospital for soldiers of both the North and South.

In Eighteen-sixty-six, the Legislature of the State of Texas made appropriation for the removal of General Johnston's body from New Orleans; Sheridan and Griffin, for the United States army, prohibited a funeral procession in Galveston, and when the remains reached Houston the emotion and sorrow of Texas rose to an uncontrollable and appalling pitch. The city was covered with placards, "Our honored dead must and shall be respected." Every house was draped from street to roof with crêpe and illusion, every store was blank, Houston was a vast memento mori. The coffin lay in state at the Academy, with tall silver candlesticks, burning candles; it was banked in rich flowers. Above hung portraits of Mr. Davis with General Lee on his right and General Jackson at the left; in the center there was a framed representation of The Weeping Confederacy. The funeral cortège was escorted by five hundred ladies on foot, the procession of gentlemen reached for a mile. The hearse bore six pairs of large black plumes equally spaced, it was drawn by six milk-white horses. Johnston had said, "When I die I want a handful of Texas earth on my breast."

If he had lived it is probable that the battle of Shiloh would not have been finally lost to the South. If he had lived, perhaps even the Confederacy might have survived for a period, long or short, of its own choosing. Men like Albert Sidney Johnston, men of honor and of valor, calm with decision, have limitless power over events.

SHADOWS ON THE SEA

SHADOWS ON THE SEA

AT THE AGE OF THIRTEEN, precocious even for naval gentlemen in the year Eighteen-thirty-two, John Newland Maffitt was commissioned midshipman by the United States. His commission bore the date of February, twenty-fifth. He reported in March and in September he was ordered to the U. S. sloop-of-war St. Louis. The St. Louis cruised to the West Indies; in December she was anchored at Pensacola, overhauling ship and getting in stores; she stood away for the Windward Islands with Havana for the next port of call. January, Eighteen-thirty-four, John Maffitt obtained leave of absence, and later in the same year—he was then fifteen—he was ordered to the Boston Navy Yard. In Eighteen-thirty-five, February, he was on board the frigate Constitution, flagship of the squadron under Commodore Elliot fitting out for a three years' cruise to the Mediterranean. He presented his orders to the commanding officer of his ship, they were countersigned, and he proceeded forward—wholly familiar with his small and intricate and rigid world—to the steerage and quarters of the younger officers.

He found the midshipmen at their dinner in the port messroom, and there were exclamations in proper keeping with the romantic gravity of their prospects. "John Maffitt, by all the rosy gods!" The bottle was then passed and Maffitt's health secured a complete attention. A brief period of seasickness followed with the midshipmen, but on the first Saturday night out there was a bowl of hot punch. There were toasts. "Well, gentlemen," this was Benton, a Kentuckian, "fill up and we'll drink to a jolly cruise, a happy return and a speedy promotion." A song was demanded, a guitar produced. What should the nature of the music be—love, murder or choragic? The next acknowledgment, it was pointed out, was by custom—on Saturday night—sweethearts and wives. "We'll take," Benton asserted, "a pull at the sentimental halyards first."

At Piræus, Maffitt, who was the Captain's aide, was ordered to prepare the barge to bring on board the King and Queen of Greece. This ceremony was interrupted only by a single minor accident—the ice-cream freezer was allowed to fall in the sea. It was recovered—without comment by the boatmen—but the Queen, it was politely evident, did not enjoy the consequent flavor of salt. She was known, however, to cherish a passion for dancing, and Captain Bruin ordered part of the ship's band to the quarterdeck. It played a most animated waltz, the Queen looked wistfully at the Captain, and he was obliged to admit that he was no waltzer. He beckoned, he said, to one of his aides, Midshipman Maffitt, who was quite an adept at the business, presented him to the Queen—they were at the same age, fifteen —and motioned to him to be off.

Twenty couples, including the King, soon followed them. Dusk floated over the harbor, awnings were spread, the muskets of the marines were ranged around the capstan with lighted candles in their muzzles. The dance continued until two o'clock in the morning, when the King proposed his return to shore. The boats were manned, the masts and yards of the Constitution illuminated, and a salute of twenty-one guns was fired. The Queen of Greece, leaving the ship, promised that she would give a ball in return; she said this to Mr. Maffitt, together with some other and undiscoverable things, and departed with his cloak wrapped about her shoulders. Invitations arrived for Captain Bruin, General Cass and his family, and for John Maffitt; only the captain on a British frigate was invited; and when Maffitt asked permission to attend the Queen's ball it was refused. If he went, Bruin pointed out, it would not only damage the feelings of the young men who had been neglected, but probably result in complaint from the English Ambassador.

The frigate sailed from Piræus the next day, and at Cape Colonna the young gentlemen visited the temples of Minerva and Jupiter Olympus. They were carried to Smyrna and Scio, to Tenedos and Syria and Candia, and then returned to the familiar Harbor of Port Mahon. At Malaga, Maffitt met the two lovely daughters of General Obergrand, and never forgot them. He attended a masque ball in Lisbon, to celebrate the marriage of the Prince of Saxe-Coburg with Donna Maria of Portugal, in the costume of an Indian squaw. He was ordered to the U. S. schooner Shark for passage home, and displayed great energy and ability—he had a large part in putting down the threat of a mutiny, and, although he was not a regular watch officer, on several occasions he was given charge of the deck. The Shark docked at Newport and Maffitt went to Baltimore, where he prepared for examination to obtain the rank of passed midshipman. In June, Eighteen-thirty-eight, he was promoted, and ordered to the government packet Woodbury.

He was on the U. S. sloop-of-war Vandalia by November. In Eighteen-thirty-nine, Maffitt was concerned with gales in the Gulf of Mexico. He saw, at Vera Cruz, the French fleet that stormed and took the celebrated fortress at San Juan de Ulua. At Matamoras he came near to drowning on the bar, and in March he was appointed lieutenant. In June he left Vera Cruz for Tampico and continued on to Pensacola. He had been assigned to the frigate Macedonian, but he was first granted a leave of absence for three months.

He had met, in Pensacola, Miss Mary Florence Murrell, the daughter of a Virginia gentleman who had removed to Alabama, and they were very soon married. Two years later, acting master of the Macedonian, he was ordered back to Pensacola, to the Navy Yard; and there his first child, a girl, was born and baptized on the frigate. He was detached again and placed on waiting orders. On the twenty-first of November, Eighteen-forty-two, John Maffitt was ordered to the rendezvous at Baltimore. The May following he was with the Coast Survey. Maffitt brought his family to Baltimore, where he rented a house and engaged a long-known Irishman to take care of his interests.

This was in Eighteen-forty-four, when his first son, Eugene Anderson, was born, and when tragedy overcame his house. What, exactly, that was, is lost in the past. His biography, the only available intimate source of information, was written by Emma Martin Maffitt, his third wife, and her comment is at once poetic, final and obscure. "Upon this period of his life," she wrote, "let silence fall; the broken threads of his life were gathered up and its warp and woof rewoven, but the scars remained." It does not seem improbable that the catastrophe, which involved Mary Florence, included as well the long-known anonymous Irishman.

Lieutenant John Maffitt's work in the Coast Survey was highly important: it was connected—and always without accurate instruments—with the hydrographic plotting in Boston Harbor and at Nantucket, and in command of the vessel Gallatin, a topsail schooner, at Charleston. He made a reconnaissance south of Cape Hatteras, and of Bull's Bay, northeast of Charleston, and discovered a new channel, Maffitt's Channel, across the Charleston Bar. He surveyed Beaufort Harbor and charted Rattlesnake Shoals, off the limit of the available sheets. He mapped the Savannah Bar, the Savannah River from Cockspur to Shad's Chimney, and the North Edisto Bar and river. In Eighteen-fifty-one, he was stationed, with the Gallatin, at Smithville, North Carolina, at the mouth of the Cape Fear River.

Smithville, deserted in winter, in summer was filled by the polite society of Wilmington; it was, consequently, a place of cultivation and gaiety. The officers of the Coast Survey lived in the barracks at Fort Johnson, they were invited to the selectest parties, and John Maffitt organized a dramatic company. There were, as well, games in which everyone took part in the Garrison grounds—football and prisoner's base, especially when there was a moon, and the flying of kites. Picnics along the beaches, sea bathing, occupied the days; tableaux and dancing ornamented the nights in brilliant illuminated houses and balconies, Chinese pagodas and gardens.

* * *

On one occasion the Arundle cotillion was followed by a scene from the Bride of Lammermoor; a Cotillion Waltz was supported by Dombey and The Nipper; there was a march from Norma, a Grand Promenade, and a Scene: Pickwick and the Middle Aged Lady; a Cotillion, Beautiful Boy, was followed by An Elopement in High Life; the Polka Cotillion was followed by the appearance of Mr. and Mrs. Caudle; a Curtsey Cotillion preceded A Gypsy Encampment; the Basket Cotillion exhibited, at its end, Samuel Weller and the Pretty Housemaid; the Sociable Cotillion, An Artist's Studio; a Cotillion, Miss Philadelphia, showed a scene entitled The Gold Diggers. All this began at a quarter past eight; when the last figure was completed four sky rockets were sent up, a gong sounded and there was a wild strain of Arabic music. At one thirty a reel was danced in the costumes of the tableaux.

Eighteen-fifty-two, in St. Paul's Church at Charleston, John Maffitt married Mrs. Caroline Laurens Read, the widow of Lieutenant James W. Read; they returned to Smithville, where they lived in a house on the Garrison grounds; and Maffitt continued his hydrographic work: he noted important changes on the Cape Fear Bar and in the Gulf Stream; with the schooners Bancroft and Crawford he completed the preliminary survey of the entrance to Port Royal and the Broad and Beaufort Rivers; he established the shore line of St. Helena Sound and inside soundings between the coast and Martin's Industry.

Lieutenant Maffitt was detached and ordered to command the brig Dolphin; this was interrupted by a confusion of orders; a political Retiring Board arbitrarily placed him on the indefinite furlough list, finding he was incapable of performing promptly and efficiently his duty ashore and afloat; but that was so obviously unjust, so ridiculous, that, after a brief hearing, he was immediately restored to the Dolphin. His duty now was the capture of pirates and slave ships, and, cruising on the north coast of Cuba, running down the shore line between Sagua la Grande and Cardenas, he grew suspicious of a vessel laying the same course. The Dolphin went in pursuit and, drawing close, hoisted an English flag and fired two blank cartridges. This had no effect and the Dolphin fired a solid shot across the other's bows; a second shot was more effective—and American colors were raised. Maffitt hauled down the English flag, he showed his own, and fired a shot through the main topsail of the vessel he was overtaking. That brought her to, and Lieutenant Bradford was ordered aboard: she had no papers or national flag. A cargo of negroes was stowed in a temporary deck forty-four inches high. She was the Echo; Putnam, New Orleans, was half painted out on her stern; and she was brought into Charleston.

Maffitt, in Eighteen-fifty-four, bought land on the James River, in Virginia; he removed with his family there; and, except for the failure of his wife's health, a short happy period followed. In Eighteen-fifty-nine, he sold his Virginia property and bought a house in Washington, on K Street. Mrs. Maffitt died, and he was obliged to place his children at appropriate schools and in the care of a cousin, Mrs. Hybart, at Ellerslie. Lieutenant Maffitt was, then, in command of the U. S. steamer Crusader. His duty again was to cruise off Cuba and intercept slave ships and pirates. In the old Bahama Channel, not far from Nuevitas, a questionable square-rigged ship was reported from aloft. A shot was fired to windward of her and she showed the French colors at her peak. As the Crusader came alongside the peculiar and sickening stench of a slave ship was heavily perceptible; there was a continuous audible moaning and murmur of human voices.

Before a boat could bring up from the Crusader the close battened hatches of the slaver were broken open and hundreds of shouting liberated negroes filled the deck. They climbed along the rail, they hung on the shrouds, and swarmed up the rigging. They burst into bread barrels and water casks, and decorated themselves in everything their hands came on—some fastened belaying pins to their wrists and others paraded with copper ladles hung about their necks. Naked black women—Maffitt's marines clothed them with the ends of canvas—many with babies in their arms, stood entranced. The captain of the slave ship was French, the crew French and Spanish, and the negroes had been selected from three thousand prisoners of war taken by the King of Dahomey.

John Maffitt captured the Echo; the Bogota; in July, Eighteen-sixty, he took the slave ship Kibly; on the fourteenth of August, he brought to an end the career of the pirate Young Antonio. He was ordered to sail for New York; and, unable to get money at the Bank of Havana for the necessities of his ship, he took the sum from his private funds. Maffitt turned the Crusader over to the navy, but the money he had furnished was never repaid by the government. He began to be considered Southern in his sympathies.

John Newland Maffitt's father, an Irishman, had been a Methodist preacher in New London, Connecticut. He had preceded his family to America; his wife Ann, then beautiful and young, impetuously followed him; and John Newland was born at sea. In Eighteen-twenty-four his uncle, Doctor William Maffitt, who lived near Fayetteville in North Carolina, visited his brother in Connecticut; he found the preacher in greatly reduced circumstances, and he adopted John, then five years old. When he was nine Doctor Maffitt sent him North to a school at White Plains, New York; he entered the United States navy from there; but the four years he spent at Ellerslie, his uncle's place, bound his imagination and allegiance to North Carolina. The suspicions of the authorities of the Union were correct—when North Carolina seceded, Maffitt followed with his adopted state.

On the fourth of June, Eighteen-sixty-one, his resignation from the navy was accepted to date from May second; but it was doubtful if he could escape from Washington. He succeeded, however, through the sympathetic understanding of a Federal officer, in crossing the Long Bridge, although it was closely guarded by a company of artillery. Maffitt stayed for a night in Alexandria, and then went on to Richmond and the Confederate capital at Montgomery, Alabama.

John Maffitt saw Mr. Davis, he offered his services to the South, but the President informed him that he did not contemplate forming a navy. Maffitt was so discouraged that he returned to his hotel and was packing his trunk for Europe when Robert Toombs, with Benjamin Hill and others, arrived direct from a discussion with Jefferson Davis and insisted that the South would not agree to his loss. He received, finally, a lieutenant's commission and orders to report to Commodore Tatnall at Savannah. General Beauregard had politely invited Maffitt to join his staff, but the Secretary of War refused the necessary permission.

The Confederate government, immediately after this, was forced to maintain some protection on the waters along its coast, and it purchased, without any reference to their essential fitness, what steam vessels were available. They were, mostly, aged and dilapidated tug boats and flimsy passenger steamers with neither speed nor the tonnage to support suitable ordnance. Maffitt arrived at Savannah May ninth, where he was to take command of the Savannah, a former passenger boat on the inland route to Jacksonville, Florida, and she was, he said abruptly, an absurd abortion. The fleet consisted of the Sampson, an old tug; the Resolute, an old tug; and the Lady Davis, an iron tug. John Maffitt made a number of invaluable suggestions for the improvement of the Confederacy on the sea; they were all refused sanction but one, and that was accepted too late to be put into action. In November he was attached to the staff of General Lee, in South Carolina, in the capacity of Naval Aide, to map roads and construct inland forts.

* * *

In April, Eighteen-sixty-one, Mr. Lincoln proclaimed a military and commercial blockade of the South extending from the capes of Virginia to the mouth of the Rio Grande; this was, in effect, hardly better than a paper blockade; the Paris Congress of Eighteen-fifty-six had ruled that a blockade, to be binding, must be effective; and the Union, with only four warships immediately available, concentrated at the main ports of the Confederacy—Charleston and Savannah and the entrance to the Cape Fear River. The first Federal ship to appear on the Cape Fear station, July twentieth, was the Daylight. She was soon followed by others—the number of blockaders off the New Inlet and the Main, the Western, Bar of the river was rapidly increased to more than thirty. At night they formed in the shape of a crescent, with the points so close to land that it was practically impossible for the smallest boat to pass without discovery; armed picket barges patrolled the waters and often came under the walls of the Confederate forts.

A second cordon was maintained outside Nassau and the Bermudas, the chief ports of delivery and loading for the South; and the Federal cruisers there were quite capable of ignoring the internationally guaranteed safety of all vessels within three geographical miles of neutral land. Still a third cordon of fast steamers later patrolled the edge of the Gulf Stream, where, after a hard night's run with only a glimmer of light at the binnacle, the blockade runners appeared with the early morning.

In the face of such preparations and vigilance, heedless of extraordinary hardship, imminent danger, the blockade was run throughout the war. It was run by swift steamers, tremendous for their day, and by pilot boats and insignificant yawls sailed by mere boys with a cargo of two or three bales of cotton; boats so small that when they were captured they were hooked to the falls of Federal davits and, with cargo and crew, ignominiously hoisted on deck. The successful trips of blockade runners brought enormous profits: a steamer carrying a thousand bales of cotton realized a quarter of a million dollars in an outward and inward trip of two weeks. Cotton could be bought in the Confederacy for three cents gold a pound and it was frequently sold in England for a dollar. The steamer R. E. Lee, under Captain John Wilkinson, ran the blockade at Wilmington twenty-one times; he carried abroad seven thousand bales of cotton worth two million dollars gold. She brought back to the Confederacy equally valuable cargoes. The steamer Siren ran the blockade sixty-four times and her profit was millions.

An immediate, very special, and optimistic industry was begun in Liverpool. Gere's General Advertiser published notices of regular lines of steamers intending to sail between England and the Southern States. "A first class steamship will be dispatched from Liverpool to Charleston on or about the 15th of July next. A monthly service will be established. Goods and passengers for New Orleans, Mobile and Savannah, can be forwarded by this line, Charleston having direct railroad communication with all the Southern and Western cities." This, however, was early in the war; the blockade rapidly became effective; large commercial or political plans for evading or ignoring it were abandoned. Only the fastest steamers, the most skillful and courageous, the most fortunate, commanders, were eventually successful.

The schooner yacht America, winner of the international races off Cowes, England, in Eighteen-fifty-one, was hauled out on the Thames River, rebuilt, and ran the blockade more than once with invaluable cargoes of quinine, morphine, ammunition and surgical instruments. The Banshee, built for a Liverpool firm, was the first steel ship to cross the Atlantic. She was a side-wheeler of remarkably fine lines, two hundred and fourteen feet long and twenty feet in beam, and drew only eight feet of water. The Banshee was five hundred tons gross tonnage, with an anticipated speed of eleven knots, and a crew of thirty-six hands all told. In Eighteen-sixty-four, however, the Colonel Lamb, commanded by Thomas Lockwood of North Carolina, developed a speed of sixteen and four-fifths knots an hour. She was the fastest vessel afloat.

These were, almost wholly, private enterprises. Food for the half-starved Southern armies, essential medicines, and the importation of munitions of war, formed the great necessity for eluding the blockade; and Wilmington was the best situated port for that since the two entrances to the Cape Fear River had thirty miles of sea and shoals, and Smith's Island, between them. From Smithville, midway of the bars, both blockading fleets could be easily seen and an outward-bound vessel chose her most promising course; inward-bound she had a selection of entrances following the wind and the weather. The approaches to both bars were clear of obstructions; the soundings were so regular that the coast could be followed for miles at the edge of the breakers.

Wilmington, during this period, was completely disorganized. It was filled with speculators from all parts of the South attending the weekly auctions of imported cargoes; desperate characters and acts of violence made life and property precarious; it was not only unsafe to go about at night—there was a constant murderous fighting between the drunken crews of steamers and the soldiers stationed on land through the day. The civil authorities were powerless. Agents and employes of different blockade-running companies lived magnificently in houses rented from permanent residents who had retired to the country—houses where, in the past, John Newland Maffitt had danced so many cotillions—and fabulous sums were paid for quarters of lambs and fresh vegetables and tea. Across the river the steam cotton presses occupied a low marshy flat, and there the ships took on and discharged their cargoes. Sentries were stationed on the wharves to prevent deserters from leaving the country.

Notable and romantic individuals, as well as the questionable, were familiar to Wilmington: Captain Roberts, of the Don, was in reality son of the Earl of Buckinghamshire and a port captain in the British navy; the Condor, one of a fleet of fast three-funnel boats, was commanded by the celebrated Admiral Hewett, knighted by Queen Victoria and special envoy to King John of Abyssinia; Burgoyne, lost with the iron-clad Captain in the Bay of Biscay, was an English officer and blockade runner. The Falcon made one trip under Hobart Pasha. The native commanders and pilots, however, were far more significant; they were not engaged in adventure but in a continuous danger and monotony of hardship.

James William Craig, pilot on the steamer Annie, cleared with his ship from Nassau and fell in with a hurricane; they were obliged to heave to for forty hours and lost their reckoning; they were without lunar or solar observations for three days. He was on the Lynx in a hurricane when her paddle-boxes, sponsons and bridge-deck were swept away. The Lynx was chased by the very fast Federal cruiser Fort Jackson and her safety valves were weighted down with the iron tops of the coal bunkers. John William Anderson, piloting the Mary Celeste and dying of yellow fever, hung by the wheel in the arms of two strong sailors. His face was the color of gold and his eyes shone like stars. "Hard starboard," he said. The wheel spun quickly and a shot from the bow gun of a pursuing blockader passed over the pilot-house. "Steady," Anderson said, with the breakers on the coast of North Carolina before him. The Mary Celeste came under the protection of Fort Fisher; she crossed the bar and her engines slowed down in safe water; Anderson was dead.

* *
*

In January, Eighteen-sixty-two, John Maffitt was ordered to the steamer Cecile to run the blockade. The Cecile, engaged in commercial blockade running, had been transferred to the Confederate government by her owners, Frazier, Trenholm and Company of Charleston. She was reported uncommonly fast and could stow to advantage seven hundred bales of cotton. Maffitt took on her cargo at Wilmington and dropped down the Cape Fear River in time to anchor off Smithville at sunset. They watched, through the twilight, the blockading fleet come to position outside the bar. The channel, the Federal attitude announced, was closed for the night. It was clear, with moonlight, and Maffitt was forced to wait until the moon had disappeared; finally he got under way and—he was sailing by the Western Bar—without lights, with nothing white showing, and in dead silence, the Cecile slipped past Fort Caswell and Fort Campbell. The only audible sounds were a rising northeast wind and the faint unavoidable splash and dripping of the paddle wheels.

Night glasses swept the horizon and suddenly, with a lowered voice, an officer announced the presence of steamers lying ahead. The thin phantom of the blockading fleet emerged out of the dark. The Cecile passed between two ships, so close that it seemed impossible to escape discovery; Maffitt went by other floating shapes; it was the pilot's opinion that they were free, when there was a white glare of Drummond lights. The sea was as bright as midday. Captain Maffitt shouted for full speed, and there was an immediate increase of pressure and revolutions. A roar of heavy guns surrounded him, flights of iron shot tore through the Cecile's rigging; the steamer hung quivering after a heavy shock. A shell, Maffitt was informed, had knocked overboard several bales of cotton and wounded two of the crew. They had, however, escaped; the first cordon of the blockade had been run.

The morning was beautifully clear and serene, the Cecile ran felicitously until far in the afternoon, when a sail was reported from the mast-head. Could she be made out? "Yes, sir, a large steamer is heading for us." Maffitt changed his course, he was followed, and chase began. The engines of the Cecile were being overhauled, her fires cleaned, and at first her speed was inconsiderable. The steamer came up rapidly, under the flag of the United States, but night was swifter—there was a brief gold sunset and the dusk thickened. Then an actual derangement of his engine put all hope of escape from Maffitt's mind. In the face of disaster he sent for the chief engineer and inquired if he had a convenient quantity of coal dust. He had. "Be ready," Maffitt said, "in fifteen minutes to feed it. Have clean fuel ready that will not smoke."

The Federal ship drew nearer, the coal dust was shovelled in and dense volumes of sooty blackness rolled out of the Cecile's funnels, drifting on a northeast wind to the south and west. The pursuing steamer turned and followed the bank of smoke, and, with clean coal, Maffitt continued uninterrupted on a northward course. At sunrise he lay in Nassau Harbor discharging his cotton and received his return cargo.

The Cecile sailed at evening and the following morning encountered three Federal men-of-war. She left them behind, but her bulwarks had been badly damaged, her spars splintered by round shot. There was an even greater necessity than common for speed and caution: nine hundred barrels of powder formed part of the supplies for the Confederacy in the hold. Sail was reported again, two steamers ahead standing for the Cecile, but they were lost after an elaborate course of zig-zag running. A burning vessel was then seen, four miles off and enveloped in smoke; Maffitt was obliged to go to her assistance. She was a Spanish barque, her ensign at half-mast and the crew and passengers gathered helplessly in the stern. Ladies were among them. An officer was sent aloft to keep sharp lookout for the enemy, and the chief mate was dispatched to the barque in a cutter. The passengers, he found, were superior in calmness to the crew; the officers from the Cecile succeeded in extinguishing the fire; and Maffitt proceeded on with all possible quickness.

The next day, the last at sea, was undisturbed, and Maffitt decided to go ahead at full speed for sixty miles and then run slowly into the fleet off Cape Fear; all lighthouses had been abandoned, and the most exact navigation, a wide knowledge of currents and of the coast, were indispensable for approaching any Southern harbor. At last, after a headlong rush through the dark, the Cecile was slowly and carefully navigated with the guiding lead. Grim floating shapes came into view through a bank of cloud. A rocket swept with a sparkling rush into the sky, and the calcium flare of Drummond lights distinctly illuminated the sea for miles. There was a hail. "Heave to, or I'll sink you." Captain Maffitt acknowledged the direction and continued in a loud voice, "Stop the engine." He heard, from across the water, the shrill note of a boatswain's whistle, the calling away of the cutters, the tramping feet of the boat's crews. "Back your engine, sir," he was ordered; "stand by to receive my boats." Maffitt whispered to his engineer:

"Full speed ahead, sir, and open wide your throttle-valve."

The Federal officers first thought the Cecile was backing, then, with a salt cursing, command was given to fire. Drummond lights were burned. But, Maffitt related afterward, a radiant mist apparently raised the hull of the Cecile above the line of vision, and a broadside, instead of exploding the gun powder destined for Albert Sidney Johnston and the battle of Shiloh, passed harmlessly through the rigging.

Captain Maffitt had taken a chance so desperately slim that it could scarcely have been said to exist. The Cecile, followed by bursting shells, with a speed of sixteen knots an hour, bore up at the white lines of breakers and quickly found the smooth water of the channel.

Maffitt discharged his cargo, took on cotton, and made the run to Nassau with no more incident than a few shots outside Cape Fear. Nassau, a somnolent resort of invalids, had suddenly assumed the air, the stir and excitement, of an important city. The magical blue harbor was filled with shipping, with deep cargo steamers from England and fragile blockade runners, painted pale blue, out of Wilmington. The warehouses, the wharves and quays, were piled with cotton and merchandise, together with great guns and small-arms and ammunition, for the Confederacy. Captain Maffitt returned there again in the Cecile, and then, in April, he was ordered to the ship Nassau—she had been the Gordon—continuing on the same duty. He wrote in his private journal:

"May 4: I arrived in Nassau with the Gordon and twenty minutes after anchoring the steamer was crowded with visitors. I landed Mr. and Mrs. De Leon, my daughter Florie, who took rooms at the Royal Victoria Hotel.

"At 11 p.m. Mr. Low, provisional master C. S. N., informed me that he had come over on the Confederate gunboat Oreto and at the same time handed me a letter from Commander J. D. Bulloch that I would at once assume command and send Mr. Low back. I immediately surrendered the Gordon and informed Adderly and Co., to whom the Oreto was consigned, that, as a Southern officer, it was my duty to become custodian of the lone Confederate waif upon the waters until the pleasure of the Navy Department should be expressed. The response to my communication brought three young inexperienced officers, strangers to the sea, with instructions for me to assume command, equip, fit out and immediately proceed to sea as a Confederate cruiser."

The Gordon—the steamer Nassau—returning, was captured and Maffitt's daughter, who had again taken passage on her, was sent to New York, where, he records, she was treated with the greatest courtesy.

* *
*

The Oreto had been purchased in England, and sent out under bond, but it was proved that she had left unarmed, and on the eighth of August, Eighteen-sixty-two, she steamed into the Queen's Channel, the English colors were hauled down and the palmetto flag was raised on the Confederate cruiser Florida. The first day at sea two of the crew developed a raving yellow fever. There was no physician aboard and the duty of caring for them fell upon Maffitt. He was forced to give up all thought of active duty; he brought the Florida to anchor off Cardenas; the crew had been reduced by the epidemic to a single engineer and two seamen; and soon, refused all aid by the governor, Maffitt himself was overcome. After a week of hideous suffering he was conscious of three sombre-looking individuals in his cabin. One held a watch. "It is now twenty minutes after nine o'clock. I am convinced, from careful investigation, that the captain cannot survive beyond meridian."

He was, Maffitt informed him, a liar. He had too much to do, he continued, and could not afford to die. He recovered and sailed for Havana, and, unable to secure proper supplies there, he determined to fetch the Confederate port of Mobile. This was a perilous undertaking—Maffitt was still very feeble, the decimated crew was no better, and the entrance to Mobile Harbor was so difficult he'd have to make his attempt by daylight. He hoisted English colors, but the U. S. ship Oneida ignored them; followed by two other vessels of the blockading squadron she poured such a terrible fire into the Florida that every hope of escape fled from Maffitt's mind. One gunboat hung on his port bow and another at his port quarter, and their cannonading was as rapid as it was precise. He ordered the English flag down and raised his own colors. The loud explosions, the roar of shells and crashing of spars, were accompanied by the moaning of the sick men on the Florida.

Everything, then, depended on the engines and on the engineers; they, fortunately, performed their duty without interruption, and Maffitt, slowly, with a splendid cold determination, brought his ship successfully into Mobile. He refitted the Florida, escaped the blockade again, and at sea, on January nineteenth, Eighteen-sixty-two, he captured the Union brig Estelle. It was her first voyage, she was returning from Cuba with honey and sugar for Boston; Maffitt removed a few necessities and set her on fire. He coaled at Havana and on the twenty-second destroyed two Yankee vessels. Then he found that the coal taken on at Havana would not make steam, and he was obliged to go in to Nassau. Running for the New England coast he encountered a hurricane, it drove him across the Gulf Stream and badly damaged his ship. "The Florida unfortunately stows but nine days full steaming coal," he wrote. "I deeply regretted the capacity and badly cut sails that do so little justice to her beautiful hull."

In February he made a prize of the Jacob Bell of New York, with a cargo of tea to the value of a million and a half dollars. A message came from the captain that he had ladies aboard, and Maffitt surrendered his cabin to them. They remained on the Florida five days, and then Maffitt transferred them to the Danish brig Morning Star, bound for St. Thomas. On the sixth of March he ran alongside the Star of Peace, of Boston, from Calcutta. She was about a thousand tons register and had an invaluable cargo of saltpeter for the Federal army. Maffitt took on board Captain Hickly and his crew and burned their ship. He steamed away to the east and, twenty miles distant, the saltpeter ignited: Maffitt was certain a more beautiful panorama was never witnessed on the ocean. He captured the schooner Aldabaran, New York to Marenham, Brazil, and burned her. Sixteen days later he captured the Boston barque Lapwing, bound for Batavia; she was a fine vessel and Maffitt put two howitzers aboard and ordered Lieutenant Everett to command her with two officers and a crew of fifteen.

He took the barque Colcord, from New York to Cape Town, and burned her on April fool's day; on the seventeenth he captured the ship Commonwealth, for San Francisco; the ship and cargo were valued at three hundred and seventy thousand dollars and were, inevitably, burned. Maffitt took the ship Oneida of Bedford, from Shanghai to New York—this was April twenty-fifth—her cargo of tea was worth a million dollars in the United States, and her captain, Maffitt thought, was rather an odd fish—he expected to have the rings on his fingers stolen. He captured and burned the Henrietta of Baltimore, receiving her passengers and crew on the Florida; and on the sixth of May overtook the brig Clarence from Rio de Janeiro. Lieutenant C. W. Read, of the Florida, proposed to take the Clarence, with her papers and cargo intact, to Hampton Roads and attempt to cut out a gunboat or burn one of the merchant vessels assembled there. Maffitt agreed to that; on the eighth of May he was off the port of Pernambuco.

He applied to the governor there for permission to repair damages to his ship and take on coal; the governor refused; but Maffitt argued him into an agreeable attitude. On the thirteenth of May, Maffitt captured and burned the fine vessel Crown Point. He then captured the Southern Cross, a thousand tons, loaded with logwood, and added her to his victims. He kept the Red Gauntlet of Boston, for Hong Kong, with ice, coal and musical instruments, beside him for a number of days in order to transfer her coal to his own bunkers. He spoiled all plans for the Benjamin Hoxie, from the west coast of Mexico. Her destination, the captain asserted, was Falmouth, England; but his clearance was very irregular, his destination was not secure; and, after taking on board the officers and crew and silver bars to the amount of a hundred and five thousand dollars—he was obliged to reconsign the silver to its English owners—Maffitt fired her.

Soon afterward he captured the whaling schooner V. H. Hill, of Provincetown, and, bonding her for ten thousand dollars, he put his prisoners on her at the captain's promise that he would land them in Bermuda. The Sunrise, bound for Liverpool, came next; she had a neutral cargo on board, a very few passengers, and Maffitt bonded her for sixty thousand dollars. On the eighth of July he sighted a Federal side-wheel man-of-war. She had four funnels and was identified as the U. S. steamer Ericsson. When she came within range the Florida opened on her with a starboard broadside and the Ericsson changed her course and bore off without returning a shot. Immediately afterward, within sixty miles of New York, Maffitt took the brig W. B. Nash, with lard and staves, and the whaling schooner Rienzie, and burned them both in the wake of the Ericsson. He entered the harbor of St. Georges, in Bermuda, and was honored by the first salute paid abroad to the Confederate flag.

In May, John Maffitt had been appointed commander, for gallant and meritorious conduct on the steam sloop Florida; he continued his cruise until his engineers notified him that the vessel's shaft required relaying, the machinery would have to be overhauled; Maffitt was in the English Channel and he determined to run into the harbor of Brest. Admiral Comte Guedon received him warmly at his palace. He was happy to inform Commander Maffitt that the French government extended to him the hospitality of Brest. There were extraordinary rumors about the Florida: her hull was filled with gold captured from the enemy; Maffitt was a sea vulture with an insatiable thirst for blood; his officers were pirates and his crew a set of cut-throats; outside the roads corpses had been seen to hang from the Florida's masts. A great crowd gazed at her from the quay when she was towed in and docked in charge of the engineers of the French arsenal. The young officers of the Florida, in bright new uniforms, attended the opening of the theatrical season, and it was universally agreed that they were too young, too handsome and too modest, to be guilty of any crimes.

* *
*

The Florida was not large. She mounted only eight guns —six 48-pound Blakeleys, with a stern and bow chaser; she had been forced to leave Mobile with an insufficient crew, and the oldest of her staff of officers, except for her commander, was twenty-seven. The London Times was informed by its correspondent that he had no difficulty in making out the Florida as she lay at anchor among some of the giants of the French Navy—a long, low, black, rakish-looking craft—a pigmy among these monsters, and yet a formidable pigmy, even to the unpracticed eye, the palmetto flag flying proudly from her mizzen. John Maffitt was described as a slight, well-knit man of about forty-two, a merry-looking man with a ready determined air, full of life and business. His plainly furnished little state-room was like a merchant's office. A round table in the center was occupied by books and manuscript, shelves were filled with account books and charts. Maffitt's cabin, every part of the Florida, appeared to have been built for use rather than ornament. "We never seek a fight," Maffitt explained, "and we don't avoid one. You see, we've only two vessels against fifteen hundred, so we should stand a poor chance. Our object is merely to destroy commerce, so as to bring about a peace. We have taken, altogether, seventy-two prizes and estimated the value at fifteen million dollars." However, he continued, there was very little actual treasure on board the Florida: the papers of the burned prizes were all kept, and a valuation made, in the expectation that when peace was restored the Confederate government would make an equable appropriation of money to the captors. The captain and officers of the Florida were working on the faith of the future solvency of the South.

The Florida was soon ready for sea, but a severe attack at Maffitt's heart compelled him to apply for leave. This was in September, Eighteen-sixty-three; he was sent for rest and travel in Sweden; but he was extremely impatient to return to active duty; and he took command of a cargo ship sailing for the Confederacy. In June of the next year he was sailing from St. Georges in charge of the blockade runner Lilian. The voyage for three hundred and fifty miles was uninterrupted, and then he sighted a Federal ship enveloped in dense clouds of white smoke from her Cumberland coal. She was dropped astern and, the following morning, Maffitt prepared to lay to between the outer and inner cordon of blockaders, waiting for the dark. At half past one an impressive steamer with immense paddle-wheels and lofty black hull appeared at full speed from the direction of Wilmington. Before steam could be got up on the Lilian the enemy was uncomfortably near, and Maffitt ordered the mail bags to be brought up, and weights attached, so that they might be sunk in the event of capture.

The pressure of steam on the Lilian rose from fifteen pounds to twenty, from twenty pounds to twenty-three; the pressure increased to twenty-six and the revolutions of the paddle-wheels mounted from twenty-six to twenty-eight, to thirty-three, in the minute; and within two hours the tall Yankee ship was low on the horizon. It was necessary, then, to change the course of the Lilian, to run around her pursuer; but Maffitt drove his vessel so fast that he came within sight of the blockaders off Cape Fear before sunset. Night, fortunately, fell quickly; silently and with infinite caution the Lilian was worked in, past ship after ship, almost under their rails; there was no hail, no blaze of Drummond lights; once more Maffitt successfully came into a Southern harbor.

Soon after this, greatly to his satisfaction, he was ordered to Wilmington and the blockade runner Owl. On the twenty-first of December, Eighteen-sixty-four, Maffitt received on board the naval steamer Owl seven hundred and eighty bales of cotton, and, with three other vessels, ran clear of the Federal sentinels without the loss of a rope yarn. At St. Georges, Bermuda, he found a number of vessels waiting intelligence of the outcome of a Federal expedition under General Butler against Fort Fisher, at the mouth of the Cape Fear River. Fort Fisher was reported to be safe, and six ships cheerfully departed for Wilmington; Maffitt had a second assurance that Fisher was intact and he laid his course for Cape Fear. But when he approached the channel there he was amazed to find only one boat on guard. He fetched around her without trouble; there was a conflagration on Bald Head and no response to signals; Fort Caswell, however, seemed quiet, natural, to Maffitt, and he decided to continue up the river.

When he came to anchor he learned that a second Union attack, under General Terry and Admiral Porter, had reduced Fort Fisher and that Cape Fear was in possession of Federal forces. It was imperative for Maffitt to leave immediately, Union gunboats were within hail of him, and he had already ordered the anchor chain slipped when the pilot on the Owl begged permission to go ashore, if it was for no more than ten minutes. He had left his wife ill and without means of support. This request Maffitt could not refuse; and, while the pilot was absent, steam was raised and the anchor chain unshackled. The Owl, running out, was pursued by the solitary blockader. "His artillery," Maffitt wrote, "palled under the reverberation of an explosion that rumbled portentously from wave to wave in melancholy echoes that enunciated far at sea the fate of Caswell."

The cargo of the Owl was exceedingly important to the South, and, with Wilmington closed to the Confederacy, Maffitt determined to land it if possible at Charleston. That port was more closely guarded than ever, and he accommodated his speed to arrive off the Charleston Bar at dusk. Throughout the day he was pursued by vigilant steamers along the coast: they would sight the Owl, fire up and make a dash for her; but the blockade runner drew off with such speed that the Federal boats almost immediately gave up chase.

At nine in the evening he was close by Maffitt's Channel, the channel that, in the service of the U. S. Coast Survey, he had discovered and charted. At the western end of Rattlesnake Shoal the Owl encountered streaks of mist and fog; they lifted suddenly and Maffitt saw that he was about to run into an anchored blockader. There was barely room to put the helm hard aport, the ships missed collision by less than fifteen feet. The Federal officer on deck cried the familiar order, "Heave to or I'll sink you." The command was disregarded, and the Owl received his entire broadside. The turtle-back was cut away, the bulwarks in front of the engine room torn up, and twelve men were slightly or severely wounded. Rockets were fired, and Drummond lights illuminated a fleet of animated vessels, but the Owl passed swiftly out of range and retired into the night.

It was useless to make any further attempt to land his cargo in Charleston, and Maffitt determined to proceed to Galveston, Texas. On the fifth of May, it was an exceedingly fine morning, Maffitt successfully ran through the fleet of sixteen vessels blockading the port of Galveston, but at the entrance to the harbor, at a point within range of the Federal guns, he unfortunately grounded on Bird Island. In the harbor there was a Confederate fleet commanded by Captain James H. McGarvey, two gunboats, the Diana and Bayou City, and four transports; and McGarvey and a volunteer crew went to the assistance of the Owl. Under a heavy fire, and directed by Maffitt with an exact coolness from the exposed bridge of his steamer, the blockade runner was floated; the people of Galveston, on the roofs of the houses fronting the harbor, gave a great cheer and the Owl—it was impossible for Maffitt to proceed with his design—escaped to sea. Later he was at Havana; from there he sailed to Halifax; the last hope for the Confederacy was exhausted, and, following his final official orders, he delivered the Owl to the agents of Frazier, Trenholm and Company at Liverpool. Mr. Lincoln's blockade had reduced the South to a poverty that left no other course than surrender.

*   *

*

John Maffitt took command of the British steamer Widgeon, trading between Liverpool and South America. January, in Eighteen-sixty-seven, he wrote to his daughter

Florie that, as soon as his engagement in England ended, he'd return to the United States and see what could be done about the recovery of his property. He was unsuccessful in that—the North seized his estate of seventy-five thousand dollars and, a disgraceful performance, never returned it to him. David McRae, an Englishman, encountered him in Eighteen-sixty-eight; he had heard a very great deal about Maffitt in the North, where he was widely regarded as the ablest naval officer in the service of the Confederacy; it was said that if he had remained with the Union he would have occupied Admiral Farragut's place. John Maffitt, McRae found, was a cultivated and gentlemanly man, with a fine-cast head, a keen dark eye, a strong tuft of black whiskers on his chin, and firm little mouth that seemed to express the energy and determination of his character. McRae remembered him well as he stepped about in his short military cloak, dignified and stern-appearing. He was, then, in reduced circumstances, but, like so many of his old military and naval associates, he was endeavoring to make a living and reconcile himself to the new order of things.

"The Confederate navy," Maffitt explained, "minute though it was, won a place for itself in history. To the Confederates the credit belongs of testing in battle the invulnerability of iron-clads and of revolutionizing the navies of the world. The Merrimac did that. And though we had but a handful of light cruisers, while the ocean swarmed with armed Federal vessels, we defied the Federal navy and swept Northern commerce from the seas. If only," he added, "the old usage in regard to sea prizes in neutral ports had been still in vogue, we should have done more, and the pecuniary gain to the officers and men of the Confederate government would have been immense—but a Confederate cruiser out upon the ocean was a lonely knight-errant. Her nationality was unrecognized; her facilities for supplies and repairs hampered by neutral proclamations that affected only her. She had to do everything for herself, live upon the enemy, and contend friendless and alone in the world. Well, it is all over now."

When it was clear that his property was lost Maffitt returned to Wilmington, to North Carolina, where his daughter Florie lived. He managed to secure a farm of two hundred and twelve acres on the sound at Wrightsville Beach; he called his house The Moorings, and gathered there a stepdaughter, Mary Read, and Colden Rhind, one of his younger sons. Another son, Eugene, married a Miss Kate Martin, they lived with his father, and Kate's sister, Emma, came to see them there. Captain Maffitt and Emma were caught in a cold January rain, and he wrapped about her shoulders his antique faded blue cape, the military cloak of McRae's report. It would shield her, Maffitt said, as it had shielded him in his wanderings over land and sea for many years. Its silent folds, she replied, must hold a romantic history. Her conjecture, Maffitt assured her, was true: it had served him in Italy and France, in England and Germany and Palestine, and among the Pyramids. Years ago the Queen of Greece had worn it around her shoulders.

At Piræus Maffitt, who was the Captain's aide, was ordered to prepare the barge to bring on board the Constitution the King and Queen of Greece. The Queen was known to cherish a passion for dancing, and Captain Bruin ordered part of the ship's band to the quarterdeck. The Queen looked wistfully at the Captain, and he was obliged to admit that he was no waltzer. He beckoned to one of his aides, Midshipman Maffitt, who was quite an adept at the business, and presented him to the Queen—they were the same age, fifteen. Dusk floated over the harbor, muskets were ranged around the capstan with lighted candles in their muzzles. The Queen of Greece, wrapped in Mr. Maffitt's cloak, whispered to him.

Emma Martin and Maffitt determined to write a book together and call it Oreto, or the Adventures of a Midshipman's Cloak; they changed the title to Nautilus, or Cruising Under Canvas; in November, Eighteen-seventy, they were married. Maffitt became a practical farmer: he raised grapes of different varieties, but especially the scuppernong, which he grew in great perfection. He had orchards of peaches and apples and cultivated pears and figs, blackberries and strawberries and raspberries. A flower garden was carefully tended; he especially delighted in constructing arbors for climbing roses. His evenings with Emma were literary; they projected a great many books and papers; their description of Raphael Semmes was printed in The South Atlantic Monthly.

Mr. Cleveland was elected to the Presidency in Eighteen-eighty-four, and friends of John Maffitt's nominated him for a position in the Custom House at Wilmington; the President refused to confirm the nomination; and Maffitt's spirit was shocked. He had moved from The Moorings into Wilmington, both because he was now unable to superintend his farm and for the education of his children. He failed rapidly. "The ship is ready," he said, his mind far from the actuality of dying, "the sails are set and the wind is favorable; all we are waiting for is Mr. Lambert to come and ask God's blessing upon us; then we will heave anchor and away on the billows."

His old age had been darkened by hardship and sorrow—both Florie and Eugene, his favorite daughter and his son, died before him—but his youth was a splendid panorama of romantic adventure. His life was bright with danger. It was performed with honor, sustained by courage. War and the sea possessed him, the two great enemies of monotony and fear; through the years of his maturity he had death to face—hurricanes in fragile iron ships, pestilence, and Federal shells in the white glare of Drummond lights. He literally sailed through battle fleets, without the privilege of returning a shot, when the sea was crushed with the weight of explosions showered upon him; he sailed through fleets cunningly in the dark, with a glimmer at his binnacle and not a whisper along his deck, and lost not as much as a rope yarn. He took seventy-two prizes in a steam sloop with a crew of scarcely better than boys, over all the western ocean, and such were his exploits, his character and determination were such, that he compelled the assistance of France, the courtesy of the port of Brest, against all the influence of the United States.

John Maffitt was a midshipman, when he was thirteen, on the Constitution, when she was a man-of-war of the line; he danced, when he was lieutenant, the graceful and gay cotillions of a lost world; he was a commander in the days of the Confederacy. What happened in his old age, even his sorrow and loss, must have been remote compared with his memories. Nothing could detract from the dignity of his step on the changed streets of Wilmington. No other garment in the world owned the sustaining magic, the beauty, of his faded cloak. The blockade runners, the shadows on the sea, stayed vivid and recompensing in his mind. The sea and, appearing above the horizon, the smoke of Federal cruisers! Rising speed and the sting of salt spray, the white town of St. Georges against the low sage-green Bermuda hills, the indigo harbor of Nassau, ineffable blue noons on the Gulf Stream, nights of stars and the regular beat of paddle-wheels, all preserved him against the sense of futility, the vain regret, that in ordinary men and times bring life to an empty close.

The Florida was captured by Commander Napoleon Collins, of the United States Navy, at Bahia, Brazil. This was in defiance of all decency, the Florida had received permission to remain in port forty-eight hours. The Brazilian government demanded her return but she was arbitrarily sunk.

THE GOOD FIGHTER

THE GOOD FIGHTER

General Nathan Bedford Forrest was a legacy to the Civil War from the American frontier. He was born in the deep South and fought for the Confederacy; but he belonged, by tradition and spirit and habit, to all the United States. He was native to it in a sense that was uncommon even in Eighteen-sixty; Forrest spoke with an early American idiom—to the end of his life he said fit when he meant fought, he said mout instead of might. Betwixt and fetch were frequent in his vocabulary. "I never see a pen," he once said, "but what I think of a snake." His written order at Brice's Crossing is a perfect expression of provincial simplicity. "Tell Bell to move up and fetch all he's got." That valid color of English speech has been lost; education and the infusion of other languages have killed it; it was killed by the destruction of localities of men and habits and of place. Forrest was fortunate:

He was born on the thirteenth of July, Eighteen-twenty-one, in a log cabin, a frontier settlement, of what was then middle Tennessee. The cabin was primitive even for cabins—it had but one room with a shallow loft, an end was filled by a great fireplace, there were two doors swinging on wooden hinges at the middle of opposite walls, and there were no windows. Light and air came through the chinks of hewn cedar logs and down the wide chimney. Outside there was a patch of cleared land—a very few acres—enclosed with a straight stake fence of cedar; short inner fences divided the yard at the rear from a garden and young orchard of peach and apple trees, pears and plums. A public road ran by the yard so newly cut through the forest that the stumps and roots of trees had not been removed.

For three generations Nathan Bedford Forrest's family had followed the restless course of pioneers. Shadrach Forrest moved from Virginia in Seventeen-forty to the colony of North Carolina. There he married and lived and reared a large family of children. Nathan, his second son, wedded a Miss Baugh, of Irish descent; in Eighteen-six they removed to Tennessee and two years later settled in the Duck River country, then Bedford County; their first child, William, who became a blacksmith, was General Forrest's father. But that, today, is a wholly misleading statement: blacksmiths—where they exist at all—are regarded as meritorious, but small, inferior, members of society. At the beginning of the Nineteenth Century, when William learned his trade, they were both important and highly esteemed. Early in the Eighteen hundreds no free American was inferior save in morality or industry. Outside a few cities, a few plantations, there was small consciousness of social differences; there literally was no leisure class. No rich men existed whatever, and where there are no rich there are no poor. Where there is no money, but only labor, labor in the place of money is the measure of personal weight and social importance.

William Forrest was following his vocation when, in Eighteen-twenty, he married Marian Beck. Only a little is known about him; General Forrest's mother was Scottish in blood; her family had emigrated from South Carolina to Caney Springs, near the Duck River. She was almost six feet tall with a powerful muscular frame and weighed an hundred and eighty pounds. Her hair was dark, her eyes bluegrey; she had prominent cheek bones and a wide forehead; her face was deeply lined and her expression, her voice, were gentle. Bedford Forrest cherished for her an immeasurable affection.

His boyhood was happily obscure; he had great physical courage and an indomitable will; when he was a child—like the infant Hercules—he killed a tremendous snake. In Bedford's case it was a rattlesnake. He rode skillfully, mostly bareback, but once, suddenly attacked by dogs, his horse pitched him through the air. He landed disconcerted but on his feet, the dogs fled, and long afterward Forrest insisted that that was his first lesson in the value of direct assault. When he was sixteen his father died, and the burden of supporting the family fell upon him: he labored with his brothers at clearing land; he raised corn and wheat, oats and cotton, and supported a drove of cattle and various other stock. Bedford toiled all through the day and at night sat up making buckskin leggings and shoes and coonskin caps for the smaller boys. Nearly everything, then, was homemade: his mother and sisters spun yarn and cotton thread; they wove cloth on wooden looms and cut and sewed together clothing.

In Eighteen-forty-one Bedford Forrest joined a company of volunteers who offered their services in the Texas struggle for independence. There is a description of him, by General James R. Chalmers, at that period. "A tall blackhaired and grey-eyed youth, scarce twenty years of age, who then gave the first evidence of the military ardor he possessed." The company arrived at New Orleans; many of the volunteers, soon discouraged, returned from Louisiana to their homes; but Forrest went on to Houston. He found no need for his presence there, his small store of money was quickly exhausted, and he worked on a farm until he was able to go back to the Duck River country.

In Eighteen-seventeen Bedford County had become part of the new State of Mississippi, and in Eighteen-forty-two

Forrest moved to the northern part of the state, to the town of Hernando, where, with an uncle, Jonathan Forrest, he speculated in horses and cattle. They were immediately successful; every year Bedford added to an increasingly comfortable sum of money. In Eighteen-forty-five a dispute rose between Jonathan Forrest, who was an aged man, and four members of a neighboring family. They brutally shot Jonathan down, and Bedford, alone, instantly attacked them. He was wounded, but not seriously, by a fire of pistols, and with a double-barrelled pistol he disabled two; a bystander then put a bowie knife in his hand and the two remaining assailants not only fled but permanently left Hernando. That year, he was twenty-five, he married Mary Montgomery.

He found her on a Sunday morning in a carriage sunk in a mud hole. Two men on horse standing at the side of the road had made no effort to assist her, and Bedford Forrest, dismounting and wading through the water and mud, asked permission to carry her to firm ground. He did this; then, after he had assisted the driver in freeing the carriage, he characteristically undertook to correct the indolence of the other men. They avoided an imminent violence by riding rapidly away; Forrest introduced himself; he asked permission to call on Mary Montgomery and his appearance almost immediately followed. He encountered, on her porch, the inert spectators of his first meeting with Mary Montgomery and ordered them off the place; their retreat was no less obligingly prudent than before; and at once Bedford Forrest successfully proposed marriage.

The sale of negroes, at that time, had become an important industry in the deep South, and Forrest brought his affairs in Hernando to a close—he removed to the young city of Memphis and became a broker in real estate and speculator in slaves. He was, apparently, an extraordinary slave dealer

—when Forrest purchased negroes he delivered them to his body servant, Jeremiah, with instructions to bathe them and put them in fresh comfortable clothes. It was a fact that, in the face of the vicarious generosity of abolitionists, his slaves venerated him. He was invariably kind to them.

Bedford Forrest was always engaged in heated personal or impersonal contention: he determined to save a citizen of Memphis threatened with lynching, and placed himself between the jail and an attacking mob; he stood at the door with a knife held high in his left hand and swore to kill any man who approached him. He was, ordinarily, grave and dignified; but anger completely transformed Forrest; during paroxysms of rage his face changed color, its capillaries were so charged with blood that he grew bright scarlet; the blood vessels of his eyes were flaming red. His voice became harsh, metallic rather than human. Later, in battle, it could be heard clearly above the massed roar of cannon.

He was elected to the Memphis Board of Aldermen, but resigned to devote all his time to the cultivation of cotton— he had purchased invaluable uncleared cotton lands along the Mississippi River and two wide plantations in Coahoma County. In Eighteen-fifty-nine he brought his real estate operations in Memphis to an end and gave up the slave market; two years afterward his properties made a thousand bales of cotton; he had an annual income—tremendous for his period—of thirty thousand dollars.

* *
*

His distinguishing career, his true justification, began on the fourteenth of July, Eighteen-sixty-one, when he enlisted as a Confederate private in Captain Josiah White's Tennessee Mounted Rifles. A few days after his enlistment some notable citizens of Memphis proceeded to Nashville, where they conferred with the governor of Tennessee, Isham Harris, and General Leonidas Polk. The result was that Forrest was given authority to raise a battalion of cavalry for volunteer service. He immediately placed an advertisement in the Memphis Daily Appeal: "Having been authorized by Governor Harris to raise a battalion of mounted rangers for the war, I desire to enlist 500 able-bodied men, mounted and equipped with such arms as they can procure—shot guns and pistols preferable—suitable to the service. Those that cannot equip themselves will be furnished arms by the state. When mustered in, a valuation of the property in horses and arms will be made, and the amount credited to the volunteers. Those wishing to enlist are requested to report themselves at the Gayoso House, where quarters will be assigned until such time as the battalion is raised."

Bedford Forrest equipped himself from his own resources; he secretly made a trip into Ohio and Kentucky where supplies for his battalion might be procured; and while he was absent Captain Charles May recruited a splendid company in Memphis called the Forrest Rangers. By October, eight companies of mounted volunteers were assembled, the battalion was organized, and Forrest elected lieutenant colonel. Before the end of October he was ready for duty. Colonel Forrest and his men—armed principally with double-barrelled shot guns—were ordered to the headquarters of General Lloyd Tilghman at Hopkinsville, Kentucky. At the village of Sacramento, however, Forrest decided to overtake and attack a body of Federal cavalry. Riding into action, a Kentucky girl, mounted on a superfine horse, galloped at his side and cheered his rangers forward. "Her untied tresses," he wrote in his official report, "floating in the breeze, infused nerve into my arm and kindled knightly chivalry in my heart." He seized a rifle from one of the volunteers and fired the first shot of the engagement.

He charged with no particular order other than a command for his troops to hold all fire until they were within close range; that, he saw at once, was a doubtful method of attack; and he developed his famous movement by flank and rear. Forrest kept back his men on horse, he threw forward a number on foot as skirmishers, and then advanced with his mounted force from points unobserved by the enemy. Single troopers, behind logs and trees and fence corners, kept up a sharp fire, a column swung into view from the right and another fell on the Union left flank. Forrest, standing in his stirrups, his sabre in the air, seemed to be a foot taller than any other man in the world. The Federal cavalry broke and fled.

At Fort Donelson, leading the advance against Pillow's attacking column, Forrest was in his full accomplished glory: he rode erect and easy at the head of his command, his deep-set eyes alert beneath the wide slightly upturned brim of a soft felt hat. His broad high forehead, his shaggy brows and high cheek bones and bold assertive nose, were all stamped with tenacity. About his ears and neck half-curling locks of black hair hung so stiff and stubborn they were scarcely moved by a persistent cold wind. His dark moustache and short beard were solid, grey, with frozen moisture. Forrest's compressed lips, the deep flush over his face, were ominous. A heavy grey overcoat, with a cape, was close-buttoned at his throat and hung to his knees, buckled over it there was a broad black belt, supporting two navy sixes and his long heavy sabre, ground—against all military ruling—to a razor-keen edge. His words were few and sharp, like pistol shots.

During the battle a shell crashed through his horse, just behind Forrest's leg, and he ran on foot until he came up with his command. He had, throughout the war, twenty-nine horses shot from under him—two at Fort Donelson, one was pierced by seven bullets; at Monterey his horse was killed and Forrest badly wounded in the hip; at Munfordville his horse was shot and his shoulder dislocated from the fall; in the second engagement of Dover two horses were killed under him; at Thompson's Station, Roderick, his favorite war mount, was slain; in the pursuit of Colonel Abel Streight, of Indiana, three of his horses were shot; at Chickamauga, Highlander, another cherished horse, was killed; at Rossville his horse was shot through the neck in a charge, and Forrest, realizing that the animal was rapidly bleeding to death, held his hand over the wound until he reached a place of comparative safety. A second horse was killed in the same action, and Forrest continued on King Philip, a large dapple-grey animal, slow as a dray horse except in the excitement of battle; King Philip was wounded several times at Okolona, but he survived the war; he was with Forrest when he surrendered. At Fort Pillow he had two horses killed and a third wounded; at Plantersville his mount was fatally wounded; at Selma another was slain.

General Bedford Forrest was not a soldier in Lee's elevated sense, he had none of Beauregard's formal military splendor, he was without Albert Sidney Johnston's fine melancholy humanity—Forrest was, simply, a good fighter. There wasn't a better fighter in the North or South. He was, at the same time, an able and successful leader; Forrest was not innocent of tactics or empty of thought; but sheer battle changed him into a simple and terrible agent of destruction. He was totally without caution.

Early in the war he was so disdainful of ordinary prudence, he was so reckless in personal exposure, that no one thought he could continue to live. His passion of combat was so fierce that his sabre was equally fatal to his friends and enemies; in battle, however, he owned a genius that rose to meet every emergency. His use of artillery, for example, often moving his guns forward to the skirmishing line, would have been an act of sheer madness in an ordinary commander, but it was overwhelmingly successful with Forrest. "War means fighting and fighting means killing," he repeated again and again. It is a fact that alone and hand to hand he fought and routed thirty Union soldiers. It is probable that, in all the wars of the world, no commanding officer ever killed so many enemy.

Forrest was especially ruthless with any form of cowardice: at Murfreesboro he shot the color-bearer of a stampeding regiment and rallied the troops. In a fight near West Point he jumped from his horse and with his stick thrashed a trooper who had left the line. All his officers were ordered to shoot any man who flickered. He was fully appreciated in the Union army. Sherman said, "Keep Forrest away from me, and I will attend to Johnston and cut the Confederacy in two." He was strictly temperate, he never took a drink except when he was wounded; Forrest didn't know brandy from whiskey and called them both liquor. He was, as well, deeply religious—there was preaching at his headquarters on Sunday, prayers in his tent at night. Always, before he went into action, he drew up his men and all stood with uncovered heads while a chaplain asked God's blessing on them. He released a terrified Federal chaplain explaining that he would keep him to preach if he were not needed so much more by the sinners of the other side.

*　　*
*

At Shiloh, the second day of battle, Colonel Forrest's horse carried him far into the line of Federal reserves; he was surrounded by Union soldiers firing at him and shouting,

"Shoot that man! Knock him off his horse!" An infantryman shoved his musket practically against Forrest's side and discharged it; the ball entered his left hip and disabled him for weeks. On his forty-first birthday, in July, Eighteen-sixty-two, by an extraordinary mixture of effrontery and military skill he captured Murfreesboro. His original battalion was transferred to another officer and, hiding his chagrin and indignation, Forrest opened a recruiting office in Murfreesboro. Within six weeks he had gathered about him a fresh formidable body of men. The Fourth Tennessee cavalry, under James W. Starnes and a cavalry regiment from Alabama joined Forrest.

He spread rumors everywhere about the large number of his troops, and maintained a constant beating of kettle drums to lend an effect of closely supporting infantry. He pursued the Federals and captured Trenton, he captured Union City, he won the battle of Parker's crossroad. Forrest forced a thousand of his horses to swim the Tennessee River when there wasn't time to ferry them over. He took a fortified Union camp at Brentwood together with five hundred prisoners; he overwhelmed a strong stockade and captured two hundred and thirty prisoners; he destroyed Harpeth Ferry; but Forrest was defeated at Franklin. Captain Freeman, his foremost artilleryman, was killed there. The Union command determined to destroy two important Southern railroads leading out of Chattanooga, one to Atlanta and the other to Knoxville, and Colonel Abel D. Streight of Indiana was given charge of the expedition. He chose, for his advance, a mountainous and thinly inhabited country, and where—always following the mountains—there was a marked Union sympathy; the hills were so rugged, the roads so wretched, that Streight put his men on mules.

He proceeded by the Cumberland River to Palmyra; he

sent his troops on in boats up the Tennessee to Fort Henry; Streight arrived before his force and continued, with every mule he could discover, to Eastport. He had two thousand picked men, and the Union General Dodge, twelve miles away at Bear Creek, had five thousand and five hundred more. At Eastport the Confederates stampeded the Federal mules: they crept, in the fashion of Comanches, into the corral and with hoots and yells and the firing of guns scattered four hundred of the best animals. Streight filed out of Eastport in April, this was Eighteen-sixty-three, and, harassed by General Roddey, he reached Tuscumbia. Here he had disturbing information:

Forrest, in pursuit of him, had crossed the Tennessee River.

That, in reality, did General Forrest less than justice— he had, by a series of forced marches, night and day, almost come up to the Union advance. He had joined Roddey, and, beyond the Tennessee River, he held a position across General Dodge's course. There were a number of minor engagements in which Dodge was successful; and, on the twenty-eighth April, James Moon, a considerable citizen of Tuscumbia, rode through the Federal lines to bring Forrest the information that a large body of Union troops had passed Mount Hope in the direction of Moulton. It was understood, Streight explained later, that in the event Forrest took after him, Dodge and a force of cavalry were to follow Forrest. Streight's lightning brigade marched out of Tuscumbia, over almost impassable roads, in a night of hard rain and mud and impenetrable darkness. His progress was extremely slow, but he had the cheerful news from General Dodge that he had turned Forrest back. Streight rested his weary column at Moulton and then moved eastward toward Blountsville.

Again his information about Bedford Forrest had not

marched with the fact: Forrest threw Roddey and his Alabama regiment, a Tennessee regiment and Julians' battalion, between Dodge and Streight; and then, with incredible rapidity, he fell upon Streight. The Confederates attacked on the side of Sand Mountain; they had, there, less than a thousand men, and the Federal soldiers forced them down the small deeply worn beds of creeks where the steep sides were dense with laurel. Forrest lost two personally cherished guns and his temper rose accordingly. He rode among his cavalrymen beating them with the flat of his sabre and cursing amazingly; Forrest ordered every man to dismount and hitch his horse to a sapling. He would recover his guns, he asserted, if it destroyed his entire command. He forced a battle on a mountain ridge an hour before dark and the fighting continued until past ten o'clock; it was all at close range, there was no light except the flash of pistols and carbines.

The Federal force was in a desperate position, it could not return to the Union base at Tuscumbia, Streight was forced to keep on—a hopeless endeavor—toward the Confederate arsenals at Rome in Georgia. He transferred his supplies from wagons to pack mules, and burned the wagons, and—the smoke was still rising—Forrest, at the head of his column, arrived in a whirlwind of dust. A scout came galloping up to Forrest with the excited report that a heavy force of Union cavalry was overtaking them. Forrest asked, "Did you see the Yankees?" No, he replied; he had been in a blacksmith shop; someone had told the scout that he had seen them. Colonel Forrest seized him by the throat with both hands; he dragged him from his horse and beat his head against a tree. "Now, damn you," he said, "if you ever come to me again with a pack of lies you won't get off so easily." At the fording of the Black Warrior River two of the Federal mules were drowned, and some Confederates, stripping off their clothes, recovered the hard-tack from the dead animals. A freckled and powerful youth stumbling up the bank with a heavy soaked box expressed their appreciation. "Boys, it's wet and full of mule hair, but it's better than anything the old man is giving us now."

The Union advance had become a retreat; it was, in reality, no better than an orderly flight. Forrest, after a fourth relentless night's march, again overtook Streight at the bridge over Black Creek. There Black Creek is a crooked and sluggish stream; it has its source, however, in a plateau on Lookout Mountain; it falls by a series of crystal and pure cascades over rocks to the stained water of the lowlands. The bridge, in Eighteen-sixty-three, was wood, rude and uncovered; there was no other known means of crossing the creek except by a long abandoned structure two miles distant; and Colonel Streight planned to destroy the Black Creek Bridge and delay Forrest until he could reach the Chattooga River near Rome.

By nine o'clock, on the morning of May second, in spite of Forrest's rapid movement, all the Federal force except a rear vidette had crossed the creek. Streight put howitzers in position on the east bank, he piled fence rails on the bridge and fired it. Bedford Forrest, with his attending cloud of dust, was too late. He halted beside the road where there was a farmhouse, built after the primitive habit of that section in one story with two rooms on either side of a wide passageway. A widow named Sansom with two daughters lived there; Mrs. Sansom's only son, who had supported them, had long ago joined the Confederate army; and, without slaves, the women were struggling to stay alive. Emma Sansom—she was sixteen—saw that General Forrest was a Southern officer; she realized, she wrote afterward, that they were in the midst of their own men; and she told Forrest there was an old ford on her mother's farm where, when the water was low, she had seen cows walking through the stream. She believed his horses could cross there; no one else knew of this lost ford; she, Emma Sansom, could guide him to it.

Emma, all knowledge of her is pleasant, was born at Social Circle, in Georgia. In Eighteen-fifty-two her father had moved to Black Creek, Alabama, and he died there seven years later.

* *
*

She was at home, the morning of the second of May, when a company of men wearing blue uniforms and riding mules galloped past the house and went on toward the bridge. Pretty soon a great crowd came along, and some of them stopped at the gate and asked for water. Emma and her sister each carried a bucketful to the gate and a soldier asked Emma where her father was. She told him he was dead. He asked if she had any brothers and—liberal with the truth—she replied six. He asked where they were and Emma said in the Confederate army. He continued:

"Do you think the South will whip?"

"They do."

"What do you think about it?"

"I think God is on our side and we will win."

"You do! Well, if you had seen us whip Colonel Roddey the other day and run him across the Tennessee River, you would agree God was on the side of the best artillery."

The Federal soldiers began to dismount, Emma and her sister went into the house, but they were followed. A search began for men's saddles and firearms, only a side saddle was discovered, the skirts were cut off that, and a loud voice said from the road, "You men bring a chunk of fire with you and get out of that house." Fire was secured from the kitchen, the soldiers left, and an officer put a guard around the house for its protection. Soon Emma saw smoke rising and knew that the bridge was burned. At her mother's suggestion they went to save their rail fences; but it was too late—the rails were already piled on the bridge. They returned to find a Yankee riding furiously up the road; there were men behind him shouting, "Halt!" and, "Surrender!" The fugitive stopped and held up his hands. His gun was seized. The officer then in charge continued, "Ladies, do not be alarmed, I am General Forrest, I and my men will protect you from harm. Where are the Yankees?" Emma's mother replied:

"They have set the bridge on fire and are standing in line on the other side, and if you go down that hill they will kill the last one of you."

The main body of Forrest's command had arrived, a general shooting began, and Mrs. Sansom with her daughters—Emma, she admits, was in the lead—ran back to their house. It was then Forrest asked where he could cross the creek; Emma explained about the ford and said that if he would put her saddle on a horse she could guide him to it. "There is no time to saddle a horse," Forrest told her; "get up here behind me." He rode close to the bank along the road and Emma lightly obeyed him. Just as they started off her mother came up about out of breath. "Emma," she gasped, "what do you mean?" Forrest answered for her. "She is going to show me a ford where I can get my men over in time to catch those Yankees before they get to Rome. Don't be uneasy. I will bring her back safe."

They rode into a field where there was a small branch and ravine with a thick undergrowth which, for a short distance, kept them hidden from Federal observation; the branch emptied into Black Creek just above the burning bridge and soon Emma Sansom said, "General Forrest, I think we had better get off the horse, as we are now where we may be seen." They both dismounted and crept through the bushes; they reached the ford, Emma happened to be first, and Forrest quickly stepped between her and the Yankees. "I am glad to have you for a pilot," he explained, "but I am not going to make breastworks of you." The howitzers and muskets were firing fast then, Emma pointed out where Forrest must cross the water and they returned to the house.

Bedford Forrest asked Emma her name; he asked her for a lock of her hair. "The cannon balls," she wrote, "were screaming over us so loud that we were told to leave and hide in some place out of danger." Soon the firing stopped and Emma returned to her home. On the way she met Forrest. He asked again for a lock of her hair. He had written a note to her and left it on a bureau. "One of my bravest men has been killed," he continued, "and he is laid out in the house. His name is Robert Turner." General Forrest wanted her to see that he was buried in some graveyard nearby. "He then told me goodbye and got on his horse and he and his men rode away and left us all alone. My sister and I sat up all night watching the dead soldier, who had lost his life fighting for our rights, in which we were overpowered but never conquered." Forrest's note, written in pencil on the stained leaf of an old pocket memorandum, was rigidly self-contained.

"Hed Quaters in Sadle
May 2, 1863
"My highest regards to Miss Emma Sansom for her gallant conduct while my posse was skirmishing with the Federals across Black Creek near Gadsden Alabama.
N. B. Forrest
Bry Genrl
Com. N. Ala—"

Emma Sansom was a mountain girl and Forrest had been born in the mountains. He belonged to them; they were in his voice and heart and memory; their rocks and cold water and dark silences had entered into his bearing. He asked her twice for a lock of hair. She sat up through the night, in a silence doubly still after the alarm and firing of guns, watching a dead soldier. A dead soldier and a soldier from the mountains who had ridden off! A soldier on the side of God who was whipping the Yankees. General Forrest. N. B. Forrest. The N might be this and the B might be that. She learned what they were. Afterward. He had ridden off. A dead soldier with his hands folded at peace and his grey face at peace. Grey was the color of the South. General Forrest had worn grey. Her brother, who had gone to war long ago and was in the Nineteenth Alabama infantry, wore grey. Like General Forrest. A dead soldier in the smoky light of an oil lamp. It might have been the smaller light of a tallow dip. His name was Robert Turner and he had been one of General Forrest's men. Beyond Robert Turner sat her dimly perceived sister. War left a dreadful silence after it. A terrible emptiness. For women. Robert Turner didn't mind it. He was so young she would rather call him Robert. General Forrest wasn't young. He was tired. His face was as grey from being tired as Robert's was grey with death. Black hair that was almost curly and a sword and two pistols around his waist. Pistols that belonged to God. It was hard to think after war had passed over you. Passed over you and right through your heart. It was harder to feel. Your heart was left numb. That is if you were a woman.

You were a girl and then you were numb and you were a woman. All at once. Sometimes, when it was hot, in June or August or September, the cows stood in the ford. They stood where the water wasn't high and then they went over to the other bank. She was first and General Forrest stood between her and the Yankees. The shots screamed loud but she could hear his voice clear over them. She could hear it now and her mother crying after her, "Emma, what do you mean?" There was nothing for her mother to worry about for wasn't she with General Forrest. He would bring her back safe. A swift rebellion stirred and tore at her numbness. She didn't want to be brought back. She didn't want to be safe. It sank. The terrible emptiness and pain after war. Her brother gone and it didn't seem likely he would come back, and her mother, so bothered and old, with the farm. Now there wasn't no fence and it would be worse.

The Yankees had burned their fence and the Black Creek bridge, but she had taken General Forrest to the ford. He had crossed with his men. He had left a note for her on a bureau. And her hair. A lock of her hair. She hated whippoor-wills and wished they would stop their loud racket in the dark. Not that she cared if the morning didn't never come now.

* * *

Immediately after General Forrest's arrival at Black Creek the Confederate cannon were brought up, the Federals driven from their position on the opposite bank, the Sansom ford was cleared and made more easily passable. The cavalry went over carrying by hand the ammunition from the caissons, an advance guard hurried after the Union raiders, and drove them out of the town of Gadsden before any serious damage could be effected. Both columns were in a state of complete exhaustion—Forrest continued his unrelenting tactics of harassment, Colonel Gilbert Hathaway, Streight's finest soldier, was seriously wounded. That was an irreparable loss for the North. Near Turkeytown, Streight sent two hundred of his best mounted men, under Captain Milton Russell, ahead to seize the Rome bridge in preparation for the arrival of his main force; but Russell found Rome so closely barricaded that he concluded not to attack.

The Federal position became hourly worse: Colonel Streight, urging forward his exhausted command, arrived by starlight at the Chattooga River. There the ferry boat had been concealed, and he had to march a number of additional miles upstream to a bridge. They were forced, he said, to pass an old coal-chopping, where timber had been cut and hauled off for charcoal, leaving a confusion of wagon roads running in every direction. His men continually fell asleep. Forrest's column, however, was refreshed with ten hours' rest. He overtook Streight; the Union commander tried desperately to make his men fight; but further effort was impossible—they fired their guns with both eyes closed; they fell fast asleep lying in line of battle under a heavy skirmishing fire. Forrest sent out a flag of truce, there was a short consultation, and the Federal force surrendered; the men stacked their rifles and moved into a clearing.

Bedford Forrest was met with an unrestrained acclaim in Rome; the Roman citizens presented him with the most valuable saddle horse in the country. The whole South was revivified by Forrest's extraordinary pursuit and capture of a force three times greater than his own. The fighting in the barren hills, the mountains, of North Alabama was peculiarly impressive: the thunder of artillery, the discharge of muskets, rolled and returned in infinitely multiplied echoes; the narrow valleys were loud with the shouted clangor of orders, the cheers and Rebel yells of the men, the inarticulate agonies of wounded animals. The roads of pursuit were strewn with saddles and bridles and broken boxes of crackers, crockery and kitchen utensils, blankets and shoes and plated ware and hastily discarded embroidered skirts and looted feminine trifles. In Blountsville the uproar of battle so appalled the inhabitants that women and children crouched hiding in ash-hoppers, horse-troughs and in the recesses of chimneys.

Near Warrior River two young girls—they were seventeen and eighteen—poorly but neatly dressed in homespun and with bare feet, appeared leading three accoutred horses and driving before them three Union soldiers. Each of the girls bore a shotgun on her shoulder. They delivered their captives to Forrest, and asked permission to go forward with the Southern troops; but they were satisfied—rather they were delighted—with a gift of two horses.

In September, Eighteen-sixty-three, General Forrest was in the battle of Chickamauga; his cavalry fought dismounted as infantry; he behaved with great coolness and gallantry and was complimented by General D. H. Hill. He fired both the opening and closing gun of that great engagement. Forrest had a collision with Braxton Bragg expressed, as it was customary with him, in words no less violent than his acts. "I am not here to pass civilities or compliments with you," he proceeded. "I have stood your meanness as long as I intend to. You have played the part of a damned scoundrel, and are a coward, and if you were any part of a man I would slap your jaws and force you to resent it. You have threatened to arrest me for not obeying your orders promptly. I dare you to do it, and I say to you that if you ever again try to interfere with me or cross my path it will be at the peril of your life."

General Bragg relieved him from duty; but Jefferson Davis, after a conversation in Montgomery, assigned Forrest to an independent command in the West. He proceeded from Atlanta with four pieces of artillery and two hundred and seventy-one men; with five hundred men he crossed the Trocha and invaded western Tennessee. He established recruiting stations there, gathered up a large herd of cattle and marched South.

After that he was involved in continuous and picturesque battle. He pursued General William Sooy Smith, who was endeavoring to join Sherman, and defeated him at West Point and again at Okolona. He invaded Tennessee a second time, and, with the fragments of three Kentucky regiments of infantry, a third time. He stormed and took Fort Pillow after a desperate resistance in which liquor was freely distributed to the garrison. Sherman was again highly complimentary: he offered a major general's commission to any brigadier who succeeded in killing Forrest. "It must," he wrote, "be done if it costs ten thousand lives and breaks the treasury." General S. D. Sturgis was sent to accomplish this—after seven hours of combat his force was driven, an abject mob, from the field; Forrest pursued him for fifty miles and captured eighteen pieces of artillery and two hundred and fifty wagons. Twenty-six hundred and twelve Union soldiers were killed or captured. General A. J. Smith and General Mower were moved against Forrest. They marched by day in line of battle, at night they slept on their arms, there was a constant skirmishing and, near Tupelo, a final engagement. The Confederates, under General Stephen D. Lee, were repulsed with a great slaughter; the Federal forces held a strong position but the South retained its line of battle. Forrest made a night attack, the Union generals retreated the following day, and Forrest was painfully wounded at Old Town Creek.

He profanely declined to go to the rear for treatment; instead he had a buggy so arranged that he could drive about with a leg elevated. General Lee was transferred and Dabney H. Maury placed in temporary command. Sherman sent Smith back after Forrest. There was a report that General Forrest had died of lockjaw following a wound. Instead, with two thousand picked men, he rode around General Smith's army and fell on the city of Memphis, held by the

Union. This was in August, Eighteen-sixty-four. Forrest individually forced his way into the center of the city; General C. C. Washburn was constrained to escape from his residence at noon in a nightshirt. Colonel Starr engaged Forrest in a personal encounter, he was badly injured, and Forrest returned to his command. Washburn was very bitter with Smith for permitting Forrest to escape; Smith was ordered to retreat; Mississippi was abandoned to the Confederacy.

Mr. Davis saw, at last, the necessity of allowing Forrest's assaults to fall unchecked on Sherman's lines of communication. War had changed him—his stubborn black hair had become grey. He was a tall stalwart man, a contemporary description continued, with a mild countenance, slow and homely of speech. Forrest surrounded the Federal military post at Athens and it surrendered at once; he captured the Union stockades near Athens and the forts at Sulphur Trestle. He took the Elk River block house, drove the enemy into Pulaski, and diverted thirty thousand Northern soldiers from the Georgia campaign. Forrest asked for leave of absence, it was denied, and he moved once more into Tennessee. He laid masked batteries along the Tennessee River, and captured the transport Mazeppa, the gunboats Undine and Venus, and the J. W. Cheeseman. He put crews of his cavalry on the Venus and Undine, they attacked the Union flotilla, but—not unnaturally—the cavalrymen were ignominiously defeated. The Venus was recaptured, with two of Forrest's guns, 20-pound Parrotts; the Undine was destroyed.

He then descended on Johnsonville and burned a great quantity of boats and general mill supplies. They represented a value of over three million dollars, and the loss was a serious charge upon Sherman. Forrest was, then, given command of all cavalry in the army of Tennessee. At the end of the disastrous Nashville campaign he organized the famous rear guard of the Southern army. It made possible the safe crossing of Rutherford Creek and the Duck River; Forrest with double teams saved the wagons and artillery. He escaped through a barren country in the depth of winter, a country without sustenance or shelter or hope.

*　　*
*

In the spring, Eighteen-sixty-five, seventy-five thousand Union soldiers were gathered to invade Forrest's department. General Wilson, with an advance force of fourteen thousand, and the best equipped cavalrymen the war had seen, moved from Waterloo to Selma. He detached Croxton's brigade—it was lost from his army for two months—and Croxton missed an opportunity to destroy Jackson's wagon train and artillery; Wilson, with great skill and courage, took Tuscaloosa; he captured a courier with invaluable dispatches from General Forrest. Forrest, moving forward, court-martialled and shot two men at Sipsey Bridge for desertion; with two hundred and seventy-five men he charged the rear guard of Wilson's command and put it to flight. Forrest made a detour through the night and placed himself before Wilson at Bogler's Creek. There was a desperate engagement; a Captain Taylor and Forrest had what was believed to be the bloodiest personal encounter in the war. Taylor was killed.

Forrest relied upon immediate support. Chalmers was unable to reach him, and only the informal appearance of Armstrong—he became the hero of the battle of Selma—saved him from instant destruction. Selma followed. It fell and the South was defeated. Armstrong and Bedford Forrest literally cut their way out of the conflict. After the surrender at Gainesville, Forrest made his farewell address to the Seventh Tennessee cavalry. They grounded, he said, their arms with honor. At dusk they gathered about the staff in front of the regiment headquarters, and the silk of their bullet-torn flag, bearing a blue cross, was cut into fragments, a keepsake for each man. A young bride in Aberdeen, Mississippi, had made it from her wedding dress.

Forrest returned to Memphis, and there were reports of his arrest; Maury and Colonel Sam Tate advised him to leave his plantation, they prepared letters of credit on Europe; but he refused to move. "This is my country," he asserted. "I am hard at work on my plantation, and carefully observing the obligations of my parole. If the Federal government does not regard it they will be sorry." Nothing, it appeared, could restrain the arrogance of his courage. The triumphant weight of the whole Federal Union was powerless to force even a reasonable caution upon him. Forrest's reputation did not end with the war— the most extravagant rumors of his exploits and valor and inhumanity persisted in the North and in the South. He became interested in the politics of his section: Forrest devoted himself to the restoration of the autonomy of his state; and he was subjected to a bitter Northern abuse.

In the Presidential campaign of Eighteen-sixty-eight, General Kilpatrick, a renowned Federal cavalry officer, accused Forrest in several political speeches of atrocities committed in war. General Forrest, he declared, at Fort Pillow had tied some negroes to a plank fence and then set fire to the fence. This was, apparently, no better than libel: Forrest, when his anger was excited, was an exceedingly fierce man, but he had shown no evidence of unnatural barbarity. It is probable that, without further cause, he would have ignored Kilpatrick's charges; but another Federal officer, General Shackelford, not only remonstrated with Kilpatrick, declaring his utter disbelief in such assertions, he sent Forrest a copy of them with a record of his own proceeding. Bedford Forrest, because of this, felt obliged to act publicly—he printed a letter in the Louisville Courier-Journal that was, perhaps, the ultimate model for all violently unrestrained expressions of indignation. It was concluded by the request for General Kilpatrick to consider Forrest's remarks in the light of a challenge to combat.

The peculiar conditions then prevailing, he continued, might excuse him from a regular and more formal transmission of a cartel; he hoped Kilpatrick would waive that and immediately communicate with General Basil W. Duke, who was authorized to make all necessary arrangements for him. This created a serious difficulty in Duke's mind—it was necessary, he realized, for Forrest to fight in Kentucky, where both men would have sympathizers and the benefit of a general willingness to let them fight in peace; Forrest was not safe north of the Ohio River; the great part of the South was under a Federal military supervision that, with opportunity, would deal relentlessly with him. The statutes of Kentucky, however, were extremely severe about duels; lawyers who participated in them were disbarred from practice for a period not less than five years; and Duke, who had come out of the war with a family but no property, had just entered upon the career of attorney at law.

General Duke, though, had no thought of failing Forrest—he requested Doctor James Keller, of St. Louis, a recognized authority on the duello and warm supporter of Forrest's, to act publicly in his place. Keller arrived in Louisville almost simultaneously with his reception of Duke's telegram; and—Forrest had expressed a desire to fight on horseback—Basil Duke, desiring to obtain the best mount available, called upon Captain Bart Jenkins, formerly of the Fourth Kentucky Confederate cavalry, now proprietor of a livery stable with a number of very fine horses at his disposal.

Captain Jenkins, Duke found, was desperately ill, but he was allowed to see him. He was taken up to a small room above the office of the livery stable, where Jenkins lay on a lounge. He had, he said, in a whispering voice, pneumonia; he was unable to rise from the couch and his illness, he thought, must end fatally. Duke prepared to withdraw at once; he had come, he admitted, to discuss an affair between Forrest and a General Kilpatrick; but that, in the present circumstances, was impossible. Jenkins' voice grew perceptibly stronger. "I want," he said, "to hear about it." Oh, well, Forrest wished to fight on horseback with sabres. Jenkins interrupted him. "That's right," he agreed, rising to a sitting position; "that's right." He got up and began putting on his clothes. "I've got the very animal you want." Duke protested, "Don't do that, Bart. You've just told me the doctor insists that you be very careful."

"The doctor be damned!" he replied. "Do you think I'll let a doctor interfere with important business like this? I want to show you my brown mare, the finest in the state and has taken the blue ribbon at every fair in the center of Kentucky. She's sixteen hands high, built just right for a man of Forrest's weight, and as quick on her feet as a cat. Place the men sixty yards apart, and tell Forrest that when you give the word he must drive in the spurs and ride straight at the other horse. She'll knock him off his feet and Forrest can cut off Kilpatrick's head before he touches the ground. And," Jenkins added, "I must see the fight." It did not, however, occur:

General Duke received no word from Kilpatrick; instead Kilpatrick later published a statement in the Eastern papers —a Congressional Committee, he asserted, had declared Forrest guilty of the alleged massacre of negroes at Fort

Pillow; and therefore he, Kilpatrick, could not regard him as a gentleman. General Shackelford, a gallant and persistent man, then published it as his opinion that, while the report of a Congressional Committee might be valuable for many things, no one could consider it conclusive of a man's standing as a gentleman. He strongly urged Kilpatrick, after wantonly assailing Forrest, to meet him.

Bedford Forrest engaged himself in the building of a railroad from Selma, Alabama, to Mississippi. A rapid and startling change fell on him—he grew greatly emaciated; the thinness and pallor of his face brought into relief the extraordinary fineness of his brow and head. Any harshness vanished from his expression; a curiously patient and gentle manner filled him. He said to General Morgan, "I am broken in health and spirit and have not long to live. My life has been a battle from the start. It was a fight to achieve a livelihood from those dependent on me in younger days, and an independence for myself when I grew to manhood, as well as the terrible turmoil of the Civil War. I have seen too much of violence, and I want to close my days in peace—"

General Nathan Bedford Forrest had, at last, a desire for tranquillity; he was, he firmly believed, at peace with his Maker.

BELLE BOYD, OR THE FEMALE SPY

BELLE BOYD, OR THE FEMALE SPY

A FEMALE SPY is an engaging creature, but in crinoline she has an especial, a romantic and absurd, charm. Belle Boyd, the most famous woman concerned with official secret activities in the Civil War, not only was enveloped in a cloud of crinoline, she wore it with grace and elegance; she had a great many talents; she was carefully educated; and—of far more importance—she had the daring that is the property of beauty. She had all through her life the beauty of daring. It is difficult to write about Belle Boyd exactly because, although she was both a celebrated and important figure in the war she ornamented, there are almost no records of her. Only a very little was written or preserved about her life and affairs. Her principal activity, of course, was closely guarded, hidden, by the Confederate government. Her value depended upon the privacy of her movements and on the discretion of her public conduct. Privacy and discretion, it is clear, were not fundamental in her character; actually she regarded one with indifference and the other with disdain; beauty and courage supported her; and so, fortunately, through the necessary official silence, she appears in her proper person at absorbing and highly dramatic moments. It is precisely as though the smoke of battle lifted to disclose her in swift clear flashes—a perfumed girl in the widest of skirts, a ridiculous hat like a garnished plate set at an absurd angle on a coiled wealth of hair, and a brilliant face.

Belle Boyd was born in Martinsburg, when it was still

Virginia, the May of Eighteen-forty-four. In Eighteen-sixty-one, when she first visited a camp of Southern soldiers —at Harper's Ferry—she was seventeen years old. That was in May, or perhaps it was June. Anyhow, in July, the same year, she shot and killed a Federal soldier. Her father, then a private in the Confederate army, was absent in the field, the Northern soldier assailed her mother, and Belle killed him with a revolver. That served to introduce her to the world of war. It gave her daring a great prominence, both in her own consciousness and with others; in short, it made her into a female spy. Her beauty, not necessarily a desirable quality, at once helped her and was a source of trouble. Of danger really. If it got her out of trouble, prevailing over the susceptibilities of Union generals and the governors of Northern prisons, it equally led her into difficulties.

A more desirable quality in a spy, male or female, is to be and to remain inconspicuous, to proceed unnoticed about the business of spying; and it was one of the triumphs of Belle Boyd's determination and wit that while she was by nature, appearance, a conspicuous individual she was at the same time an invaluable spy. One thing is evident, her success was not the result of an effort to be as good as any man, or to be better: Belle wisely proceeded wholly upon the fact that she was a woman. An attractive woman. She didn't envy or copy any doubtful masculine privilege; on the contrary she took shameless advantage of the limitations, the disabilities, of women. During the Civil War they were at once heavier and more binding, and less burdensome, than they are now. In Eighteen-sixty-one, and for a few years after, a woman, a charming woman, was definitely feminine; she was not a creature who had given up wide powers for an inappropriate masculine authority in impersonal and frequently ridiculous affairs. Charm then and grace were very potent, and Belle Boyd, who had them in large degrees, made no mistake in the historic and infallible manner of their use. She dressed beautifully, she was always, as I have hinted, sweet-scented; she used her grace, her voice, her eyes, a purely feminine wisdom; and gave little thought to logic or an equality of justice—clumsy and impracticable qualities compared to the arbitrary masked batteries, the stratagems and surprises, contained in her person.

The women of the traditional South, the South destroyed by the changes of time and improvement, never realized that they were inferior beings; the qualities of allegiance and devotion, of fidelity to what they knew as love, were not regarded as marks of servitude; women then, even lovely women, were domestic and maternal. They were not, however, because of that, stupid. Varina Howell, who married Jefferson Davis, knew as much about the intricacies of national government as her husband; she prepared and transcribed a great many of his papers. But her knowledge only supplemented the fact—the inferior fact—that she was a woman. She was a woman and Jefferson Davis' wife. Belle Boyd, who had a very different character and fate— she was neither conspicuously domestic nor maternal— owned the unfortunate limitations of her period: she couldn't, unhappily, vote; she couldn't hold public office; she could only influence, assist or undermine, the men who did occupy important places in government. In the capacity of a spy she affected and controlled great events indirectly.

That, naturally, is the sphere of a spy; it is, or at least it was, the sphere of women; and in Belle those two suitable consummations met perfectly. They were fused, given a gem-like hardness and brilliancy, by the fire of her Rebel sympathies. Through all the South there was no more ardent Confederate. She gave the cause of the South all the tenderness and passion and belief she possessed. Where it was concerned she was—deeply feminine—illogical, bitterly partisan, unfair, without any necessity for truth, plausible, tireless, heroic and petty. She sang to it and nursed it, she smiled at it and wept over it; she went repeatedly to prison for it; and when the hope of the South sank into the coldness of imminent defeat, when her cause was plainly lost, she loved and cherished it more than ever. That, then, was her maternity; the whole South was her domestic hearth.

The actual records of Belle are not only inconsiderable, all that exists is scattered and, in the succession of events, contradictory. There is no agreement about the terms she served in prison: one account says two periods of three and seven months each; another seven months and ten months; a third, The Official Records of the War of the Rebellion, is totally different and no more conclusive. Her memoir, Belle Boyd In Camp, is equally uncertain where her various sentences and months under close guard are concerned. It is certain, however, that at the age of twelve she was sent to Mount Washington Female Seminary, and that in Eighteen-sixty, when she was sixteen, she was formally presented to society in Washington. The following year Belle became a spy.

The spring of Eighteen-sixty-two she was captured and taken to Baltimore but released by General Dix. In May, the twenty-second, of the same year, she was detained by Colonel Beale but liberated immediately. The next day she bore important information to Jackson, and on the twenty-fifth she was arrested by the Union General Kimball. A General Shields, on an unknown date, set her free. But at the end of July Mr. Stanton ordered her apprehension and she was conveyed by Cridge, a detective in the Secret Service, to the Old Capitol Prison. The spring, Eighteen-sixty-three, was occupied by a tour through all the Southern States. In August she was again arrested and confined in

Carroll Prison at Washington, once a block of dwellings known as Duff Green's Row. On the first of December Belle was removed to Fortress Monroe. She made a second tour of the South early in Eighteen-sixty-four, and May eighth she sailed with important dispatches for England on the Greyhound. The Greyhound was captured by the U. S. S. Connecticut, and Belle Boyd was once more made a prisoner. She finally, in the private capacity of a woman, succeeded in reaching England, and August twenty-fifth— it was still the year Eighteen-sixty-four—she married a Mr. Hardinge, a Federal officer her charms had seduced away from his country. He died and Belle became an actress; she married again and secured a divorce; she married for a third time and died at Kilbourne, Wisconsin, in Nineteen hundred.

* *
*

Spies throughout the Civil War were in even greater danger than is common to the hazards of their lives. This, mainly, was the result of the incompetency of the officers, the armies and governments, they served. The ciphers arranged for them, in which their messages were transferred, were crude and easily made out; the arrangements for their movements were inadequate. A great many spies were captured and executed; the information they secured was often misinterpreted or entirely ignored. The South, however, with almost none of the resources of the North, was better served than the Union; the celebrated Allan Pinkerton, with the best will in the world, furnished Mr. Lincoln with some surprising misinformation. At the beginning of the war the city of Washington, the government, were distinctly Southern in sympathy; when the members of the government from the South departed home numbers of their wives and daughters remained for short or long periods. The South was handsomely supported by its men but it was worshipped by its women; they were fanatical in its service; no sacrifice was too great; every Southern woman who remained in the capitol was a potential or actual spy. They were, most of them, important socially, charming in appearance, schooled in personal and political tact. It is probable that their information brought about the Federal defeat at the first battle of Manassas. One of them, Mrs. Rose Greenhow, became openly defiant, she declared that, instead of loving and worshipping the old flag of the stars and stripes, she saw in it only the symbol of murder, plunder, oppression and shame.

The Assistant Secretary of War desired Mr. Pinkerton to keep a close watch upon her; she was arrested and held at the Old Capitol Prison; but Mrs. Greenhow too—like Belle Boyd—was indiscreetly released; she continued her secret activities in America and England until, running the blockade outside Wilmington, North Carolina, the ship that bore her, the Condor, went ashore on the New Inlet bar. Mrs. Greenhow insisted on being taken to land, and her boat was overturned. Everyone else escaped—she was drowned by the weight of her heavy black silk dress and a bag full of gold sovereigns.

That is all very simple, very direct, compared with the variations in the accounts of Belle Boyd. There is even a lack of agreement about the date of her birth: in Vol. XI of the Southern Historical Publications, Richmond, it appears that she was born about Eighteen-thirty-five. This is plainly incorrect. The same authority asserts that she married and divorced a Federal officer in London; and that, as well, is an error. She didn't divorce Mr. Hardinge, he died. The details of her existence, ornamented by the spirit and floral style of her time, are engagingly set down in her memoir. Belle agrees, with the best opinions, that she was born in Eighteen-forty-four. There was, she thought, no tract of country in the world more lovely than the Valley of the Shenandoah. No prettier or more peaceful little village than Martinsburg existed. Many beautiful houses gave it a degree of importance; the Baltimore and Ohio Railroad had begun to build the vast machine shops that General Jackson—to prevent their capture by the advancing Yankees—was soon to destroy.

"Imagine," Belle Boyd proceeds, "a bright warm sun shining upon a pretty two-storied house, the walls completely hidden by roses and honeysuckle in luxuriant bloom. At a short distance in front of it flows a broad, clear, rapid, stream; around it the silver maples wave their graceful branches in the perfume-laden air of the South." Her childhood, she remembers, was all golden; she was surrounded by loving, by beloved, parents and brothers and sisters. "I believe," she adds, "I shall not be contradicted in affirming that nowhere could be found more pleasant society than that of Virginia. In this respect the neighborhood of Martinsburg was remarkably fortunate, populated as it was by some of the best families of the Old Dominion, descendants of such ancestors as the Fairfaxes and Warringtons."

At twelve—it was, Belle says, the custom of her country—she was sent to Mount Washington Female Seminary, and cherished a most grateful recollection of the principal, a Mr. Staley. At sixteen her education was held to be complete, she made her entrée into the world in Washington City with all the high hopes and thoughtless joys natural to her time of life. It is impossible to ignore the stilted charm of her own description of that existence. "Washington is so well known to English people, I need not pause to describe its gaities. In the winter of 1860–61, when I made my first acquaintance with it, the season was preëminently brilliant. The Senate and Congress halls were nightly dignified by the presence of our ablest orators and statesmen; the salons of the wealthy and talented were filled to overflowing; the theatres were crowded to excess, and for the last time for many years to come the daughters of the North and South commingled in sisterly love."

When Virginia, at once firm and reluctant, seceded the call for troops was instantly and fully met. Belle Boyd's father was among the first to enlist; he was offered, she explains, a grade in the army proper to his social position, but he declined all privilege—he preferred to serve in the ranks and give to a needier man an officer's pay. He joined a regiment—the Second Virginia—armed and equipped by subscriptions raised by Belle and other ladies in the Valley. Its colors were inscribed, Our God, Our Country, And Our Women. The regiment was attached to the corps commanded by Colonel Nadenbush, it belonged to the part of the army afterwards known as the Stonewall Brigade, and it was ordered at once to Harper's Ferry.

Martinsburg, when the troops had marched away, fell into a state of melancholy, a mood of deserted and silent depression. Belle occupied the long summer days with reading and the packing of easily carried provisions for her father. But, against all her efforts at reasonable contentment, she found her life very monotonous. It was not in accord with her temperament, and she decided—her phrase is coûte qui coûte—to visit her father's encampment. Belle had little difficulty in persuading others to join her, and they found an animated scene at Harper's Ferry. The ladies, married or single, in the society of husbands, brothers, sons, and lovers, had cast their cares to the winds, and seemed, one and all, resolved that whatever calamity the future might have in store for them, it should not mar the transient pleasure of the hour.

That "insouciance" however did not last for long—the

Federal army was reported to be advancing, and General Jackson, with five thousand men, marched out to observe its progress. The Southern troops withdrew to Falling Waters, near Martinsburg and nearer to Williamsport, and the battle of Martinsburg—in the July of Eighteen-sixty-one—followed. Belle heard the dull thunder of the artillery, the sharp roll of muskets, in her pretty two-storied house. She was informed that the Yankees, under General Patterson and General Cadwalader, were moving in force; but it was only a Federal advance guard; a skirmish followed that lasted five hours.

At ten of the morning General Jackson's troops, in full retreat but admirable in order, passed through Martinsburg. Jackson was endeavoring to join the main body of General J. E. Johnston's command, and his rear was protected by a few horsemen under Colonel Ashby. The Confederates vanished and immediately the shrilling of Federal fifes, the roll of Federal drums, filled the town. Twenty-five thousand Union soldiers made for Belle Boyd a sad but imposing sight. Their colors passed her bright on the air; the bayonets glittered in the sunlight; she saw the dancing plumes of the cavalry and heard the rumbling of the gun-carriages; she is certain, far worse, that her ears were filled with hellish shouts.

* * *

The Fourth of July in Martinsburg was, inappropriately, brilliantly clear; Union flags hung in numbers of windows; Belle Boyd was forced to listen to the harassing strains of Yankee Doodle. Whiskey flowed liberally amid, she noted, a motley crowd of Americans, Dutchmen and other nations. The Irish element predominated. The doors of houses were broken in, rooms were forcibly entered by inebriated soldiers, glass and other fragile objects largely destroyed.

Shots were fired through windows; chairs and tables were hurled out into the streets. A squad of soldiers, Belle asserts, even more violent than their companions, forced their way into the Boyd house hunting for the Rebel flags that, they had been informed, decorated Belle's room. Her negro maid, however, had already destroyed the Confederate emblems on her walls; the soldiers contented themselves with petty acts of destruction. They prepared to raise a large Federal flag over the house. Belle Boyd's mother could not support so much. She stepped quietly but resolutely forward and said, "Men, every member of my household will die before that flag shall be raised over us." Belle's further account is circumstantial:

"Upon this, one of the soldiers, thrusting himself forward addressed my mother in language as offensive as it is possible to conceive. I could stand it no longer; my indignation was roused beyond control; my blood was literally boiling in my veins; I drew out my pistol and shot him. He was carried away mortally wounded and soon after expired." In a note she adds that, since all male relatives were away with the army, ladies were obliged to go armed in order to protect themselves from insult and outrage. Perhaps. It all has the sound of a too harrowing and conventional drama. And yet, where Belle's record of events can be corroborated, she is usually proved to be truthful. There can be no doubt of her passionate willingness, her entire ability, to kill any man in such circumstances.

The soldiers streamed out, but they were hardly gone when the servants rushed in, crying that the house had been set to burning. Belle, together with the others, was naturally terrified, but she managed to send a message to the Federal officer in command. It had been reported at headquarters that she had shot a Union soldier, and at first, she says, great indignation was felt and expressed about her.

The Federal commander, with several members of his staff, conducted an investigation at the Boyd dwelling: he examined witnesses, inquired into all the circumstances, with a strict impartiality, and finally declared that Belle had done exactly right. He placed sentries before the house, and every day Federal officers called to see if Belle had any further reason for complaint. She hadn't, but she came to know some of the officers very well—a knowledge which, when she had become a Rebel spy, was immensely useful.

That occupation she entered upon at once. Her residence within the Federal lines, her increasing acquaintance with Northern officers, brought her invaluable information about the position and designs of the enemy. Everything she learned Belle wrote down and, with opportunity, sent by secret dispatch to General J. E. B. Stuart. She was successful for a while, and then, either through accident or treachery, one of her messages fell into Yankee hands. She was not, yet, writing in cipher, her handwriting was identified, and she was summoned to appear before a colonel whose name she forgot. She remembered, though, a Captain Gwyne who escorted her to headquarters. There she was reprimanded and threatened, the Article of War concerning secret activities was read to her with a severe emphasis and the caution that it would be carried out to the letter:

"Whoever shall give food, ammunition, information, to, or aid and abet the enemies of the U. S. Government in any manner whatever, shall suffer death, or whatever penalty the honorable members of the court-martial shall see fit to inflict."

Belle listened coldly; she was not frightened; she felt within her, her memoir explains, the spirit of Douglas, from whom she was descended. At the end of her examination she made a low bow and—satirical in intent—she said, "Thank you, gentlemen of the Jury." From that moment she was a suspect; all the circuitous damage done to the Federal cause was charged to her; a great deal of it, she asserts, with entire justice. Whenever it was possible she confiscated and hid the swords and pistols of Union officers; they searched for them in vain never dreaming they had been robbed by Belle Boyd and that she was smuggling their weapons into the Confederacy.

At the approach of the first battle of Manassas she was visiting her uncle and aunt at Front Royal. "To this romantic retreat," she proceeds, "they had fled from Washington. Their Southern sympathies were too strong and too openly expressed to allow of their remaining in the Northern capital. They left a magnificent house, replete with handsome furniture, a prey to the Yankees." Orders soon arrived from the battlefield that a military hospital was to be established at Front Royal; Belle had a part in the preparations for the reception of the wounded soldiers; she was appointed a matron at the hospital. But after eight weeks nursing she was obliged, in the interest of her own well-being, to return to Martinsburg and rest. Later, with her mother, Belle visited her father at Manassas. They stayed in a large house at the center of the camp, a tenement that was the temporary home of many officers' wives and daughters, and there Belle acted as courier between General Beauregard and General Jackson and their subordinates.

That was a happy experience, but she was soon obliged to return to Martinsburg, and the winter advanced slowly and with but a single adventure. She was riding in the evening with two young Confederate officers, a cousin and a friend, when her horse became unmanageable and carried her within the Federal lines. Her companions had not dared to follow her and she rode up to the officer in charge of the picquet, asking permission to return to Martinsburg.

"We are exceedingly proud of our beautiful captive,"

he replied; "but of course we cannot think of detaining you. May we have the honor of escorting you beyond our lines and restoring you to the custody of your friends? I suppose there is no fear of those cowardly Rebels taking us prisoners?"

"I scarcely hoped," Belle assured them, "for such an honor. I thought you would probably give me a pass; but since you are so kind to offer your services in person, I cannot do otherwise than accept them. Have no fear, gentlemen, of the cowardly Rebels." Two officers started back with her and Belle's companions suddenly rode out of ambush. There was a moment, she admits, of embarrassed silence, and then she spoke to her friends, "Here are two prisoners I have brought you." She turned to the Union officer. "These are some of the cowardly Rebels whom you hoped there was no danger of meeting." The Federals looked inquiringly at Belle. They demanded:

"And who, pray, is this lady?"

"Belle Boyd, at your service," she replied.

"Good God, the Rebel spy!"

"So be it," she said, "since your journals have honored me with that title."

The Yankees, Belle confesses, reproached her bitterly for her treachery. "But when it is considered that their release followed their capture within an hour, that they had in the first place stigmatized the Rebels, when none were near, as cowards, that they had immediately afterwards yielded without a blow to an equal number of these self-same cowards, I think my readers will admit that their spirit of bravado merited a slight humiliation." Belle consoled herself with the reflection that all was fair in love and war.

*   *
*

It is necessary to realize, in the face of Belle's elegantly artificial phrases, that she lived surrounded by a very actual and brutal hazard. She was invaluable to the Confederacy because her situation, close to the Federal lines, brought her in contact with Union men and plans; she remained there—as Belle would have unquestionably described it—after she was a marked woman; at first she could have escaped, removed to the deep and safe South, but she chose to stay in the Valley of the Shenandoah at the constant peril of her life. Her father, in reality, who was home on sick leave, strongly advised her to go further south, and to please him she returned to Front Royal. While she was there, however, the Confederates lost the battle of Kearnstown, close by, and the Northern troops moved into Front Royal. Her uncle and aunt, taking one daughter with them, again fled from the Yankees, this time to Richmond, and left their other daughter Alice—who was Belle's age and more beautiful still—her grandmother and Belle to take charge of the servants and house.

When Belle found that the Confederates had retreated far down the Valley—her father was with them—she became anxious about her mother and determined to return to Martinsburg. She had managed to get a pass from General Shields, but at Winchester she was detained and charged with active spying. She had already taken her seat in a train, it was ready to depart, when a Federal officer, Captain Bannon, stopped beside her. Was she, he inquired, Miss Belle Boyd? She was, she replied; and, apologizing, Bannon explained that he was the assistant provost. He had orders for her arrest. Belle showed him her pass, he deliberated for a moment, and then said that he would assume the responsibility of conveying her to Baltimore with other prisoners in his charge. In Baltimore she was lodged at the Eutaw House, a large and expensive hotel; she was treated with great courtesy and allowed to see her Maryland friends; and after a week General Dix, who declared he could discover nothing specific in the charges against Belle, released her.

In Martinsburg—it was in the hands of the Federals— she was placed under a strict surveillance and forbidden to leave the town; Union officers were prohibited the Boyd house; she was, Belle says, so watched and harassed that her mother sought relief from the Provost Marshal, Major Walker. Belle was granted permission to go on to Front Royal by way of Winchester, with the understanding that she would join her family in Richmond. It was, over the harried ground between the two armies, a difficult trip; she succeeded in reaching Winchester, but, facing the Shenandoah River at dusk, she found that all the bridges had been destroyed. She prevailed on a Federal officer, a Captain Everhart, to ferry her across, and proceeded to a little cottage occupied by the part of her uncle's family that had remained in Front Royal. Their more appropriate residence had been taken by General Shields and his staff.

Belle sent her card to General Shields and he returned that practical courtesy by a call in person. He was, she says, charming to her, he immediately gave her a pass through his lines and introduced her to the officers attached to him. To one of them, an Irishman, she was indebted for some very remarkable effusions, some withered flowers, and last, not least, for a great deal of highly important information, which she carefully transmitted to her countrymen. "I must," Belle Boyd admits, "avow the flowers and the poetry were comparatively valueless in my eyes, but let Captain K. be consoled: these were days of war, not of love, and there are still other ladies in the world besides the Rebel spy."

The night before Belle's departure General Shields held a council of war with his officers in what had been her aunt's drawing-room; immediately above there was a bedroom with a closet that concealed a hole in the floor, and Belle was able to overhear the entire conversation below. She remained there until one o'clock and then, careful in the darkness of the courtyard, returned to her room and put down in cipher all she had heard that was important. She saddled a horse and galloped in the direction of the mountains. Federal sentries stopped her twice but, with passes given to her on other occasions, she managed to continue; at last clear of interference she rode for fifteen miles to the house of a Mr. M. It was in darkness and she knocked loudly at the door.

"Who is there?" she was challenged.

"It is I."

"But who are you? What is your name?"

"Belle Boyd. I have important intelligence to communicate to Colonel Ashby: is he here?"

She returned safely, and a few days later, Belle continues, Colonel Shields marched south, laying what he supposed was a trap to catch "poor old Jackson and his demoralized army." Her mother returned home, but Belle stayed at Front Royal, waiting, it appeared, for an opportunity to go on toward Richmond. She was, now, annoyed by the persistent attentions of the correspondent for the New York Herald; he was living at the Federal headquarters, and, in consequence, his pursuit of her was so official that once, sitting in a room with her cousin, she was obliged to bolt the door against him. His dispatches about her to New York, after that, were filled with a nonsense of detraction.

On the twenty-third of May, in Eighteen-sixty-two, Belle, sitting at a window in her aunt's house, saw a great confusion on the street. A Union officer told her that the Confederates were approaching in force under General Jackson and Ewell; he hurried away and the correspondent for the Herald appeared in a panic, demanding what had happened. "Nothing to speak of," Belle assured him, "only the Rebels are coming, and you had best prepare yourself for a visit to Libby Prison." He rushed into the room where his papers were kept and began feverishly to destroy them. The key to his door, Belle saw, was on the outside: she locked him in to secure for him the beneficial restraints of a Confederate prison. She then hurried to a balcony and, with opera glasses, saw an advance guard of Southern troops marching rapidly toward the town.

Belle had been waiting with important news for General Jackson, it was now imperative news, and she asked a group of men standing at the door, sympathetic to the South, if one of them would bear a message to Jackson. With complete accord they all replied, "No, no. You go." She put on a white sunbonnet and ran down the street, through throngs of Federal soldiers, and reached the open fields beyond. Belle wore a dark blue dress and a small frilled white apron, the contrast of color made her conspicuous, and a retreating Union picquet opened fire upon her. Volleys were discharged at her from the long façade of the hospital. Bullets repeatedly pierced her dress. The Northern guns, commanding the Confederate approach, were in action; the Southern artillery dropped a hail of iron about her; a Federal shell exploded within twenty feet and covered her with débris and earth. Belle's escape was miraculous.

As she approached the Confederate line she waved her sunbonnet, and the First Maryland infantry and Hay's Louisiana brigade received her with a great cheer. She discovered a friend, Major Henry Douglas, and explained that the Union General Banks was at Strasburg with four thousand men, that General White was marching from Harper's Ferry toward Winchester, Fremont was just beyond the Valley, and that the massed weight of their troops was to be flung against General Jackson. Major Douglas galloped in search of his commander, and, acting rapidly upon Belle's information, the Confederates won a wide victory. General Jackson sent Belle a note: "Miss Belle Boyd, I thank you, for myself and for the army, for the immense service that you have rendered your country today. Hastily, I am your friend, T. J. Jackson, C. S. A."

* *
*

The Northern journals were now filled with extravagant accounts of Belle's great beauty and ingenuity and daring: it was asserted that she directed the firing on the field of battle, she alone sustained the wavering counsels of Southern generals, and that with a sanguinary sword she led the attack of armies. The Confederate forces made a short thrust north in the Valley; the South again occupied Front Royal; and a woman who was, she said, the wife of a soldier in the Michigan cavalry, was put in Belle's charge. When the Federals, under General Geary returned, she accused Belle of dangerous secret activities. Geary placed Belle under arrest, there were sentries around her house, but when General Shields arrived—General Geary's superior—he released her immediately. Belle then decided she was no longer useful in the Valley of the Shenandoah; she was willing to go into the deep South. General Banks was again in her uncle's house, and she applied to him for permission to depart.

While Banks was deliberating Belle saw two soldiers in Confederate uniform standing near the provost marshal's tent; she asked them to have dinner with her; and, although a servant from the kitchen warned her that they were Union spies, she gave one a letter to carry to General Jackson. A Federal officer told her that the messenger was a Secret Service agent on his way to Harrisburg, and she immediately tried to correct her dangerous mistake. She wrote a careful description of her letter and the man bearing it, to Captain Henry Gilmore; it went by the underground-railroad, within the case of a large silver watch; but the spy had already delivered Belle's message to General Sigel. He sent it to Mr. Stanton, the Secretary of War. Another Federal officer then warned Belle that his government had determined to meet any further misconduct of hers with the severest punishment.

She prepared to leave Front Royal at once for Richmond, it was Tuesday, a pass had been promised her for Thursday; but, in the meanwhile, she sent an additional note to Major Gilmore, informing him of a Union cavalry movement. On Wednesday she rose early; standing in the cottage door she saw several Yankee soldiers open a coach house and drag out a carriage; they harnessed a pair of horses to it and then waited at headquarters. That was not extraordinary, but Belle was conscious of a persistent curiosity about the purpose of the carriage.

She was, at once, summoned to the drawing-room, where, in addition to a Major McEnnis, familiar to her, there was a Major Sherman and the detective from the Secret Service Department, named Cridge. Cridge, Belle said, was "low in stature, coarse in appearance, with a mean, vile expression of countenance, and a grizzly beard. All his features were repulsive in the extreme, denoting a mixture of cowardice, ferocity, and cunning." Major McEnnis explained to Belle that she was under arrest. Major Sherman continued in a tone of apology—he was executing the command of Mr. Stanton. Cridge produced the written order: "War Department. Sir: You will proceed immediately to Front Royal, Va., and arrest, if found there, Miss Belle Boyd, and bring her at once to Washington. I am, respectfully, Your obedient servant, E. M. Stanton."

Her room was searched, her dresses were flung in a fantastic pile on the floor; her underclothing followed; her portfolio was minutely examined. Some incriminating papers had just been burned, but others, unhappily, far from innocent, were discovered. Cridge took these, together with a handsome pistol, complete with its belt, given to her by a Federal officer in recognition of his admiration at the spirited manner in which she had defended her mother. The news of her arrest spread quickly, the streets were filled with people, and Belle was driven away with an escort of four hundred and fifty soldiers: fifty scouts were detached in skirmishing order to prevent all surprise on the right and fifty performed that same duty on the left. At Winchester, surrounded by the whole body of more than five hundred men, she was marched with solemn procession through a silent throng. At Martinsburg Belle's mother vainly begged Major Sherman to release her. She was lodged at Raemer's Hotel, guarded by twenty-seven sentries; but Belle at least succeeded in having the odious Cridge removed from her immediate vicinity—a Lieutenant Steel, of the Twelfth Illinois cavalry, was detailed to accompany her.

A large crowd had gathered at the depot in Washington to see her, but she was immediately and roughly dragged to a carriage and driven to the Old Capitol Prison. There, however, a Mr. Wood was polite: he promised to make her as comfortable as possible; and Belle was conducted through a narrow hall, up a flight of stairs, and lodged in cell No. 6. It contained a washstand, a looking-glass, an iron bedstead, a table and two chairs. She could see, through its windows, over Pennsylvania Avenue and, farther, the house of General Floyd, who had been Secretary of War, where she had been part of many gay and fashionable parties. She was provided with a negro servant, an "intelligent contraband," and her dinner, at least, was generous: Soup, beefsteak, chicken, boiled corn, tomatoes, Irish stew, potatoes, bread and butter, cantaloups, peaches, pears and grapes. At eight o'clock the Chief of Detectives and Mr. Wood appeared and tried, but without success, to force a confession from her.

A narrow open space behind the prison was used as an exercise ground, and Belle saw, passing her door in the direction of that limited freedom, familiar figures from the Army of Virginia. She scooped a hole through the plaster of the wall separating her from the prisoners in the next cell and exchanged notes with them. Several gentlemen from Fredericksburg, confined in the room above her, managed to loosen a plank in the floor and talk to her. On the fourth morning of her confinement a little Frenchman gave her a half length portrait of Jefferson Davis; Belle promptly hung it on her wall with an inscription, Three Cheers for Jefferson Davis and the Southern Confederacy; and for that offense she was kept in close confinement.

It is impossible to discover how long she was detained in Washington; she was, eventually, one of two hundred prisoners who were exchanged; they formed in line on the street, but Belle was escorted to a carriage by a Major Fitzhugh, who accompanied her to Richmond. They proceeded directly to the steamer Juanita, and soon passed up the James River to her destination. Belle went to the Ballard House; she drove by the encampment of the Richmond Blues and the company presented arms; in the evening she was serenaded by the city band. She soon left the hotel for a boarding house on Grace Street; General and Mrs. Joseph Johnston, General Wigfall and his family, were staying there: they had a part in the presentation of a gold watch and chatelaine, elaborately enamelled and set with diamonds, given to Belle in token of the affection and esteem of her fellow prisoners in the Old Capitol.

Her father arrived in Richmond to take her home,

Martinsburg was again occupied by the Confederates, and General Jackson greeted Belle very warmly. She visited him at his headquarters and he rode in for tea with her. On the following day Jackson sent her word that he was preparing a retrograde movement upon Winchester, and that he could spare an ambulance in which she might precede his retreating army. Belle accepted his offer, and in Winchester she was commissioned captain and made honorary aide to General Jackson. She was present on his staff when the Southern troops were reviewed before Lord Harrington and Colonel Leslie, and again when General Wilcox's division was inspected by General Longstreet and by General Lee.

* *
*

The anonymous author of a volume of Southern War memoirs, edited by Myrta Lockett Avary, A Virginia Girl in the Civil War, describes in detail a meeting with Belle Boyd. It was at Culpepper Court House, and she was seated in a room lighted by two tallow candles on the bureau when there was a knock at the door. She was asked if a lady, who had arrived unexpectedly, could share her room. A heavy snow was falling; a high wind was blowing it into drifts; Mrs. Rixey's house was filled with Confederates who either wished to be near the army or were waiting an opportunity to slip through the lines. The evenings were gay:

"When I entered the parlor there was, as usual, a merry party, and I did not catch my room-mate's name. She seemed to be nineteen, or perhaps twenty, rather young, I thought, to be travelling alone. What made her an object of interest to every woman present was that she was exceedingly well dressed. It had been a long long time since we had seen a new dress. She was a brilliant talker, and soon everybody in the room was attracted to her, especially the men. She talked chiefly to the men—indeed I am afraid she did not care particularly for the women—and at first we were a little piqued; but when we found she was devoted to The Cause we were ready to forgive her everything.

"She soon let us know that she had come directly from Washington, where she had been a prisoner of the United States. She showed us her watch and told us how the prisoners in Washington had made up the money among themselves and presented it to her. I got sleepy, slipped quietly out of the room and went upstairs to bed. My room-mate got undressed and got to bed so quickly that I did not wake. The next morning, when the maid came in to make the fire, we woke up face to face in the same bed, and then she told me that her name was Belle Boyd, and I knew for the first time that my bedfellow was the South's famous female spy. When she got up she took a large bottle of cologne and poured it into the basin in which she was going to bathe. It was the first cologne I had seen for more than a year, and it was the last I saw until I ran the blockade. Later in the day a ragged unkempt Confederate soldier appeared. As he stood in the hall ready to go back to camp, Belle Boyd came down the staircase, carrying a large new blanket shawl. 'You must let me wrap you up, lieutenant,' she said, putting the shawl around his shoulders and pinning it together. He blushed and objected. A shawl like that was too much—it was a princely gift, a fortune. 'I can't let you go back to camp in this thin jacket,' she insisted. 'It is serving our country, lieutenant, when it protects her soldier from the cold!' She did not spend another night with us. She seemed to feel that she had the weight of the Confederacy on her shoulders, and took the afternoon train for Richmond."

Early in January—Belle's memoir says it was Eighteen-

sixty-two, but that is impossible, it must have been later—
she was in Charlottesville; she was anxious about her mother,
and she wrote General Jackson, asking if it would be wise
for her to return to Martinsburg. It would not, he replied,
addressing her as his dear child. It would be better for her
to go to her relatives in Tennessee. He was truly her friend,
T. J. Jackson. She followed his advice, and at Knoxville
Belle was met with great attention: she was serenaded at
night by a band and a large crowd; there were insistent calls
for her appearance on the balcony. At last she came forward
with the briefest of words. "Like General Joe Johnston, I
can fight but I cannot make speeches, but my good friends,
I no less feel and appreciate the kind compliment you have
paid me tonight."

In the spring she resolved to make the classic wartime
tour of the whole South, and her progress Belle describes
as an unbroken ovation. She was anticipated by telegrams
at each town. Belle visited the cotton plantations of Alabama.
There was a long delightful period at Montgomery, and
she went on to Mobile. In Mobile she heard of General
Jackson's death, and for thirty days—the time allotted to
the mourning of a soldier—she wore crêpe on her arm.
At Charleston she had dinner with Beauregard; one of his
staff presented her with a great basket of fresh fruit newly
arrived on a blockade runner from the West Indies; he also
gave her an especially handsome parrot that she took back
to Richmond.

Her father was now in Martinsburg, useless from the
effects of his long hard campaigning; after Sharpsburg the
town was turned into a vast hospital; and when the retreating
Confederates moved south down the Valley, Belle remained
caring for the wounded. The Union forces reappeared, an
entire regiment stopped outside the Boyd house, and two
officers entered in search of Belle. Four days later an order

was issued for her arrest. Her mother was ill, and she was allowed to remain at home, but guards were again stationed about the house; she was not permitted even to go out on a balcony. This was in July, Eighteen-sixty-three; her confinement became so wearisome that she succeeded in getting permission from the commanding officer to take a walk. It read, "Miss Belle Boyd is allowed to walk out for half an hour, at 5 o'clock this P.M., giving her word of honor that she will use nothing which she may see or hear to the disadvantage of the United States troops."

She had gone, however, only a few blocks when she was rearrested and sent back. A note from headquarters repeated the fact that she was not allowed to promenade freely in Martinsburg. She remained under guard for a month, and then Major Walker, the provost marshal, called with a detective and said she must prepare to go to Washington at once. Mr. Stanton had ordered it. She was, this time, lodged in Carroll Prison, together with blockade-runners, smugglers, spies, criminals under sentence of death, hostages and a large number of Federal officers and contractors convicted of defrauding the government. She spent the monotonous days of prison life gazing listlessly through her barred window and exchanging, through a hole in the wall, notes with four men who had been captured trying to get South to join the Rebel army. She was standing at the window, singing "Take me back to my own sunny South," when an arrow winged by her and fell on the floor. It was from a C. H., he expressed a great admiration for Belle, and begged her to sew an answer in a rubber ball and throw it out the window. A correspondence followed that was both romantic and practical—she learned from it a great deal about the movements of the Federal troops.

Her court-martial, meanwhile, was progressing under Judge Advocate T. C. Turner; and, on the first of December, it was decided that Belle should be transferred to Fortress Monroe. There she was escorted into the presence of Butler. He was seated at a table, and, looking up, he said, "Ah, so this is Miss Belle Boyd, the famous Rebel spy. Pray be seated."

"Thank you, General Butler," Belle replied, "but I prefer to stand." He noted that she was agitated and trembled, and he repeated, "Pray be seated. But why do you tremble so? Are you frightened?"

"No, ah, that is, yes, General Butler. I must acknowledge that I do feel frightened in the presence of a man with such a world-wide reputation as yourself." This, she relates, seemed to please him immensely, and rubbing his hands together he smiled benevolently. "Oh, do be seated, Miss Boyd. But what do you mean when you say that I am widely known?"

"I mean, General Butler," she explained, "that you are a man whose atrocious conduct and brutality, especially to Southern ladies, is so infamous that even the British Parliament commented on it. I naturally feel alarmed at being in your presence." He ordered her immediately from the room, she was conducted to a hotel, and then sent again to Richmond.

* *
*

Two Saratoga trunks and a hat box belonging to Belle were first searched: they were found to contain two suits of gentlemen's civilian clothes, a uniform for a Confederate major general, a great many useful bagatelles of military existence, and a pair of field glasses that had belonged to General Jackson. How she had accumulated so much, even by the mysterious processes of the underground-railway, remains an enigma. It was all, of course, confiscated; she entreated the Federal authorities for the privilege of keeping

Jackson's field glasses; but, to her intense mortification, they were presented to General Butler. She managed, however, to avoid a search of her person, and in that Belle was fortunate—she had concealed about her body twenty thousand dollars in Confederate notes, five thousand in United States greenbacks, and a thousand dollars gold.

At Richmond she proceeded to the Spottswood Hotel, a dinner party was given for her on a Saturday, and the following Monday she learned that her father was dead. Belle applied for permission to go to her mother, it was—not unnaturally—refused, and instead she again visited the deep South. Upon her return to Richmond she determined to go to England: she was now in a precarious state of health. Jefferson Davis approved of her design, the Confederate Secretary of State was instructed to make her a bearer of dispatches, and she sailed from Wilmington, North Carolina, on the Greyhound, commanded by Captain George Henry Bier—he is, in Belle Boyd's memoir, transformed into a Captain Henry—the May of Eighteen-sixty-four.

The deck of the Greyhound was piled high with cotton, the blockade-runner was almost free of the Federal ships, when she was sighted by a fast Northern steamer. There was a broadside, shots followed in rapid accurate succession, and the cotton bales on the deck of the Greyhound were rolled overboard. Even relieved of this weight Captain Bier could not avoid capture, a hundred-pound iron bolt passed between Belle and himself, and he brought his ship to. Belle Boyd destroyed her dispatches and Bier dropped over the rail a keg containing thirty thousand dollars. The Federal steamer was the Connecticut; her men took what pleased them from the Greyhound; they consumed Captain Bier's private stock of wines and even forced their way into Belle's cabin, and insulted her negro maid.

Belle noticed a young officer who had just come over the side. "I confess," she writes, "my attention was riveted by a gentleman—the first whom I had met in my hour of distress. His dark brown hair hung down on his shoulders; his eyes were large and bright. Those who judge of beauty by regularity of feature only would not have pronounced him strictly handsome, but the fascination of his manner was such that my heart yielded." Later he asked permission to enter her cabin for a minute. It was Lieutenant Hardinge; Hardinge explained that he was now in command of the Greyhound; but he begged Belle to consider herself a passenger rather than prisoner.

The second evening after her capture, Belle proceeds, she was seated by the wheel with Captain Bier and Hardinge. "The moon shone beautifully clear, lighting up everything; a slight breeze swept the surface of the ocean until it was a vast bed of sparkling diamonds." Captain Bier withdrew. "Mr. Hardinge quoted some beautiful passages from Byron and Shakespeare. Then, in a decidedly Claude Melnotte style, he endeavored to paint the home to which, if love could but fulfil its prayers, this heart would lead thee! And from poetry he passed on to plead an oft told tale."

In that romantic situation, under the moon, Belle admits that she remained purely practical; Hardinge might, she realized, be very useful; when he asked her to marry him she replied that his question involved serious consequences; he must not, she explained, expect an answer until they arrived in Boston. The Greyhound called at New York, Belle was allowed to go on shore, and she was able to transfer to safety a great weight of gold—it was both hers and Captain Bier's—she had secretly carried. On the further passage to Boston she surrendered her wisdom to romance. She promised to marry the headlong Mr. Hardinge. Very soon indeed after that, in Boston Harbor, Captain Bier escaped. Belle is careful to keep the whole doubtful credit for that. She was taken to the Tremont House, and treated with great courtesy; crowds continually waited to see her; all her movements were followed in the newspapers. Mr. Hardinge, with letters to influential men, had gone to Washington to procure, if possible, her release.

Instead he was arrested for complicity in the escape of Captain Bier. Belle had applied to Gideon Welles, Secretary of the Navy, for permission to go into Canada, and Welles sent her a telegram: Miss Belle Boyd and her servant were to be escorted beyond the lines into Canada. If she was again caught in the United States, or by the United States authorities, she would be shot. She was anxious, however, first to see Mr. Hardinge; Hardinge was paroled until sundown for that privilege; and Belle left for Niagara Falls immediately. She continued on to Quebec, and sailed from there to Liverpool. She saw Mr. Hotze, the Confederate agent in London, reported to him the destruction of her dispatches at the capture of the Greyhound, and all her connection with the Civil War came to an end.

The personal details of Belle's life are as engaging as her official and more extraordinary acts. Mr. Hotze gave her a letter from Hardinge: he was in Paris searching for her; she sent him word of her presence in London, and, August third, Eighteen-sixty-four, they were married at St. James' Church, Piccadilly. Their wedding had the full attention of the London newspapers. It was, the Morning Post asserted, a romantic episode in the fratricidal war now raging on the American continent. "Miss Belle Boyd, whose name and fame are deservedly cherished in the Southern States, pledged her troth to Mr. Sam Wylde Hardinge, formerly an officer in the Federal naval service. The wedding attracted to the church a considerable number of English and American sympathizers in the cause of the South, anxious to see the lady whose heroism has made her name so famous, and to witness the result of her last activity, the making captive of the Federal officer under whose guard she was being conveyed to prison."

The bride, it was further related, was attended at the altar by Mrs. Edward Robinson Harvey. Mr. Hardinge was supported by Mr. Henry Howard Barber. The services were read by the Reverend Mr. Paull; the Reverend Frederic Kill Harford gave the bride away. "At the conclusion of the ceremony the bride and bridegroom and their friends proceeded to the Brunswick Hotel, Jermyn Street, where a choice and well-arranged breakfast was partaken of; and at a fitting moment, Mr. Barber, in a most eloquent speech, proposed the health of Mr. and Mrs. Hardinge, eulogizing the services the lady had performed and prognosticating that the bridegroom would soon win fame in the services—the services are unexplained—on which he is about to enter. The toast of 'The Queen' was afterwards given. 'President Davis and General Lee' and many other toasts followed in due order, till the growing hours warned the bride and bridegroom that it was time to depart for Liverpool. Mr. Hardinge proposes in a few days to leave for the South, whither, in spite of the blockade, he intends to convey a goodly portion of the wedding cake for distribution amongst his wife's friends."

Hardinge succeeded in landing at Wilmington, he distributed the wedding cake as he had promised, but in Baltimore he was arrested, now charged with being a deserter, and finally taken to the Old Capitol Prison. When the war ended he was released; he returned to the damaging seductiveness of Belle.

GOLD SPURS

GOLD SPURS

GENERAL J. E. B. STUART wore gold spurs and a rose with his war jacket. Ladies in Maryland gave him the spurs and ladies wherever he chanced to be gave him the rosebuds. It was not uncommon for him to have a girl, but always lovely, mounted on one of his finest horses, galloping beside him over the roads that led to battle. Naturally he was in the cavalry. He was different, in everything except ability, from the other great cavalry leaders of the South—Jeb Stuart was without the black fury of General Forrest; he had none of the illogical severity of Jackson's spirit. Stuart wore a brown felt hat looped up flat with a gold star and sweeping black plume; his double-breasted jacket was invariably open, buttoned back on a grey waistcoat; his boots in action were heavy, but afterwards he changed them for immaculate boots of patent leather worked with gold thread; but he danced as well as fought in his spurs.

On the march he wore a graceful cape, lined in brilliant red, his arms were a light French sabre and a single pistol in a black holster. He kept strapped on the pommel of his saddle an oilcloth poncho for rain. In rain, curiously enough, his spirits were always highest. He sang continually in all downpours. Stuart wrapped a beautiful yellow sash around his waist, he arranged it so that the tassels would fall in full view on the left side, and over that his belt was buckled. He never moved out of the company of a bright red battle flag, ignoring the fact that it might and frequently did draw the enemy's fire, and he was never without the presence of his banjo player, Sweeny. Sweeny was an inmate of the general's tent, he rode behind him in the field, and accompanied General Stuart upon all social occasions. Stuart wrote practically all his important dispatches to the rattle of Sweeny's strings; often he would interrupt the most serious concerns by singing, in a loud and sonorous and correct voice, a sentimental or robust chorus.

The songs preferred by Sweeny and General Stuart were: The Bugles Sang Truce, for the Night Cloud was Lowered. The Dew is on the Blossom. Sweet Evelina, and humorous catches: If You Get There Before I Do. The Old Grey Horse. If You Want to have a Good Time, Jine the Cavalry. Stuart led his men at Chancellorsville singing, Old Joe Hooker, will you come out of the Wilderness? Sweeny himself took especial pleasure in, Oh, Johnny Booker, Help This Nigger. And, Oh, Lord, Ladies don't you mind Stephen.

In winter quarters General Stuart's tent was a large affair; there was a good chimney with a cheerful fireplace; but in summer, on more active service, he had an informal piece of canvas hung over a rail and open at both ends. There were a chair and desk, his red blankets were laid on the ground, his two setters, Nip and Tuck, stayed at Stuart's feet. He carried them, whenever it was necessary and possible, on his saddle. Unofficially he was gay with moments of unaccountable temper. Stuart, in his personal relationships, was both tender and highly sensitive; all misunderstanding made him acutely miserable; but where his position, his authority, were concerned he was adamant. Nothing could change his convictions or designs. He never overlooked or forgot the slightest opposition to his will.

His courage was absolute, it was recklessness beyond any reason; he showed no sign of the restlessness exhibited by the bravest men in situations of extreme danger; he sat on his horse with his head up, unmoved, in full sight of the enemy. The sharp passage of bullets—at Fredericksburg they cut off locks of his hair and pierced his clothes—did not even distract his attention. Bravery, rather than the result of a strong will, in Stuart seemed to be the product of indifference. An immense animal vitality danced in his brilliant blue eyes—he was not tall, rather his frame was low and powerful, closely-knit and capable of enormous endurance. He had a broad high forehead, instinct with imagination, a heavy nose and large delicate nostrils; a chestnut brown moustache was curled up at the ends above a great brown beard.

His mind was active and determined rather than learned—his education and preferences were those of a gentleman rather than of a scholar—Stuart read very little. He was familiar with the volume of Napoleon's Maxims and with a translation of Jomini's Treatise on War. When he read at all it was in the subject of his profession. He was a born, an ideal, leader of cavalry. His perceptions there were faultless; he was never known to make a tactical error. His plans were formed instantly with no more than a single sweeping view of a complicated battlefield. At times, however, nothing but his unconquerable resolution, a cold desperation, saved him from destruction. General Stuart was often forced to depend upon sharp-shooting but he enormously preferred pure cavalry fighting; but when his men were dismounted in skirmishes he remained stubbornly beside them, buoyant with encouragement and songs.

His great ability was in raiding, in rapid flank movements, charging and falling back with horse. His extraordinary energy was practically inexhaustible; Stuart almost never slept. He needed, it seemed, little if any rest. On the night of the second battle of Manassas he gave comprehensible orders when he was asleep. After days and nights without interruption in the saddle he would stop by any roadside and lie down, safe or in the enemy's country, without picquets or videttes. He did this at Carlisle, Pennsylvania; wrapped in his cloak he rested for an hour against a tree; and then he remounted completely refreshed. Through moments of extreme peril he sat with a leg thrown over the pommel of his saddle, drumming with his fingers on a knee. He was often begged not to expose himself so recklessly; he must, it was pointed out, be killed; but his invariable response was that he reckoned not. His life did appear to be charmed: he lived untouched in a rain of shell, canister, round shot and bullets until he was hit fatally at Yellow Tavern.

He died, happily, at the moment of his greatest glory, at the last glorious moment of the Confederacy; he suffered none of the ignominy, the poverty and sadness, of defeat. For that reason he was the most satisfactory, the most wholly romantic, soldier of the Civil War. Nothing about him, nothing in his career, was disappointing; it was all handsome, all ingratiating, like his yellow sash with its graceful fringed ends. He had the immense good fortune to be born at the right time, at the right place and to the right manner; his ancestors were both distinguished and honorable. The first member of his family to reach America was Archibald Stuart, in Seventeen-twenty-six; he left Londonderry, Ireland, to escape religious persecution, and settled in western Pennsylvania. His second son, Alexander, was commissioned an officer in the Revolution; and his son, again Alexander, was a judge in Richmond and member of the Executive Council of State. Judge Stuart's son, Archibald—the family kept its own names—J. E. B. Stuart's father, was an officer in the United States army in the War of Eighteen-twelve, he sat in the Virginia Legislature, he was a member of the Constitutional Convention of Eighteen-twenty-eight and thirty, and of the Convention of Eighteen-fifty.

Archibald Stuart married Elizabeth Letcher Pannill, of Pittsylvania County, Virginia, and she brought him a beautiful estate and plantation called Laurel Hill in Patrick County. Her family, four sons and six daughters, was born there, James Ewell Brown on the sixth of February, Eighteen-thirty-three. The house he first knew was set in a deep lawn of oak trees and surrounded by beds of flowers. He spent his childhood in the shadow of oaks and in a garden with his mother. Beyond he saw against the sky the high serene beauty of the Blue Ridge Mountains.

* * *

In Eighteen-fifty-five, when Stuart was twenty-two years old, he was appointed regimental quartermaster and commissary at Fort Leavenworth. He had been second lieutenant in the First regiment, United States cavalry. Fort Leavenworth, above the great bend of the Missouri River, on what became the Iowa-Missouri border, was the most western of the forts begun in Eighteen-sixteen to protect the territory of the United States from foreign menace beyond. It was built in Eighteen-twenty-seven, and when Jeb Stuart was ordered there Leavenworth was the most important military post in the country. It controlled the hostile prairie Indians; it was a point of departure for the Santa Fé Trail and the trails to the North; and, as far as possible, it preserved a comparative order in the preliminary and local civil war that took place in Kansas Territory. In Kansas, the North and the South met in a bitter and destructive struggle.

Senator Douglas, in Eighteen-fifty-four, presented a bill that resulted in bringing to an end the Missouri Compromise, an agreement and a line dividing the states where slavery was permitted from the Northern States that were to remain free. Kansas Territory was now given the right to decide if it would become a free or a slave state, and in consequence of this there was a lawless and bloody strife. Elections were no better than battles. An organized immigration of anti-slave forces was sent from New England; armed bodies of men crossed the Missouri border—the Border Ruffians—in the interest of slave-holders. The Southerners declared that the Massachusetts Aid Societies were composed of the lowest class of rowdies, hellish emigrants and paupers whose bellies were filled with beggar's food; men of black and poisonous hearts; they were riffraff, scoundrels and criminals. The citizens of Missouri, the North asserted, were low and degraded beings, armed to the teeth and revelling in cruelty —in brief, fiends incarnate.

The result of such extravagant opinion was both immediate and serious: there were, among other things, two legislatures, two territorial governments; the ballot was soon given up for the more decisive effect of bowie knives and Sharp's rifles. That was the scene which witnessed the entrance of John Brown and his sons into history. John Brown had been living on a farm in North Elba, Massachusetts; and in August, Eighteen-fifty-four, he decided to remove to Kansas and oppose what he held to be the fatal iniquity of slavery. He was delayed, however, in starting; nearly a year later, in April, Eighteen-fifty-five, three of his sons, Owen and Frederick and Salmon, with eleven head of cattle and three horses, entered Kansas; in May they were at Osawatomie; and there two more brothers, Jason and John, joined them. John Brown reached Osawatomie in October, bringing with him, for the extending of liberty, several cases of guns belonging to disbanded militia companies of the State of Ohio, a gift of broadswords from General Lucius V. Bierce, and an assortment of carbines, revolvers, swords, powder and caps. Personally he was destitute, he owned only sixty cents in money; his sons, burning with fever and ague, had neither been able to build cabins nor cultivate their scant crops. No better than tents protected them from the local bitter winds. They had no meat, almost no sugar, the bread was made from corn laboriously ground by hand. This did nothing to reduce John Brown's fervor. "God," he wrote, "has not deserted us; & we get day by day our dayly bread; & I wish we had a great deal more gratitude to mingle with our undeserved blessings." His sons eagerly attended Free State Meetings; he was ready to meet violence with violence, to do, he declared, to the Border Ruffians what they were doing to Free-soilers. He was ready to take from the pro-slavery men their chattels, living or immobile, and even their lives.

In November, Eighteen-fifty-four, Lucius Kibby, a Free-soiler, had killed Henry Davis, a Kentuckian, with a knife. Then William Phillips, a Northern lawyer settled in Leavenworth, was warned by a pro-slavery vigilance committee to leave the Territory. He declined and the committee tarred and feathered him near Rialto, Missouri. One side of his head was shaved; after he had been stripped and the hot tar applied he was ridden on a rail for a mile and a half, and then he was sold for a dollar by a negro auctioneer. The Reverend Pardee Butler, of Atchison, was put on a raft in the Missouri River by Southern sympathizers and there stoned. His forehead was marked by the letter R and flags on his raft bore the inscriptions, Greeley to the Rescue, I have a Nigger. Eastern Aid Express. And, Rev. Mr. Butler, Agent to the Underground Railroad.

John Brown, who considered himself to be the weapon of a transcendent justice, lost no time in entering the struggle—three days after his arrival in Kansas he went with his sons fully armed to the election of a Free State candidate, but no enemy appeared. He organized a company called the Liberty Guards, with four of his sons, Frederick and Owen and Salmon and John, and others, and for the first time he received the title of captain. His fervor increased: with the assistance of four of his sons, a Henry Thompson, Theodore Weiner and James Townsley, he deliberately killed five pro-slavery men. They began that practical expression of the spirit by sharpening the cutlasses General Bierce had supplied. Young John Brown and Jason held them while the grindstone was turned by a boy named Bain Fuller. George Grant, who saw the operation, remarked to Frederick Brown, "This looks like business." Frederick replied, "Yes, it does." Near sundown a James Blood saw a wagon accompanied by a mounted man going toward Pottawatomie Creek. As it drew near to him John Brown rose up in it and called halt! The men in the wagon, Blood recalled, were armed with rifles, revolvers, knives and the sharp cutlasses.

"John Brown's manner," Colonel Blood wrote long afterwards, "was wild and frenzied, and the whole party watched with excited eagerness every word or motion of the old man. Finally as I left them, he requested me not to mention the fact that I had met them, as they were on a secret expedition and did not want anyone to know they were in the neighborhood."

That night John Brown camped near a ford called Dutch Henry's Crossing. All the following day—it was Saturday, the twenty-fourth of May, Eighteen-fifty-six—the party lay on their arms. At ten o'clock in the evening they made their way to the cabin of a pro-slavery man named Doyle. They knocked at the door and then entered. Mrs. Doyle stormed and raved; her husband said, "Hush, mother, hush." Doyle and his two sons, they were twenty and twenty-two years old, were taken outside the cabin. There was the sound of a pistol shot. Mrs. Doyle was positive about that, but who fired it is still an uncertainty: Salmon Brown declared that his father took no actual part in the killing but admitted that, if a pistol was fired, no one else pulled a trigger. The cutlasses were used for the execution. John Brown's band then divided and part of it went to the house of Allen Wilkinson, a member of the pro-slavery legislature at Shawnee Mission.

Mrs. Wilkinson, who was suffering from measles, woke up her husband and said that the dog was barking. Immediately afterwards someone outside asked the way to Dutch Henry's. Wilkinson replied when a voice said, "Come out and show us." Mrs. Wilkinson would not let him go, and she could hear whispering. Allen Wilkinson was then told that he was a prisoner and commanded to open the door. He did this, against his wife's protests, and four men entered. They searched for arms, Mrs. Wilkinson explained that she was sick and helpless, she begged them not to take her husband away and leave her without assistance. An old man, who seemed to be in command, replied, "It matters not." The next morning Wilkinson's body was found—he had been hacked to death—in a pile of brush. "We then crossed the Pottawatomie and came to the house of Henry Sherman," James Townsley related. Henry Sherman, however, was out on the plains in search of lost cattle; a William Sherman was marched down to the creek and murdered. John Brown's righteousness was satisfied.

*   *
*

Jason Brown and his brother John were arrested by a detachment of the First United States cavalry under Captain Wood; they were examined at Lecompton; and, since it was plain they had no part in the murders on Pottawatomie Creek, Jason was released. The younger John Brown, because of his political activities, was held on a charge of high treason; but he too was given his freedom in September. Their father escaped, hiding with his companions in the Kansas woods; and the troops at Fort Leavenworth were bitterly condemned throughout the South for their failure to bring justice upon the old man. Lieutenant J. E. B. Stuart had encountered him more than once, and for that reason he was selected, with Brevet Colonel Robert E. Lee, to attend a conference at the White House with the President and the Secretary of War, Mr. Floyd, when John Brown was in possession of the arsenal at Harper's Ferry. This was the year Eighteen-fifty-nine, in the autumn; Colonel Lee and Stuart, who was his aide, were ordered to join the United States marines proceeding against John Brown; they surrounded the fire engine house held by the fanatical old man and his decimated force.

Lieutenant Stuart was informed by his superior officer that he determined first to demand a surrender of the whole party at dawn, and then, in the case of refusal, to have the place taken by a few picked men with the bayonet. Stuart was deputed to read to the leader, who was called Smith, the terms of submission; if they were refused he was to leave the door and wave his cap. The storming party would then advance, batter open the door, and capture the insurgents. John Brown had some prisoners confined with him in the engine house, and Colonel Lee was very particular in his instructions about their safety. Lieutenant Stuart, in the presence of some two thousand spectators, approached the informal fortification and notified Mr. Smith that he had a communication for him from Colonel Lee. He opened the door about four inches, and placed his body against the crack, with a cocked carbine in his hand.

A long parley followed—Stuart had immediately recognized old Osawatomie Brown—in which John Brown, with an admirable tact, presented a number of counter suggestions; but it all amounted to this—the only condition upon which he would surrender was that he and his party should be allowed to escape. Stuart told him that Colonel Lee would never accede to any terms but those he had offered:

> "Headquarters Harper's Ferry,
> October 18, 1859
>
> "Colonel Lee, United States army, commanding the troops sent by the President of the United States to suppress the insurrection at this place, demands the surrender of the persons in the armory buildings.
>
> "If they will peaceably surrender themselves and restore the pillaged property, they shall be kept in safety to await the orders of the President. Colonel Lee represents to them, in all frankness, that it is impossible for them to escape; that the armory is surrounded on all sides by troops; and that if he is compelled to take them by force he cannot answer for their safety.
>
> R. E. Lee
> Colonel Commanding United States troops."

Brevet Colonel Lee, who was in civilian's clothes, stood on a slight elevation about forty feet away from the fire engine house and carefully supervised the details of its capture. He turned to Lieutenant Israel Green, of the marines, and asked him whether he wished the honor of "taking those men out." Green at once removed his hat and, simply and sincerely, thanked Colonel Lee. He then picked a storming detail of twelve men, with a second twelve in reserve, and, exactly at sunrise, Green ordered the attack. Three marines, with sledge hammers, began beating at the engine house door, but with little effect; Lieutenant Green recognized the futility of that, and, seeing a heavy stepladder lying near by, he ordered his men to use it as a battering ram. The door was broken in at the second blow.

The entrance was a ragged hole low down on the right, and Green, stooping, made his way within. He attacked John Brown, lunging at him with a light dress sword—he had neglected to arm himself properly—but, striking Brown's belt, it bent double. Then taking the bent weapon in both hands Lieutenant Green beat John Brown down to the floor. The marines followed, and Private Luke Quin was mortally shot, the man behind him was gravely wounded in the face. In retaliation, an individual hiding under an engine was bayoneted and a second was pinned to a wall. Lieutenant Green then ordered the shedding of blood to end.

John Brown, his second in command, Stevens, two negroes, Copeland and Green, and Edwin Coppoc were captured; the bodies of nine others lay in front of their fort or scattered over Harper's Ferry; seven had escaped into Pennsylvania. The eleven prisoners Brown held in the engine house, Green declared, were the sorriest lot of people he had ever seen. They had been without food for over sixty hours, and, in constant dread of being shot, stood huddled in the corner where Oliver Brown lay dead. Old Osawatomie Brown was carried to the office of the paymaster of the armory, where it was discovered that his wounds were superficial.

The governor of Virginia, Mr. Wise, arrived promptly, and there was a general interview in the paymaster's office. A. D. Stevens had been carried in and lay beside his leader; the two wounded prisoners, their hair clotted and tangled, their faces, hands and clothing powder-stained and blood-smeared, occupied two shakedowns covered with some old bedding. Near them stood the governor, Robert E. Lee, J. E. B. Stuart, Senator J. M. Mason, congressmen, colonels, reporters and gentlemen of Virginia. Colonel Lee began the interview by offering to clear the room of all visitors, but John Brown replied that he was glad to make himself and his motives clearly understood. He was asked:

"Do you consider yourself an instrument in the hands of Providence?"

"I do."

"Upon what principle do you justify your acts?"

"Upon the Golden Rule. I pity the poor in bondage that have none to help them; that is why I am here; not to gratify any personal animosity, revenge or vindictive spirit. It is my sympathy with the oppressed and wronged, that are as good as you and as precious in the sight of God." The representative for the New York Herald asked if there was anything further he would like to say. John Brown had nothing to say, only that he still claimed to be there carrying out a measure he believed to be perfectly justifiable.

"I wish to say, furthermore, that you had better—all you people at the South—prepare yourselves for a settlement of that question that must come up for settlement sooner than you are prepared for it. The sooner you are prepared the better. You may dispose of me very easily; I am nearly disposed of now; but this question is still to be settled—this negro question I mean—the end of that is not yet."

Colonel Lee requested Stuart to go with a few marines to old Brown's house, four and a half miles distant in Maryland, and see what was there. Lieutenant Stuart discovered a magazine of pikes, blankets and clothing and utensils of every sort. He had but one wagon, he was unable to carry away the pikes, and the next day he was occupied by the varied duties of an aide-de-camp. He marched, with Colonel Lee and Green, six miles and back following a false alarm among the inhabitants of a village called Pleasant Valley; John Brown was turned over to the United States Marshal;

and, with Lee and the marines, Lieutenant J. E. B. Stuart returned to Washington, unaware that he had taken part in the preliminary to his own high advancement and death.

* *
*

In the March of Eighteen-sixty-one, Lieutenant Stuart secured two months' leave; he had determined to follow the decision of his state, Virginia, when secession was proposed; he waited for three uncertain weeks in St. Louis; Virginia seceded and, removing his family to a place of comparative safety—in Eighteen-fifty-five he had married a Miss Flora Cooke—Stuart immediately forwarded his resignation from the United States army to Washington. It was accepted, he proceeded at once to Richmond, where he was commissioned lieutenant colonel in the Confederate infantry. Two months later he was made colonel of cavalry. His promotion was rapid. In September, the same year, he became a brigadier general; July, Eighteen-sixty-two, he was elevated to major general. His career in the Army of the South was brilliant from the beginning; General Stuart was particularly successful, invaluable, in the extraordinary daring of his raids.

In June, Eighteen-sixty-two, he made the rapid movement to the rear of McClellan's army that shook the confidence of the whole North in its commander. It became famous as the Chickahominy Raid—with twelve hundred cavalrymen and a section of artillery Stuart succeeded in the vastly important task of locating the right wing of the Union forces; he captured an hundred and sixty-five prisoners and two hundred and sixty horses and mules; he destroyed great stores of Federal property. The Chambersburg raid, after the battle of Sharpsburg—the Northern soldiers called it Antietam—was an even greater accomplishment. In October, Eighteen-sixty-two, General Stuart's headquarters was near Charlestown, back of Harper's Ferry; on the afternoon of the eighth he ordered his acting adjutant, Lieutenant Channing Price, to present all the official papers that required immediate attention. The morning following he assembled his men and addressed them:

"Soldiers! You are about to engage in an enterprise which, to insure success, imperatively demands at your hands coolness, decision and bravery; implicit obedience to orders without a question or cavil; and the strictest order and sobriety on the march and in bivouac. The destination and extent of this expedition had better be kept to myself than known to you. I have no doubt of its success—a success which will reflect credit in the highest degree upon your arms."

Stuart's swift advance into Pennsylvania, however, was not unobserved: the Union General Kenly, at Williamsport, discovered it, and communicated his knowledge, the line of Stuart's march, to General Brooks at Hagerstown. There was no available force of Federal cavalry sufficient to check it. The Pennsylvania farmers would not believe the Rebels had invaded the security of their land; when they appeared there was a wide consternation relieved by moments of humor. An advance guard was completely equipped with boots and shoes in a store at Mercersburg before the merchant knew whom he was refitting. He learned it from the receipt given him in conformation with General Stuart's orders. An old gentleman, deprived of the bright bay mare he was driving to a cart, insisted that the impressment of horses had been forbidden by orders from Washington. He scoffed at the assurance that he was surrounded by Confederate soldiers.

General Stuart's discipline was rigidly maintained—nothing was disturbed in Maryland, but in Pennsylvania a systematic seizure of horses began. Six hundred troopers swept the country on either side of the line of progress. Stuart reached Chambersburg at eight o'clock of the evening in a drizzling rain. Two pieces of artillery were laid commanding the town, but there was no resistance; Lieutenant Thomas Lee, with nine men from Butler's command, went forward and demanded unconditional surrender; the Rebel force marched in and was drawn up on the public square. Stuart sent Captain Butler to secure whatever funds were in the bank, but the cashier informed him they had all been removed. A military governor for the town was appointed; the pastoral quiet of Chambersburg remained unbroken through the night. Mr. A. K. McClure, then a resident of Chambersburg, had met the Confederates in a committee of citizens.

"Upon being informed who we were, and that there was no organized force in the town, General Hampton stated, in a respectful and soldierlike manner, that he commanded the advance of the Confederate troops, that he knew resistance would be vain, and he wished the citizens to be fully advised of his purpose, so as to avoid needless loss of life and wanton destruction of property. He assured us that he would scrupulously protect the citizens, and allow no soldiers to enter public or private houses unless under command of an officer upon legitimate business. He would take such private property as he needed for his government, or troops, and would give receipt for same if desired, so that claim might be made against the United States government." A squad spent the night outside Mr. McClure's door:

"In a little while a soldier entered the yard, came politely up to me, and after a profound bow, asked for a few coals to start a fire. Soon after others came and asked permission to get some water. I piloted them to the pump and again received a profusion of thanks. A communication had been established between us, squads followed each other closely for water, and promptly left the yard. I was somewhat bewildered by this uniform courtesy, and supposed it but the prelude to a general movement upon everything eatable in the morning. About one o'clock half a dozen officers came to the door, and asked to have some coffee made for them, offering to pay liberally for it with Confederate script. A subordinate officer begged of me a little bread for himself and a few men, and he was supplied in the kitchen. He was followed by others, but all politely asked permission to enter the house, and behaved with entire propriety. They did not make a single rude or profane remark even to the servants."

General Stuart, with his staff and escort of couriers, bivouacked outside the town. The drizzle increased to a steady downpour. Three times in the night Stuart woke his guide, Captain B. S. White of Maryland, and asked if he thought the rain would make the Potomac River impassable. Their position, with the concentration of Federal troops and scouts on every road, was increasingly doubtful. They marched at dawn over the direct road to Gettysburg, but when Stuart had crossed the Catoctin Mountain he turned aside through Fairfield on the road to Emmitsburg. All day details collected horses, but when the Maryland line was reached the command was assembled in close order. General McClellan had ordered Pleasonton to intercept Stuart near Emmitsburg or Mechanicstown; but Pleasonton wasted two hours; when he reached Mechanicstown, at half past eight in the evening, Stuart, within four miles of him, was moving rapidly forward. He had reached Emmitsburg at sunset, after marching thirty-one miles from Chambersburg, and he was still forty-five miles from the Potomac.

General Stuart's escape depended wholly on the speed

of his march; throughout the night his column was kept at a trot; by daylight the advance guard entered Hyattsville, thirty-three miles beyond Emmitsburg. Within twenty hours, keeping up his artillery, Stuart had marched sixty-five miles. He had, of course, a great number of horses for the guns and caissons, and during the night there were four changes of teams. He hurried on to Barnesville and then turned boldly south. Pleasonton had moved on toward Poolesville, his force was now on the road occupied by General Stuart, and the Confederate advance came into sight of the Union cavalry. The night had been cold, the Rebel soldiers were still wearing the blue overcoats secured at Chambersburg, and they were mistaken for Northerners. Stuart was riding at the head of his advance guard; he restrained his troops until they were close enough for an effective surprise and charged; and there was only one disorganized Federal volley. General Stuart now commanded the road to the Little Monocacy; he brought every man of his command safely back to Virginia soil.

* *
*

General Stuart returned with twelve hundred horses for the Confederacy; he had captured thirty officials of the United States government and sent them to Richmond; the government property destroyed at Chambersburg was valued in excess of two hundred and fifty thousand dollars. McClellan had sent all his cavalry against Stuart. "That exhausting service," he wrote, "completely broke down our cavalry horses and rendered a remount absolutely indispensable before we could advance on the enemy." Mr. Lincoln's comment was less detailed, "Stuart's cavalry outmarched ours." The Dumfries raid followed the battle of Fredericksburg—Stuart harassed the entire Federal line of communication along the Potomac. One of his men was killed, he had thirteen wounded and fourteen missing. The Union deaths were more than two hundred.

In the spring of Eighteen-sixty-three the Confederate army, although it was in close communication with Richmond, was wretchedly clothed and fed; it was practically without shoes. The Southern forces lay below the Rappahannock, facing General Hooker on the north: Hooker had the most impressive army ever assembled on the American continent. There were an hundred and twenty thousand infantry and artillerymen with four hundred cannon, twelve thousand cavalry. General Stuart, with two thousand men, had to cover a front of more than fifty miles and maintain picquets at the fords of both the Rappahannock and Rapidan Rivers. The Union advance, at the battle of Chancellorsville, began on the twenty-seventh of April. The small Confederate guard at Kelly's Ford was easily swept away, and by morning, the twenty-ninth, three Federal corps had crossed the Rappahannock. On the thirtieth they were in Chancellorsville; two divisions of the Second Corps arrived by way of the United States Ford; the Fifth and Sixth Corps under Sedgwick advanced over four pontoon bridges below Frederickstown.

General Hooker was enormously gratified by his preliminary success. "The enemy," he wrote in an order to his troops, "must ingloriously fly, or come out from behind his defenses and give us battle on our own ground, where certain destruction awaits him." With that, however, General Lee was not in complete agreement. On the morning of the thirtieth he learned that Hooker had divided his command, and, leaving ten thousand men under Jubal Early to hold the line at Fredericksburg, he marched with the rest of his army to Chancellorsville. He had Jackson's three divisions, Anderson's division of Longstreet's corps, and McLaw's three brigades—a force of less than forty thousand to meet Hooker's seventy-two thousand men.

The field of the battle of Chancellorsville was actually a woods of second growth pine and black oak; it had been, long before, a charcoal forest. It was a region fourteen miles long and ten miles wide, and, significantly named the Wilderness, its soil was poor, drained by crooked marshy streams, the few clearings were insignificant. Chancellorsville was a brick mansion set on high land a mile east of the Wilderness. The use of cavalry was made impossible by the nature of the ground, there were no positions for artillery, no range for the guns. General Stuart recognized this; he received permission to devote his men, and a small force of infantry, to the holding of an important line of communication, the road to Ely's Ford; and moving forward with the 16th North Carolina infantry he came in contact with a force of Union cavalry under Averill. Stuart was preparing to attack when Captain Adams, of A. P. Hill's staff, arrived and informed him that both Hill and General Jackson had been carried from the field wounded—the command of Jackson's corps rested upon Stuart.

General Stuart reached the line of battle at midnight, it had been impossible to conceal the fact that Jackson's condition was grave, and his troops were badly shaken by that overwhelming disaster. Stuart had no information from the commanding general about the movement Jackson had already begun; he was ignorant of the positions of the troops, the condition of the battlefield. There was no possibility, then, of receiving instructions from General Lee; the reply from an urgent message to Jackson was short, "Tell General Stuart to act upon his own judgment and do what he thinks best; I have implicit confidence in him." His difficulties multiplied—none of Jackson's staff except Colonel A. S. Pendleton reported to him; his own staff made their first personal encounters with Jackson's officers through that night and the next day.

The corps under him, Stuart learned, had had little or nothing to eat for twenty-four hours: at daybreak Lee ordered him to attack immediately. The battle opened at sunrise with extraordinary fury—Stuart, after desperate fighting, succeeded in planting thirty pieces of artillery on a ridge, and, enfiladed by their fire, the Federal line was thrown back. The bearing of General Stuart created an enormous enthusiasm on the field. A Colonel Thomas T. Lowe heard him singing, in the hottest moment of action, "Old Joe Hooker, won't you come out of the Wilderness?" General E. P. Alexander wrote at length. "I do not think there was a more brilliant thing done in the war than Stuart's extricating that command from the extremely critical position in which he found it as promptly and boldly as he did. We know that Hooker had at least eighty thousand infantry at hand. The hard marching and night fighting had thinned our ranks to less than twenty thousand. But Stuart never hesitated or doubted for a moment—he attacked at daybreak, and unlike many attacks I have seen, this one came off promptly on time, and it never stopped to draw its breath until it had crashed through everything and our forces stood united around Chancellor's burning house.

"I always thought it was an injustice to Stuart and a loss to the army that he was not at that moment continued in command of Jackson's corps. He had won the right to it. I believe he had all of Jackson's genius and dash and originality, without that eccentricity of character which sometimes led to disappointment."

General A. P. Hill, when the whole of the Federal army retreated above the Rappahannock, assumed command of Jackson's forces, and Jeb Stuart returned to his own division. There he was concerned by the familiar lack of arms and equipment: at the beginning of the war the troopers furnished their own saddles and bridles; the English roundtree saddle was in common use; and, in consequence, horses with sore backs multiplied rapidly. The government, then, furnished a saddle that saved the horses, but at the riders' painful expense. The best equipment, of course, was captured from the North. The lack of proper arms for the cavalry was more serious; a number of Virginia's counties had furnished their cavalry with pistols, but entire regiments were without them. Breech-loading carbines were even scarcer, there were never more than enough to arm one, or at most two, squadrons in a regiment. That deficiency, generally, was made up by Enfield rifles, an inferior weapon. Horseshoes and nails, and necessary forges, were as rare as they were indispensable: it was not uncommon to see a cavalryman leading his limping horse with the hoofs of a dead horse, cut off for the sound shoes on them, dangling from the saddle.

In May, however, Eighteen-sixty-three, General Stuart reviewed five brigades of Confederate cavalry on the broad fields between Brandy Station and Culpeper Court House; four thousand cavalrymen passed before him; shortly after two more brigades, one from the Valley of the Shenandoah and the other Robertson's North Carolina troopers, arrived and there was a second review of eight thousand men. In column of squadrons they walked and wheeled and charged; the guns of an artillery battalion, on a hill opposite the grandstand, lent the occasion the sound and rolling smoke and fire of actual war.

General Lee was expected to be present, he failed to arrive, but he notified Stuart that he would review the cavalry on the eighth of June. Little display was attempted; Lee was careful not to weary his troops; the artillerymen were not permitted to work their guns. The movement of

GOLD SPURS

the Army of Northern Virginia toward Gettysburg had begun.

*   *
*

On the eighth of July, Eighteen-sixty-three, the great Northern offensive of the Confederacy receded, and General Stuart covered the front of Lee's army while it waited for flood waters in the Potomac to fall. There was severe fighting between Stuart's command and Buford and Kilpatrick, at Boonsboro and Beaver Creek and on the Sharpsburg front. The cavalry of both sides fought dismounted, supported by small bodies of infantry, and Stuart reported a loss of two hundred and sixteen men. There were, as well, severe hardships; General Stuart's staff had less than half rations; for five days food was brought to them only after nightfall by the daughter of a family with Southern sympathies in Hagerstown. The cavalry moved south, Stuart reoccupied the line of the Rappahannock while Lee's main army withdrew behind the Rapidan. September promised to be a month of rest and recuperation, but on the thirteenth the Federal army advanced and occupied Culpeper County. Stuart attacked Buford's cavalry on the twenty-second, but he could make no impression upon the Union lines; he attempted to withdraw toward Liberty Mills but found himself completely surrounded by enemy; after a severe engagement he managed to retreat across the Rapidan River. On the ninth of October Lee commenced the movement around the Federal right flank that developed into the Bristoe campaign, and Stuart, protecting the line of march, led Young's command through deep woods and disorganized the whole Union position.

When Lee's army was concentrated at Warrenton, Stuart was ordered to make a reconnaissance in the direction of Catlett's Station; he immediately sent forward a brigade;

and, at four in the afternoon, he joined Lomax, its commander. He left Lomax to guard his rear, and proceeded with the rest of his force until, three miles beyond Auburn, he came upon an immense park of Federal wagons—he had penetrated, he discovered, to the center of a Union army. Stuart employed every officer in withdrawing the column to the fields on the north; almost instantly the road was empty of horsemen, artillery and wagons; at dark they were settled in a little protected valley; the artillery was masked on a hill within three hundred yards of the road where masses of the enemy were passing. Men were stationed at the head of every mule team, but, in spite of their desperate endeavors, there was an occasional loud disconcerting bray. All night Stuart listened to the multitudinous tramp of the hostile army; at dawn he recognized that a collision was unavoidable. He moved his seven guns farther over the crest of their hill and waited.

Fire opened upon him from the direction of Warrenton, and in an instant his artillery was pouring canister into a wholly surprised force. There was a short period of confusion, and, taking swift advantage of it, General Stuart again fought his way through an overwhelming opposition to safety.

On the morning of May fourth, Eighteen-sixty-four, the war in the Wilderness was renewed. General Stuart was informed that the enemy had crossed the fords of the Rapidan, and he proceeded at once to his picquet line, leaving to his staff the necessity of breaking up their pleasant winter quarters near Orange Court House. The staff overtook him late that day, and Stuart camped in the rear of his picquet reserve. The next morning he led A. P. Hill's corps over the Plank road to battle. On the sixth he renewed action in the Wilderness, a close destructive fighting that lasted into the night. On the seventh, Stuart's cavalry was engaged in repeated bitter conflicts. Grant, then, began to move his army in an effort to bring it between Lee and Richmond, his intention was soon discovered and a division thrown in front of the flanking advance. General Stuart joined it with part of Anderson's corps; and, at Anderson's request, he supported the infantry with his dismounted men, commanding the left of the line.

There was a severe fire, and Stuart exposed himself with even more than his usual indifference; the infantry officers repeatedly begged him to be careful. Stuart had but one staff officer with him, he was not even attended by a courier, and he kept sending his solitary supporter, McClellan, on so many unimportant errands to Anderson that it occurred to him General Stuart was trying to preserve his life. He said at last, "General, my horse is exhausted. You are exposing yourself, and you are alone. Please let me remain with you." He smiled at him, McClellan said, and immediately sent him away with another message for General Anderson.

The ninth of October Philip H. Sheridan with twelve thousand cavalry, strongly supported by artillery, moved to Hamilton's Crossing and on toward Richmond. His advance was promptly discovered, and Stuart marched at night against him with Gordon's brigade. At Beaver Dam Station Stuart encountered the Federal rear, but before action he rode to the house of Colonel Edmund Fontaine, close by, where his family was staying. His wife and children, he found, were safe; Sheridan had passed south to Negro Foot, and General Stuart divided his command— he sent Gordon's brigade in direct pursuit of the enemy, and he marched to Hanover Junction to place himself between the Federal advance and the Confederate capital. He reached the Junction at night, it was his intention to continue without stop, but the men under him were exhausted.

At the urgent request of their colonel he consented to let them rest until one o'clock.

General J. E. B. Stuart then took up his march toward Yellow Tavern. McClellan, still beside him, said that Stuart talked continually about affairs personal to them. He was, McClellan remembered, quieter than was his custom, his manner was softer and more communicative than usual. They reached Yellow Tavern at ten in the morning, ahead of the enemy, and in full time to draw up between him and Richmond. Stuart sent McClellan with a communication to General Bragg and when the officer returned he found the enemy in possession of the turnpike south of Yellow Tavern; to prevent capture he was compelled to make a long circle through the fields. He did not reach Stuart until two o'clock, and he learned that in his absence there had been desperate fighting. Colonel H. C. Pate, of the Fifth Virginia cavalry, had been killed; Stuart spoke of Pate's great gallantry; he seemed pleased with the information brought from Bragg and said that he intended to hold his position on General Sheridan's flank.

At four in the afternoon the enemy suddenly threw a brigade of cavalry against the Confederate extreme left, at the same time they attacked the whole Confederate line, and Stuart—it was his invariable habit—hurried to the point of greatest danger. McClellan's horse was so exhausted he could not follow his commander; but Captain G. W. Dorsey, Company K of the First Virginia cavalry, managed to stay beside him. Where Dorsey was stationed, about eighty men were collected—the Confederate line had been dissolved—and General Stuart, by his personal calmness, held them steady while the Federal troops charged entirely past their position. With his companions Stuart fired into the Union flank and rear, and then the overwhelming tide of men swept back—they had been met and repulsed by the First Virginia cavalry.

A man who had been dismounted in the encounter, and who was running on foot, turned as he passed General Stuart and shot him with a pistol.

Captain Dorsey tried to lead Stuart's horse to the rear, but the animal became unmanageable, and Jeb Stuart asked to be taken down and allowed to rest against a tree. Stuart ordered Captain Dorsey to leave him and return to his men; to drive back the enemy; he was, General Stuart explained, mortally wounded and of no further use. Dorsey replied he could not obey that order. Another horse was finally brought up, General Stuart was lifted to the saddle, and Dorsey led him toward a less exposed position; then, by Stuart's order, he was given into the charge of a private, Wheatley, and Dorsey returned to his scattered men. An ambulance was found, and as it moved from the battlefield, Stuart, dying, called out to a disorganized force of Confederates: "Go back! Go back! and do your duty, as I have done mine, and our country will be safe. Go back! Go back! I had rather die than be whipped." He left his spurs to a lady of Virginia; his sword descended to his son.

THE FOOT SOLDIER

THE FOOT SOLDIER

The Civil War in America was the last of all wars fought in the grand manner. It was the last romantic war, when army corps fought as individuals and lines of assault three miles long solidly charged the visible enemy. There will never again, in the sense of the War of the Rebellion, be cavalry; there will be no more great leaders. The necessity and field for great leaders have vanished; greatness, now, is a discreet science. Never again, it is probable, will there be a cause comparable to the necessity that arrayed the South against the Union. It was, for the generality of men, supreme in dignity and of transcendent importance. The negro, it must be remembered, was not the reason for war; the negro was a symbol: the Civil War was fought for the liberty of states and of individuals. Liberty is, of course, an ideal; there is no liberty; there never can be liberty. It isn't, perhaps, even desirable in the brief weakness of a humanity faced with universal ignorance and individual disaster.

The North conquered the South, the United States of America was preserved— a very practical, a sensible, consummation. Inevitable, really. But practicality and good sense have nothing to do with war, even with noble wars. They have, it appears, nothing to do with the ideals that lie close to the heart. The United States was saved for the future and the Confederacy was destroyed, and the dream of liberty was once more subjected to reason. But that did not detract from the beauty of what the South represented. The god of war was again on the side with the greatest number of cannon, but the motive of the Civil War had little to do with him.

Mr. Lincoln did not want war, it was an agony to his spirit, and the South didn't want war. Mr. Lincoln was the least warlike of men; and the Confederacy—a land of extraordinary soldiers—was not prepared for any military action. It had no supplies, it had no equipment, it had no arms, and very soon indeed it had no food. The Confederacy, unhappily, was not practical: it fought for an ideal that had no reality outside hope. The North, at best, fought for an ideal, for the Union, and it won. Its success was rational; the fall of the South, after a very few months, was inevitable; the negroes, the symbol of battle, were free; but the Southern States were not free; they were subjected to a government and an economic system which, they felt, were destructive to all that it was essential for them to be. When General Lee surrendered to General Grant at Appomattox Court House another of the small store of human ideals was defeated and returned to the realm of lovely impossibilities.

The result, actually, was so unanswerable, its logic so irrefutable, that there will never be another war for the same end. That dignity, or mistake, has been disposed of. There will never again, in the old sense, be nations, individual states, localities; the time may even come when there will be no wars—nations and lands are less independent every year. The world is so bound together, its interests and races are becoming so mutual, that war will soon have the ridiculous and unprofitable aspect of an individual fighting against himself. The separate pride, the handsome arrogance, for example, of South Carolina long ago subsided. South Carolina, Charleston, will never again challenge all the United States, the entire world. Its flag, except as a memorial, has lost its actuality. Sectional faith and consciousness have been absorbed by trade.

None of that was true at the beginning of the Civil War and throughout its course; the sovereign states of the South were sovereign states. The citizens of Virginia were inhabitants of a principality. They were an indistinguishable part of a soil, of tidal rivers and forests and ploughed fields. Compared with it the United States was an abstraction. Virginia was a great state complete within its greatness. Alabama was a different entity. Mississippi was a land in itself. That, in such a sense, was not true of the North; the North had advanced beyond such hopefulness. New and comparatively quick means of communication, superior railways and the electric telegraph, had drawn it together and broken down the boundaries of states, the neighborhoods of people. It was more successful than the South, more modern, and naturally it triumphed. The present and future, as it ultimately must, defeated the past.

What gave the War of the Rebellion its quality of high nobility was the fact that both the South and the North were right; that, as well, isn't sensible, but it is true. Mr. Lincoln was right and Virginia, South Carolina, Alabama, Mississippi were right. They were fighting, at best, for an incurable necessity at their hearts. The South wanted to be free and Mr. Lincoln wanted to keep the Union safe. Other reasons, for the most part sectional, were proclaimed: the Civil War, the North insisted, was brought on by the arrogance and gold of the cotton aristocracy; it was caused, the South declared, by the tariff and a commercial tyranny supported by Northern factories. Both of these charges are probably facts, but they were not, while the war lasted, important. The war created a heroism of motive and actions that clad fact in the splendor of battle flags. It was believed in and paid to the last copper for by the historic South.

The war, in addition, took place in the high, the middle and the deep South. The Confederates were fighting for their homes; they fought in fields they had planted, from the houses that had given them birth, for the cities of their traditions and blood. The Confederate army was local, it was composed of bodies of men, companions, who enlisted together, men from the same place who had known each other always. They knew each other in the line, in battle and death, by familiar names. There were no strangers, no foreigners, among them. They fought an immensely superior army of invasion by corps and regiment and company and squad, and alone, behind the piney trees and back of country fences, from streams where they had caught bullheads in the happy past. As the war progressed the Confederate soldier saw all that was invaluable to him destroyed —his family was swept from existence, his possessions and living were obliterated, his very allegiance to home became chargeable with death. A grim despair seized him; he fought more desperately than ever for his vanishing existence. Hope, through the worst of disasters, never deserted him— when General Lee was forced to surrender he was incredulous, he wept and swore and fired a last shot on his own behalf.

And, common to all causes, when the hope of the South was lost it took on a brighter, an imperishable, glow. It became a memory of pure beauty. It wasn't subjected to the impossibility of fulfilment: no one could say to the South that it had failed. It must have failed, in the sense that the North fell tragically short of its commitment; but instead of long disillusionment it died heroically; and the heroic dead are, in an immaterial and important way, quite imperishable; they cannot, later, be corrected.

There will never be another war so purely valorous because valor itself, it is beginning to be seen, is not a practical virtue. Machinery and chemical war have taken its place. Courage is not so habitual now as cunning; yes, men are sensible rather than brave. That is, beyond question, an improvement. Soon they will contrive to live by bread alone. Soon everything, even the past, will be illuminated, bathed, in a level, a colorless, light of reason. History will become a record of the defects of men. The causes that animated and sustained them, for which they died, will appear ridiculous, the emotions and mechanical reactions of inferior times. There will, then, be no individual excellence, no bright power of personal example; the world will have neither legends nor heroes nor leaders; already the grey and blue is all drab.

* * *

The generals of the Confederate army, however, were not the sole individuals who had a part in it—the common soldier, the foot soldier, kept his identity to the end. For that reason it is amazing that he was such a superlatively good soldier. There was never a question about his willingness, his ability, to fight, but his submission to discipline was open to doubt. And in a way that doubt was justified; the Confederate soldier resolutely ignored all the small niceties of military conduct. It is true that, late in the war, he was forced to ignore them—they could not exist together with rags and starvation—but at the beginning, when there was plenty of everything and victory seemed assured, he insisted on personal choice and a freedom of comment that was the reverse of formal soldiering. This was largely brought about by the fact that he did enlist with his familiars; there was nothing impersonal in his action. He had, usually, the privilege of electing the officers directly over him, and he knew them as well as he knew the men beside him in the ranks. He had seen his immediate officers too long as men—often no more highly placed than himself—to be able to regard them at once as superiors.

The fact that they were officers did not suddenly blind him to their faults, or conceal from him the fact that they might still fall into error; the foot soldier of the South saw no reason why he should not announce his whole opinion of his captain.

Later, when companies were reduced to squads—when only three members of a company were left—the men were re-formed in new regiments; for the first time the privates came in contact with strangers; they served beneath unfamiliar officers, and a greater rigidity of conduct and speech was necessary. Even then they were occasionally outspoken, humorous, but most of their gaiety had been driven out of them; their personalities had grown unimportant in the face of their great endeavor. The talent of the Confederate soldier for fighting, first and last, was always distinguished; but it became, in the final year of the war, incredible, a grim fervor for which practically nothing was impossible. At the beginning he fought without proper weapons—the Army of the North soon supplied that deficiency—and at the last he fought without food; but he never hesitated; the Rebel yell never failed to ring over the most forlorn and hopeless fields.

The South, a land almost without cities, was composed of innumerable small towns and villages; the wild there persisted long after it had retreated from the more orderly and progressive North; hunting and fishing were a reality, a means of existence, in the deep South when they had become hardly better than sports in New England. The Confederate soldier was a better shot, a better campaigner, than the Union soldier. He was, too, principally on familiar ground: it took Grant months merely to discover how to approach the fortified city of Vicksburg. General Jackson, born to the westward of the great Valley, knew its lowlands and rivers and mountains; the men of his command moved by a score of ways, a hundred high trails, where the Northern forces were ignorant of one.

The South as a people were accustomed to horses, horses were a necessity in a great part of the country; when children could yet scarcely walk they rode to the grist mill and to the crossroads store; and, in consequence, the Southern cavalry was more notable than the mounted Federal troops. It was more dashing. Ashby covering Jackson's rear with hardly more than a handful of men, the swift raids through the Union lines, the amazing night marches on horse, surpassed all the efforts of the North. The foot soldiers were hardly less mobile; they marched incredible distances in incredibly little time; they had no coffee, they had little meat, they were without salt and sugar; and yet, at the end of long forced advances, of skillful and dogged retreats, the impetus of their fighting and charges was undiminished. The fundamental discipline of their purpose held them together, the inextinguishable spirit of their individuality carried them to the last rood of battle.

The battlefield of the two armies in the Civil War was very wide; a man on horseback could not have crossed it during the battle; and a foot soldier, held in a single locality or shifted rapidly to another contracted area, knew nothing of the general engagement. He was ignorant of both the purpose and the result of his desperate efforts. He fought in wiry underbrush and charged through heavy ploughed fields; battles swept the precipitous sides of mountains where advancing troops were exhausted, vomiting with fatigue, before they reached the higher position of the enemy. Men fought in the gloom of deep forests and in treacherous swamps—the Wilderness was a woods and a swamp—and with bayonets they cleared the back yards of cities. Furious engagements raged around stately old houses set in flowers and the pastoral lawns of plantations.

The heat of July in Alabama, added to the fiery heat of battle, was incredible; the foot soldiers fainted in it, died of it, by files. Winter in the Allegheny Mountains, in the red Virginia mud, was no better. The Confederate private, except when he borrowed a greatcoat from the Union dead, was as bare as General Washington's soldiers at Valley Forge. He had less to eat; he had so little to eat that he was forced to forage in the full haversacks of the slain enemy. But if the privation was extreme the hour of relief, the winter quarters, were equally, supremely, comfortable. The messes in the Confederate army were commonly divided into groups of ten men; and when one of them, on picquet duty or scouting, came upon an inattentive and unlucky hog, the celebration, like the appetites, was enormous.

The winter quarters, compared with campaigning, were wonderfully luxurious; a woods was felled and cabins built; chimneys were constructed and chinked with clay; the soldiers, except those on short tours of duty, slept in sweet straw, rolled in their blankets, beside resinous fires. Occasionally a box would arrive from home—coffee and sugar and a ham and preserves; and everyone within call, as long as it lasted, would have something. The soldiers played the games of childhood and read and wrote letters. When mail arrived, at noon or in the dead of night, they crowded hopefully about the company headquarters. When a fortunate individual did get a letter he went off by himself and built a small fire, and in its light he went over and over the lines of reassurance or of love or despair. They prayed; a great revival swept through the whole Confederate army; the foot soldiers sang the songs of their time:

> "Aha! a song for the trumpet's tongue!
> For the bugle to sing before us,
> When our gleaming guns, like clarions,
> Shall thunder in battle chorus."

The luxury of shaving became possible; the men cut each other's hair; there were combs and brushes, mirrors, soap and towels. Boots were blacked! Baths and fresh underwear became actualities. The question of underwear bore heavily on the Confederate private's mind: at first he made an effort to carry a change of it; then, finding that increasingly difficult, he determined to occasionally wash the single pair of drawers, the solitary shirt, he possessed; but in time he gave that up as well—there wasn't a moment left between war and exhaustion, and he kept on the underwear he was so lucky as to possess. He kept it on until it fell off. In winter quarters boiled shirts made their appearance. White shirts and visitors, girls, became a reality.

The girls, however, were as much a source of distress as a pleasure: even at best the foot soldier's garb—it couldn't be called a uniform—was an affair of patches and rags. A black patch on a knee and a vivid scarlet patch over a shoulder. The pain of bashfulness struggled with the desire for a few moments, a word, of feminine charm. The rags, in reality, made little difference to the girls, except to excite their admiration and tender pity. The men could not grasp that. They listened at a distance to companions with a whole coat, or an unexampled assurance, talking to radiant creatures in freshly ironed muslin, with little bright shawls about their shoulders and flowers on their bonnets.

* *
*

There was no scarcity of military circumstance when, after the fall of Fort Sumter, John H. Worsham enlisted as a foot soldier in an old volunteer company, Company F, at Richmond. He wore an impressively fine uniform—it had a cadet grey frock coat with a row of Virginia fire-gilt buttons, there was a band of gold braid and two gilt buttons at the bottoms of the sleeves, and there was gold braid on the collar. The pants had a black stripe wider than an inch on their outer seams. John H. Worsham's cap was ornamented in black, it had two fire-gilt buttons and bore the letter F. The sergeants, in addition to a gun, carried a sword at their belts. Every man on duty was required to wear white gloves. He had a long black cloth overcoat, and he carried in his knapsack an additional short mess jacket. The knapsack was especially notable—it was imported from Paris, and made of calf skin tanned with the hair on; it was colored red and white. Inside it was elaborately divided into partitions and outside there were straps for blankets and overcoat, an oilcloth and shoes, with additional straps and hooks for additional chance purposes. Company F also imported its canteens.

John Worsham was required to report once during the day at his company headquarters, the fire bells were to ring for a general assembly, and on the twenty-first of April, Eighteen-sixty-one—it was Sunday and he was walking to church—the fire bells summoned him from all the old familiar security of his existence. John put on his uniform and proceeded to the armory. There he learned that the Union gunboat Pawnee was reported to be coming up the James River for the bombardment of Richmond. The company was marched to Wilton, ten miles below the city; at Rocketts thousands of citizens had assembled, the fields and wharves were solidly packed with humanity. Some men had shot guns, some rifles, others pistols, there were men with canes and large piles of stones handy for throwing.

The men in Company F not on duty stacked arms; they all grew conscious of the fact that no arrangement had been made for food. At nine of the evening, however, one of their officers arrived with a wagonload of hams, bread, and appropriate incidentals; there was a gay supper; and

John Worsham slept on the grass without the bother of a blanket or oilcloth. The next day—no Federal vessel had made its appearance—Company F returned to Richmond. It was received with a tremendous enthusiasm; the volunteers, it was considered, had accomplished wonders; they were covered with glory. They were moved, soon afterward, to Fredericksburg; the Yankees, they were informed, had made a demonstration at Aquia Creek. Company F was provided with a load of straw and camped on the floor and on the benches of the courthouse. Supper was provided in the private houses of the town, and the company went to bed in formal order; there was a camp guard, and lights were drummed out by taps.

That formality, however, was immediately interrupted— a supply of tin whistles and horns had been accumulated through the day, and the darkness was turned into a pandemonium. The officers commanded silence, no attention was paid to them, and the insubordinate men were ordered under arrest. Four sergeants ran about, striking matches and looking for offenders, none was discovered, and the racket was kept up until it was overcome by sleep. The next morning John was marched to the Fair Grounds, and there formal camp duty began immediately with guard mount, policing and drills. On fine evenings there was a dress parade, attended by the girls of Fredericksburg. The company messes, little groups, were formed, each with a negro cook and a mess chest. The chest John Worsham knew was oak, bound with iron, three feet long, eighteen inches wide and eighteen deep. In it were a dozen knives and forks, two or three butcher knives, a dozen plates, a dozen tea cups and saucers, several dishes and bowls, a sugar dish and cream pitcher; there were salt and pepper boxes, a tin containing a dozen assorted packages of spices, a dozen glasses, a flour sifter and rolling pin. The mess owned a frying pan, a coffee pot, a great camp kettle, a tea pot, the bread oven that the army came to know as a spider, and two water buckets.

The Fair Grounds was called Camp Mercer, and there, for the first time, John saw a soldier punished for disobedience—a member of Walker's Battery was strapped to the wheel of a cannon. It was a corrective called strapping the wheel. After three weeks Company F was ordered to Aquia Creek; their cook declined to leave Fredericksburg; and the company determined to undertake its own cooking. The result, for a few days, was not notable. A letter was addressed to a member of the company. "George W. Peterkin Esq., Dear Sir—We, the undersigned comrades in arms with yourself, have been struck with the propriety of evening prayer, and desire, if agreeable to you, that you, from this time, and so long as we may remain together, conduct that service." Company F respectfully signed its names.

At the end of May a Federal gunboat, off Aquia Creek, fired a few shots and withdrew. It was John Worsham's first experience of war. On the seventh of June three gunboats appeared and bombarded the earthworks near the wharf. It lasted several hours and the following day five vessels renewed the attack. John found the days generally very pleasant: he had lessons in skirmish drill and with the bayonet—that was called the Zouave drill—he fished from the wharf, bathed in the river and rambled idly through the woods. Then Company F was ordered back to Richmond, it became part of a regiment, the Twenty-first Virginia infantry, and was put under tents at Camp Lee. John Worsham was mustered into service, for the term of a year, the twenty-eighth day of June, Eighteen-sixty-one. He was sworn in on the Capitol Square by Inspector General J. B. Baldwin. His regiment, it numbered eight hundred and fifty men, was ordered to take the cars on the eighteenth of July; and it marched off in a thunder of cheering. The day was horribly hot, and many of the men dropped overcome out of the ranks.

John proceeded by troop train to Staunton—it required fifteen hours—and there again he marched to the Fair Grounds. Early the following morning he left Staunton for Buffalo Gap, the opening from a wide dusty green plain to the mountains of Virginia. The regiment was supported by a train of thirty-six wagons—they were four-horse mountain wagons—and when it reached the Gap a ration of flour was issued. Beef had been promised, and there was a pen of cattle in plain sight; and Company F volunteered to do the necessary killing. The cattle were shot and dressed, and John Worsham was introduced to what, at fortunate intervals, made the Confederate army ration.

The next morning march was resumed, he penetrated farther and farther into the upland, and heard the rolling echo of artillery beyond. He went into camp at Ryan's, and, at supper with his mess, he learned that a courier had arrived with the news of a great Confederate victory at Manassas. At Ryan's, Company F suffered a misfortune— the government took one of its wagons and the driver of another positively refused to go on. The oak mess chest bound with iron was left and some of the men had to carry their own knapsacks. The next day they reached McDowell —the regiment was now in the high mountains, a region of great verdant walls, deep narrow valleys, swift clear rivers, horizons of faint peaks and ranges—and there they met the men of Garnett's command defeated at Carrick's Ford. John, in spite of their forlorn appearance, scoffed at their tale of hardships and virtual starvation.

*   *
*

The following day he reached Monterey. The road there drops steeply down the mountain, in sharp angles, to the little village at the head of a narrow bluegrass valley. After three—the mountain walls are so high—a shadow falls on Monterey from the west, the hay stacks cast long shadows over the emerald-green meadows, dusk floats down the mountain side and fills the valley; the far peaks turn gold and faintly purple. John's expression for his short period in Monterey was that he lived high: his mess bought young chickens recklessly for six pence each; butter and eggs were at corresponding prices; when he preferred a local dinner its cost was nine pence. Twelve and a half cents. On the twenty-fifth of July, again in movement, the regiment crossed Napp's Creek seventeen times; it encountered General Loring, the officer in command of the expedition, and he was heard to say that, while the twenty-first Virginia was a fine looking body of men, it was not composed of soldiers. Company F met this opinion with indignation.

In camp at Huntersville a great many men fell sick with measles and typhoid fever; when John Worsham left at the beginning of August a third of his regiment remained in hospitals. The number of company wagons was reduced to one. After three days John reached Valley Mountain and General Robert E. Lee now took command of him; General Lee's headquarters tents were close to Company F; and its men were greatly pleased by his notice and politeness. Sickness increased, only a fourth of the regiment was available for duty, and John was put to work on the roads. On the ninth of September he was given thirty rounds of ammunition, this was shortly increased to forty rounds, and the command was ordered forward. It encountered the enemy at Conrad's Mill on the eleventh, there was light skirmishing together with some artillery fire, and John first saw a dead Yankee—he was lying beside the road with his emptied face turned up to the sky, in a fresh pool of blood.

On the twenty-fourth he was shifted to Middle Mountain; the column marched to its new encampment, it stacked arms there, and returned for its equipment. Company F had lost its last wagon—it left Richmond with five—and the men were forced to carry all their necessities on their backs. John Worsham left Middle Mountain in a heavy rain, the entire command now owned only two wagons, one drawn by three and one by two horses, and John gave a more hospitable attention to General Loring's remark. He came to camp on the bank of the Greenbrier River, the trees were brilliant with the scarlet of fall, and there the duty confronted him of voting for the President and Vice-President of the Confederacy. This occurred on a cloudy morning of November; the election took place at a tent where a pole marked the line between voters and judges; and in the evening it was announced that the regiment had solidly supported Jefferson Davis, with Alexander H. Stephens for Vice-President. Mr. Davis, Mr. Stephens and the Confederacy were repeatedly cheered.

Early in November John Worsham left the Greenbrier, he was marched to Bath Alum Springs, and there the regiment went into camp; it snowed and the company toted logs to their tents and built great fires; at night there were songs and tales, and John, with a comrade named Mayro, went out with their muskets and killed a deer. He left Bath Alum Springs at the end of November and proceeded to Millboro; on the fourth of December the company returned by train to Staunton. The men travelled on flat cars and suffered bitterly from the cold. They moved from Staunton to Winchester, with the right of the regiment at the fore one day and the left leading the next. The hardships of marching in the rear, John Worsham discovered, were marked. At Winchester he saw, standing in the crowd on the sidewalk, a man with full dark whiskers and long hair; he wore a uniform with a long blue overcoat and large cape; and, in military style, his trousers were inside boots that bore bright spurs. A faded grey cap was pulled down so far over his face that nothing, practically, was visible between it and the whiskers. John had a glimpse of dark flashing eyes. It was Stonewall Jackson.

Progress through the Valley of the Shenandoah was, for the foot soldiers, an unbroken feast—the countryside had just ended the winter hog killing, and every house gave them stores of fresh meat. Most of the personal and general equipment Company F had carried from Richmond was gone. Ritchie Green, who originally had refused to take anything in his knapsack but a paper collar and a plug of tobacco, was newly esteemed. General Jackson decided upon a winter campaign, and marched his foot cavalry to Unger's Crossroads. There they encountered the enemy, they engaged him until dark, and John's regiment behaved well. It snowed during the night. Jackson arrived and led his troops on horseback—as he passed Company F he ordered it to double quick, and John went forward on a run. The Yankees retreated. On the fifth of January, it was Eighteen-sixty-two, General Jackson shifted his forces toward Hancock; he sent for Company F and, an impressive compliment, directed it to lead the column across the river.

The Confederates were forced to fall back, and the return to Unger's Crossroads was terribly hard: the road glittered with ice, guns fired by falling men resulted in many accidents. John Worsham saw Jackson on foot with his men more than once. It snowed and hailed, and Company F lost its bake oven. At first, before John went to sleep, he cleared the snow from the ground; that, he discovered, made him no better than a bed of mud; the snow was far superior.

Near the end of January his regiment marched into the town of Romney, Company F occupied the bank building, and for a short while it was again comfortable. Romney was given up the third of February, a retreat was effected toward Winchester. It had been a fatally severe campaign; many men were frozen to death; a great many never recovered from the exposure and cold; the rest were rheumatic for as long as they lived. Scores of soldiers, burning their shoes in an effort to warm their feet at the camp fires, had marched barefooted through the snow. John Worsham's brigade went into winter quarters on the Berryville road; it stayed there until the middle of March; and then he was moved to the Staunton pike. The Federal army had crossed the Potomac and was advancing toward Winchester. General Banks was commanding the Union forces, he became known at once as Jackson's commissary, and the equipment of Company F was improved.

The Twenty-first Virginia regiment went into action at the battle of Kernstown; John Worsham's company was thrown forward in the skirmish line, and, close beside him, a shell struck a driver in Rockbridge's battery. It ricocheted through the company ranks, hit a stump, and spinning like a top, stopped. The Confederates, after desperate fighting, were beaten, and they retreated toward the Valley pike. At Strasburg John's mess was at supper when a shell swept over their heads; it was followed by another, soon the woods where they had bivouacked was full of falling shells; the cooking utensils and baggage were loaded on the regimental wagons in a hurry. The wagons went off at a dead run. A series of short marches and small engagements followed. On the tenth of April, John was near New Market; on the thirteenth his brigade moved to Massanuttin Mountain; the night of the seventeenth he spent at Big Spring; the next morning Jackson crossed the Shenandoah River; he was, in the Blue Ridge Mountains, safe from pursuit; all the wagons containing tents and the little baggage that was left were ordered to the rear; the command was reorganized.

* * *

Jackson was again in motion within a very few days; on the thirtieth he marched toward Harrisonburg and the second of May he was in Port Republic. The great Valley campaign, in Eighteen-sixty-two, had opened. John Worsham and his regiment proceeded across the Blue Ridge Mountains to the Central Railroad and went by train to Staunton; they marched again to Buffalo Gap; there was a small encounter at Ryan's and a battle near McDowell where the Yankees were driven back. A sergeant in the Twenty-first Virginia regiment, an old country gentleman, had carried an umbrella from Richmond, and John saw him still at the head of his men with the umbrella up when the weather was inclement. The enemy was pursued into West Virginia, and then the command returned to the Valley and joined General Taylor's Louisiana brigade. The small united force moved in the direction of Winchester; John passed a long Federal wagon train left standing beside the road, and he was amazed by the fact that the wagons, together with more appropriate equipment, held women's bonnets and dresses and shawls. Jackson captured over a hundred wagons through the night; Fremont's plan to destroy the Confederate force came to nothing; Colonel Ashby, on the sixth of June, was killed at Cross Keys; Jackson occupied the hills near Brown's Gap; he moved to the vicinity of Weyer's Cave; Fremont retreated toward Winchester and the great Valley engagement was over.

John Worsham was in the Seven Days' Campaign; he was shifted from Ashland to Pole Green Church, and immediately he was in the heaviest fighting of the war. He charged down a hill and, at its bottom, discovered a creek with high perpendicular walls. John jumped into it without hesitation but he had to be assisted up the farther bank. Then he came upon a field filled with Yankees and Confederates. The South was victorious there, John fell asleep on the ground where he stood, and when he woke up, in the morning, he was surrounded by thousands of dead men. He marched to White Oak Swamp, crossing it by a bridge of logs, and went into action again at Malvern Hill. The enemy retreated, and his division was ordered to the rear. At Willis Church he went to the spring for a drink and found a dead Union soldier lying with his face in the cool bubbling water. On the sixteenth of July he was ordered back to Richmond.

In August he was at Liberty Mills; marching to Orange Court House his regiment went into battle directly from their beds. The men fought in every fantastic state of informal undress; and after the action—John Worsham asserts that the South was again victors—there was a great shout of laughter. On August fifth he passed an old Confederate resting with a hand on a small sapling. "I don't want to fight," he explained. "I ain't mad with anybody." There was a rain of shells, the captain of Company F, Morgan, was killed, and John was part of the battle of Cedar Run. He came on a road filled with the enemy, and the two forces fought with guns, swords, pistols, knives, fence rails and rocks. The color bearer of the Twenty-first Virginia regiment knocked down a Federal color bearer and was killed at once. Another of the Confederate color guard took the flag and he was slain; a third, Roswell S. Lindsay, of Company F, bayoneted a Yankee and he was riddled with balls. Four color bearers were killed and a fifth carried the flag unharmed through the battle.

Half of John Worsham's regiment was killed or wounded; Company F carried eighteen men into the engagement, and came out with six; on August sixteenth he was prepared for another advance against General Pope. That became the battle of the Second Manassas, and the South captured immense quantities of stores and trains of railroad cars. The stores presented an extraordinary scene—Jackson's hungry men surrounded unlimited amounts of potted lobsters and ham, tongue, candy, nuts, oranges, lemons, pickles, catsup and mustard that General Jackson had decided to hold for Lee. The Federal army, however, started an offensive, Jackson was forced to withdraw, and his command was permitted to help itself. John's mess quickly deserted a kettle of soup, but a new difficulty appeared—no one could decide what to take. Some filled their haversacks with cakes, others with candy, some soldiers carried away oranges, lemons, canned goods. One addressed himself exclusively to French mustard; not contented with loading his haversack he put an additional bottle in a pocket. That was not so idiotic as it appeared—he traded mustard for bread and meat throughout a long forced march.

The Second Brigade, with John Worsham, crossed the Potomac at White's Ford; there was great enthusiasm, the bands played, the men cheered and sang, as they entered Maryland. John advanced up the tow path of the Washington Canal; at the Baltimore and Ohio Railroad depot outside Frederick City the men broke ranks and each secured a watermelon; they arrived at the city late in the evening. John was detailed to the Federal hospital to make a careful list of its inmates; he disposed of his gun and ammunition and bore his other baggage with him. He had now, in place of the original and elaborate and imported affair, an oilskin haversack, a tin cup, a rubber cloth and blanket, a pair of jean drawers and one pair of wool socks. The socks and drawers were put in the blanket, the blanket was rolled in the rubber cloth, the ends were drawn together and fastened with a short strap and it was pulled over his head and swung from a shoulder. John Worsham had become a soldier.

He remained at headquarters until the tenth of September, he marched to Harper's Ferry where the Confederates captured over eleven thousand prisoners, seventy-two pieces of artillery, caissons, horses and additional military stores, and then he came upon the desperate battle of Sharpsburg. Company F reached its low water mark—only three men were left to answer roll call, Malcolm L. Hudgins, Reuben J. Jordan and John H. Worsham. They had no officer and were ordered to report to Company D, allowed to march and camp anywhere in the regiment; they were to report daily but answer roll call when and how they chose; and, in the Maryland campaign, they were known as the guerrillas of the Twenty-first. On the eighteenth of September, Jackson returned to Virginia; his loss at Sharpsburg was larger, in proportion to the number of men engaged, than in any other of his engagements.

General Jackson's corps camped near Martinsburg; they remained in the lower Valley, mostly in Jefferson County, for a number of weeks; but they moved every few days. Jackson did not allow his men to stay long in one place: new camps were healthier than old. His soldiers now, without tents, found change easy. They had cotton flies, four feet by six, hemmed at the edges, and worked with buttonholes and buttons. Three, fastened together, made a very practical covering for three men. They were supplied by the Yankees. In November, the twenty-first, Jackson's column joined General Lee at Fredericksburg; it marched by Madison Court House and Orange Court House, through the Wilderness and by Chancellorsville, to the vicinity of Guinea's Station on the Richmond, Fredericksburg and Potomac

Railroad; and at Moss Neck, the second of December, the regiment went into winter quarters. So many men were shoeless, rude moccasins were ordered to be made from the hides of the cattle killed for the army. There were continual daily drills, camp guard duty and inspections, with, in consequence, very little leisure. John did see twenty-five hundred men engaged at one time in the unaccustomed sport of snow-balling; on picquet he had occasional ruminating talks with Yankee soldiers in similar positions.

* * *

In Eighteen-sixty-three, it was January, Company F—Malcolm L. Hudgins, Reuben J. Jordan and John H. Worsham—was ordered to Richmond to recruit a fresh force. They were stationed at Camp Lee, and beginning with squad drill they were—the result of their activities—soon able to conduct company drill. The men were conscripts now, boys and the middle aged, and it was difficult to give them a military unity. On the twenty-first of June, John was ordered to join his regiment. It was now attached to Lee's army. General Jackson had been killed at Chancellorsville; a sense of irreparable loss had fallen upon his troops. Company F moved out of Staunton the last of June, its ranks were accompanied by disorganized stragglers; they were only capable of short marches; it was necessary to keep them under a potential guard. The company had no baggage wagon, no cooking utensils and no rations. It had no nothing. John Worsham reached the Potomac River, opposite Williamsport, Maryland, on the Fourth of July. Most of the stragglers were, in desperation, released from duty; all who were left formed in line with stacked arms on a field that commanded two roads reaching into town.

The Yankees appeared promptly, they advanced out of

THE FOOT SOLDIER

a woods with eight pieces of artillery and a large body of cavalry. Captain Pegram, commanding the Confederates, moved his ridiculously small force at double quick to the protection of a group of farm buildings; he had, altogether, fifty-two men; most of them were substitutes and conscripts. One of the substitutes fainted at the approach of the enemy. Another had a pain in his belly and had to lie down. That reduced Pegram's command to fifty. A few of the remaining stragglers, however, volunteered to go into the action; ten men were added to the Southern force. They repulsed a Union charge, cleared the farmyard, and the Federal guns opened upon them. A few of the company were strung along a fence to protect the flank, and the others kept up a desperate fire on the front. At dark the enemy withdrew: Captain Pegram had been killed, one of the three men left from the original company joined Jackson under the shade of the trees. It was, John considered, their best fight: with practically nothing but new and untrained men they held a doubtful position against overwhelming odds. A substitute, he remembered long afterwards, was so frightened by the artillery fire that he ran for the protection of the wagons; a shell burst directly in front of him, tearing a fence to pieces, and he turned back wailing that no whar was safe.

The command moved to Hagerstown, it slept that night on the brick pavement of the market house, and the next morning, July eighth, joined its regiment. John Worsham had been absent from the battles of Chancellorsville, Winchester and Gettysburg and he had fought at Williamsport. The Confederate army was reduced to the extremities of destitution and hunger; hundreds of men, now, were without shoes, there were no recognizable uniforms; the bottoms of pants were in frazzles; knees were bare and elbows stuck out; hair stuck through the holes in hats; it was a gaunt army of rags and patches. The Twenty-first Virginia regiment camped at Montpelier, where President Madison had lived, until the middle of July, and then it marched once more to Liberty Mills. It returned from Liberty Mills to Montpelier and John was occupied with the making of soap—a detail gathered ashes from the fires, they put them in several barrels and formed lye; the offal from the slaughter pens was added; and the result, John asserts, was wholly satisfactory.

There was a brigade inspection, the next day there was a brigade review, and a division review immediately followed. John's regiment was presented with a battle flag. The color bearer had lost an arm at Chancellorsville, but he protested so violently against being replaced, asserting he could carry a flag with one arm as well as two, that General Johnson presented him with the new colors in the presence of a great number of spectators. The flag bore the names, the battles, of Kernstown, McDowell, Winchester, Second Manassas, Harper's Ferry, Sharpsburg, Fredericksburg, Chancellorsville and Gettysburg. The battles of Cold Harbor, Malvern Hill and Cedar Run had, through an oversight, been omitted.

On the sixteenth September, John's short period of rest came to a close; the regiment commenced a series of marches and movements that ended with Lee crossing the Rapidan and offering action. It was refused. In November John was shifted to Kelly's Ford, a rumor of the enemy's presence there was unfounded, and he was moved to Culpeper Court House. He crossed the Rapidan River at Raccoon Ford in the coldest water he ever experienced. The regiment camped at Mount Pisgah Church. On the twenty-seventh of November the column, marching quietly over a woods road, was assailed on the flank by a Yankee skirmish line. That was the action of Payne's Farm. Johnson's division fought a wing of the Army of the Potomac and the next day it joined Lee. Breastworks were thrown up against the hills occupied by Meade.

After the crushing weight of a severe cannonading Johnson was withdrawn; his troops proceeded to Morton's Ford; John Worsham was back in the familiar camp at Mount Pisgah Church the twenty-fourth of December. Some boxes with the ingredients of eggnog arrived and there was the shadow of an old-fashioned Christmas. That formed the winter quarters of Eighteen-sixty-three and four, and the familiar comfortable huts were constructed. The number of religious services increased; at times a preacher expounded the gospel and when there was none a soldier led the meetings. Three men were executed for violating the laws of the army. The firing squad of twelve men was ordered to take up twelve guns lying on the ground, six were with balls, John heard, and six without, and no man knew if he had actually executed one of the prisoners. In February the whole corps was called into activity; it proceeded to Chancellorsville, nothing happened there, and it returned to camp. The rations were reduced from almost nothing to less. Telescope rifles were served to a selected number, they shot, at practice, from one hill at a target half a mile away on another, and a mule was accidentally killed. There was, that night, for some of the men, mule steak. Hardly a boiler remained in the corps, all the bread ovens, the spiders, were gone.

In May John was flung into the last battle of the Wilderness. It was a pandemonium of death. Midway of the battle a Confederate soldier came on a Yankee in a gully, and an individual fist and skull fight followed that was watched in a momentary hush by both armies. The Confederate won, the men rolled into the gully until night, and the Northern prisoner was brought in. At sunset, on the eighth of May, John Worsham was in the line of battle at Spottsylvania

Court House, the enemy had an immense force, General Lee rode to the front and a great cry went up from his soldiers. "General Lee to the rear! General Lee to the rear!" General Gordon took Lee's bridle and gently led him back. "Those are Virginians and Georgians," he said, "and they will do their duty."

After the defeat of the Union General Wallace the road to Washington was held to be open, and on July tenth General Gordon's division passed through Urbanna, Hyattstown and Clarksburg; the following morning it reached Rockville, in Maryland; at two o'clock John was at the toll gate five miles from Washington, he stood on the Seventh Street pike. He got water from Silver Springs, the country house of Mr. Blair, a member of Mr. Lincoln's cabinet; as far as he could see there were Federal fortifications, the enemy commanded a full mile on their front; the entire Confederate force, under Jubal Early, was less than ten thousand, and it was compelled to withdraw at night. On the nineteenth of September, Eighteen-sixty-four, at Winchester, John Worsham was struck on the shoulder by a spent ball; immediately afterward he was severely wounded in the knee. The arduous days of his soldiering were done.

* *
*

He was carried in the arms of two companions from the field, but after a short distance he begged to be put down. Any further movement, he was certain, would kill him. They were still under fire, solid shot were ploughing great furrows in the earth, and he wasn't heeded. He was allowed to rest behind a large rock, but he had been scarcely laid on the ground when a cannon ball struck the rock. John was hurried on. They reached the first house in Winchester, a small brick affair at the corner of an alley, and again there was a halt—instantly a shot crashed through it and covered the three men with pieces of brick and mortar. John was carried on into the town, and met Ira Blunt, a hospital steward, who gave him a drink of new apple brandy. He felt revived, an ambulance was secured, and he was driven in search of a surgeon. The ambulance was fired upon by the enemy, the mules hitched to it ran away and dragged John through a stone wall and over an old cornfield.

The ride continued until eight o'clock the following morning, when the driver fed his mules, and John managed to get a drink of water from a branch. He consumed the breakfast in a Yankee haversack captured the day before. His boot, then, was so full of blood it was running from the top, and he prevailed on the driver to pull it off. The wound stopped bleeding and they drove, toward Staunton, until four o'clock, afternoon, stopping at a church in Woodstock. It was filled with wounded soldiers; a surgeon at last examined and dressed John's injury; he was refreshed with fruit and feminine attention. At sunset he was put in a wagon, on straw, with other wounded men, and moved up the Valley pike. They drove all night, resting for a short while at dawn, and reached Staunton in two days.

The next morning John Worsham was taken to Charlottesville; he was in Richmond, in bed, when the city was evacuated. A member of the Virginia Legislature stopped to say goodby to him and explained that the body of the Legislature was going to Lynchburg by packet boat over the James River and Kanawha Canal. The President, the cabinet and other officials of the Confederate government, with the archives, had left Richmond by the Danville Railroad. Very early of the next day there was a flash of light, brighter than the brightest lightning, in John's room, accompanied by a loud report, a rumbling and shaking of the dwelling and general crash. The sashes in a front room were blown into the middle of the floor. A powder magazine had been blown up; a great fire was burning by the river; it seemed probable the whole city would be consumed. The retreating army, John learned, had set fire to the Shockoe, the Public and the Myers and Anderson tobacco warehouses, the arsenals and military stores. The city council, in meeting with prominent citizens, had decided to destroy all liquor in government buildings and storehouses, and a flood of whiskey and brandies had been emptied into the gutters.

A great volume of smoke obliterated Richmond; chunks of fire fell on the house where John was confined; a negro stationed on the roof put out a number of small blazes. The sun was hidden. At midday there was the sound of music, of cheers and firing by a Federal body marching over the next street. The Union troops dispersed the mob that had been pillaging the burning stores; it extinguished the universal blaze. Hundreds of residents from the burned district camped in the capitol square; it was choked with household goods and busy with the small fires of supper. On Sunday, the ninth of April, a rumor reached John Worsham that General Lee had surrendered. He flatly refused to believe it, but the report was confirmed the following day. The soldiers of the Army of Northern Virginia began to arrive in Richmond; General Lee rode into the city alone; he was immediately recognized, and his old followers, forming in line, walked after him to his house. Silent and with uncovered heads they watched him vanish into his doorway.

The Confederate States of America, the separate and historic South, had ceased to exist. It had been defeated, obliterated, by changing time, by new conceptions and necessities. The beginnings of the Civil War went back to the original informal union of the colonies; it existed in the old Articles of Confederation and in the Constitution—the rights of states opposed to the rights of the Federal government. It is still present. Present but different. The United States, now, is held together by better economic understanding; it rests on a more solid and practical fact. The South has changed, grown successful; its ports are great commercial ports and its cities are great manufacturing cities. It is rich in a new and important way. The difference between the North and the South has largely disappeared; the political party of the South and the political party of the North, once so sharply divided, have merged into a common body and a single aim. The result has been success.

The deep South, compared with New England, is no longer backward; the isolation of little villages, the loneliness of cabin clearings, the forest, have been all conquered. The Wilderness has been conquered, improved; it has become a source of turpentine and shingles.

The improvement is actual; there are roads everywhere and railroads, schools back of the mountains and hospitals; poverty and ignorance and disease are diminished. Loneliness has almost become a thing of the past, since, now, the air has a voice. But if there has been a great gain there was a loss. A loss of beauty. An old serenity vanished. An individual bravery, a brave individuality, destroyed. The men who lived in the past of the South, who died in its hopeless support, were fortunate—they knew tranquillity and personal independence; they sacrificed one for the other, and when both were lost their world, all they cherished, came to an utter end. The men of the traditional South would not have cared greatly for the present, its obligations and sense of honor and courage would not have satisfied them. They would have found it, well—a little crowded, lacking in privacy, perhaps even ignominious. A gentleman of the old Mississippi River Coast, of New Orleans, of Charleston or the Virginia Tidewater, would be, today, slightly ridiculous. Provincial. No one would understand his bearing or manners; there is a danger they would excite laughter.

The women they knew and adored, at once domestic and lovely, would seem strange now. Their ideas, their incurable loyalties, appear as antiquated as their crinolines. Yes, it is fortunate that, with their land, they all disappeared together. The calamity of a war swept them from a world that would have ruined them more slowly but with no less certainty. The old bearing, the old manners, must have been killed by mockery, by the curtness of time, by practical and democratic necessities. Litigation is more reasonable than the pistol. One woman is very nearly as desirable as another. Men, now, must be rich in order to be considerable. This is so overwhelmingly true that anything else, any contrary state, seems to have been always impossible. But once it was not so. Once men held themselves more dearly than they held their possessions.

That created a state of mind, an attitude, fine and bright and dangerous. It bred remote and difficult conceptions of virtue. The virtues of candor and of chastity. Curious old-fashioned words. It was responsible, as well, for the error of pride. The men of the deep South were proud men, they were arrogant, and for that fault they were punished. Arrogant individuals overthrown by an arrogant economic rule. The Civil War was inevitable. A curtain of smoke and fire was lowered upon the mistakes, and on the beauty, of the past. The sound of spinets, the light elegance of the gavotte, were lost in the uproar of cannon and musketry; and then, in the momentary pause before the uproar of machinery again drowned a delicate music, there was a new dance to learn. They all vanished with the older measures—the eloquent Mr. Yancey; Varina Howell who loved Jefferson Davis all her life; Pierre Gustave Toutant-Beauregard,

THE FOOT SOLDIER

cast in an obligation of honor dark and ringing like bronze; Albert Sidney Johnston in the loneliness of early Texas; Captain Maffitt driving precarious steamboats, heavy with cotton, and priceless with morphia and powder and gold, into the blockaded night; Nathan Forrest charging at the head of his troops, with his great sabre ground to a razor edge; Belle Boyd, who was more dangerous, more destructive, than canister or solid shot; Jeb Stuart decorated with a rose, wound in a yellow silk sash; and John Worsham, a foot soldier with Stonewall Jackson in the Great Valley.